Ursula

CW01082725

Honoré de Balzac

(Translator: Katharine Prescott Wormeley)

Alpha Editions

This edition published in 2024

ISBN : 9789362098962

Design and Setting By
Alpha Editions
www.alphaedis.com
Email - info@alphaedis.com

As per information held with us this book is in Public Domain.
This book is a reproduction of an important historical work. Alpha Editions uses the
best technology to reproduce historical work in the same manner it was first
published to preserve its original nature. Any marks or number seen are left
intentionally to preserve its true form.

Contents

CHAPTER I. THE FRIGHTENED HEIRS.................................- 1 -

CHAPTER II. THE RICH UNCLE ....- 11 -

CHAPTER III. THE DOCTOR'S FRIENDS ....- 20 -

CHAPTER IV. ZELIE...- 29 -

CHAPTER V. URSULA ....- 38 -

CHAPTER VI. A TREATISE ON MESMERISM..................- 46 -

CHAPTER VII. A TWO-FOLD CONVERSION ....- 58 -

CHAPTER VIII. THE CONFERENCE ....- 65 -

CHAPTER IX. A FIRST CONFIDENCE ....- 73 -

CHAPTER X. THE FAMILY OF PORTENDUERE ....- 82 -

CHAPTER XI. SAVINIEN SAVED.....................................- 90 -

CHAPTER XII. OBSTACLES TO YOUNG LOVE ....- 102 -

CHAPTER XIII. BETROTHAL OF HEARTS ....- 110 -

CHAPTER XIV. URSULA AGAIN ORPHANED...............- 122 -

CHAPTER XV. THE DOCTOR'S WILL............................- 129 -

CHAPTER XVI. THE TWO ADVERSARIES.....................- 140 -

CHAPTER XVII. THE MALIGNITY OF PROVINCIAL
MINDS..- 146 -

CHAPTER XVIII. A TWO-FOLD VENGEANCE ....- 158 -

CHAPTER XIX. APPARITIONS ....- 168 -

CHAPTER XX. REMORSE..- 180 -

CHAPTER XXI. SHOWING HOW DIFFICULT IT IS TO
STEAL THAT WHICH SEEMS VERY EASILY STOLEN.- 187 -

CHAPTER I.
THE FRIGHTENED HEIRS

Entering Nemours by the road to Paris, we cross the canal du Loing, the steep banks of which serve the double purpose of ramparts to the fields and of picturesque promenades for the inhabitants of that pretty little town. Since 1830 several houses had unfortunately been built on the farther side of the bridge. If this sort of suburb increases, the place will lose its present aspect of graceful originality.

In 1829, however, both sides of the road were clear, and the master of the post route, a tall, stout man about sixty years of age, sitting one fine autumn morning at the highest part of the bridge, could take in at a glance the whole of what is called in his business a "ruban de queue." The month of September was displaying its treasures; the atmosphere glowed above the grass and the pebbles; no cloud dimmed the blue of the sky, the purity of which in all parts, even close to the horizon, showed the extreme rarefaction of the air. So Minoret-Levrault (for that was the post master's name) was obliged to shade his eyes with one hand to keep them from being dazzled. With the air of a man who was tired of waiting, he looked first to the charming meadows which lay to the right of the road where the aftermath was springing up, then to the hill-slopes covered with copses which extend, on the left, from Nemours to Bouron. He could hear in the valley of the Loing, where the sounds on the road were echoed back from the hills, the trot of his own horses and the crack of his postilion's whip.

None but a post master could feel impatient within sight of such meadows, filled with cattle worthy of Paul Potter and glowing beneath a Raffaelle sky, and beside a canal shaded with trees after Hobbema. Whoever knows Nemours knows that nature is there as beautiful as art, whose mission is to spiritualize it; there, the landscape has ideas and creates thought. But, on catching sight of Minoret-Levrault an artist would very likely have left the view to sketch the man, so original was he in his native commonness. Unite in a human being all the conditions of the brute and you have a Caliban, who is certainly a great thing. Wherever form rules, sentiment disappears. The post master, a living proof of that axiom, presented a physiognomy in which an observer could with difficulty trace, beneath the vivid carnation of its coarsely developed flesh, the semblance of a soul. His cap of blue cloth, with a small peak, and sides fluted like a melon, outlined a head of vast dimensions, showing that Gall's science has not yet produced its chapter of exceptions. The gray and rather shiny hair which appeared below the cap showed that other causes than mental toil or grief had whitened it. Large ears stood out from the head, their edges scarred with the eruptions of his over-abundant blood, which seemed ready to gush at the least exertion. His skin was crimson under an outside layer of brown, due to the habit of standing in the sun. The roving gray eyes, deep-sunken, and hidden by bushy black brows, were like those of the Kalmucks who entered France in 1815; if they ever sparkled it was only under the influence of a covetous thought. His broad pug nose was flattened at the base. Thick lips, in keeping with a repulsive double chin, the beard of which, rarely cleaned more than once a week, was encircled with a dirty silk handkerchief twisted to a cord; a short neck, rolling in fat, and heavy cheeks completed the characteristics of brute force which sculptors give to their caryatids. Minoret-Levrault was like those statues, with this difference, that whereas they supported an edifice, he had more than he could well do to support himself. You will meet many such Atlases in the world. The man's torso was a block; it was like that of a bull standing on his hind-legs. His vigorous arms ended in a pair of thick, hard hands, broad and strong and well able to handle whip, reins, and pitchfork; hands which his postilions never attempted to trifle with. The enormous stomach of this giant rested on thighs which were as large as the body of an ordinary adult, and feet like those of an elephant. Anger was a rare thing with him, but it was terrible, apoplectic, when it did burst forth. Though violent and quite incapable of reflection, the man had never done anything that justified the sinister suggestions of his bodily presence. To all those who felt afraid of him his postilions would reply, "Oh! he's not bad."

The master of Nemours, to use the common abbreviation of the country, wore a velveteen shooting-jacket of bottle-green, trousers of green linen with great stripes, and an ample yellow waistcoat of goat's skin, in the pocket of which might be discerned the round outline of a monstrous snuff-box. A snuff-box to a pug nose is a law without exception.

A son of the Revolution and a spectator of the Empire, Minoret-Levrault did not meddle with politics; as to his religious opinions, he had never set foot in a church except to be married; as to his private principles, he kept them within the civil code; all that the law did not forbid or could not prevent he considered right. He never read anything but the journal of the department of the Seine-et-Oise, and a few printed instructions relating to his business. He was considered a clever agriculturist; but his knowledge was only practical. In him the moral being did not belie the physical. He seldom spoke, and before speaking he always took a pinch of snuff to give himself time, not to find ideas, but words. If he had been a talker you would have felt that he was out of keeping with himself. Reflecting that this elephant minus a trumpet and without a mind was called Minoret-Levrault, we are compelled to agree with Sterne as to the occult power of names, which sometimes ridicule and sometimes foretell characters.

In spite of his visible incapacity he had acquired during the last thirty-six years (the Revolution helping him) an income of thirty thousand francs, derived from farm lands, woods and meadows. If Minoret, being master of the coach-lines of Nemours and those of the Gatinais to Paris, still worked at his business, it was less from habit than for the sake of an only son, to whom he was anxious to give a fine career. This son, who was now (to use an expression of the peasantry) a "monsieur," had just completed his legal studies and was about to take his degree as licentiate, preparatory to being called to the Bar. Monsieur and Madame Minoret-Levrault—for behind our colossus every one will perceive a woman without whom this signal good-fortune would have been impossible—left their son free to choose his own career; he might be a notary in Paris, king's-attorney in some district, collector of customs no matter where, broker, or post master, as he pleased. What fancy of his could they ever refuse him? to what position of life might he not aspire as the son of a man about whom the whole countryside, from Montargis to Essonne, was in the habit of saying, "Pere Minoret doesn't even know how rich he is"?

This saying had obtained fresh force about four years before this history begins, when Minoret, after selling his inn, built stables and a splendid dwelling, and removed the post-house from the Grand'Rue to the wharf. The new establishment cost two hundred thousand francs, which the gossip of thirty miles in circumference more than doubled. The Nemours mail-coach service requires a large number of horses. It goes to Fontainebleau on the road to Paris, and from there diverges to Montargis and also to Montereau. The relays are long, and the sandy soil of the Montargis road calls for the mythical third horse, always paid for but never seen. A man of Minoret's build, and Minoret's wealth, at the head of such an establishment might well be called, without contradiction, the master of Nemours. Though he never thought of God or devil, being a practical materialist, just as he was a practical agriculturist, a practical egoist, and a practical miser, Minoret had enjoyed up to this time a life of unmixed happiness,—if we can call pure materialism happiness. A physiologist, observing the rolls of flesh which covered the last vertebrae and pressed upon the giant's cerebellum, and, above all, hearing the shrill, sharp voice which contrasted so absurdly with his huge body, would have understood why this ponderous, coarse being adored his only son, and why he had so long expected him,—a fact proved by the name, Desire, which was given to the child.

The mother, whom the boy fortunately resembled, rivaled the father in spoiling him. No child could long have resisted the effects of such idolatry. As soon as Desire knew the extent of his power he milked his mother's coffer and dipped into his father's purse, making each author of his being believe that he, or she, alone was petitioned. Desire, who played a part in Nemours far beyond that of a prince royal in his father's capital, chose to gratify his fancies in Paris just as he had gratified them in his native town; he had therefore spent a yearly sum of not less than twelve thousand francs during the time of his legal studies. But for that money he had certainly acquired ideas that would never had come to him in Nemours; he had stripped off the provincial skin, learned the power of money and seen in the magistracy a means of advancement which he fancied. During the last year he had spent an extra sum of ten thousand francs in the company of artists, journalists, and their mistresses. A confidential and rather disquieting letter from his son, asking for his consent to a marriage, explains the watch which the post master was now keeping on the bridge; for Madame Minoret-Levrault, busy in preparing a sumptuous breakfast to celebrate the triumphal return of the licentiate, had sent her husband to the mail road, advising him to take a horse and ride out if he saw nothing of the diligence. The coach which was conveying the precious son usually arrived at five in the morning and it was now nine! What could be the meaning of such delay? Was the coach overturned? Could Desire be dead? Or was it nothing worse than a broken leg?

Three distinct volleys of cracking whips rent the air like a discharge of musketry; the red waistcoats of the postilions dawned in sight, ten horses neighed. The master pulled off his cap and waved it; he was seen. The best mounted postilion, who was returning with two gray carriage-horses, set spurs to his beast and came on in advance of the five diligence horses and the three other carriage-horses, and soon reached his master.

"Have you seen the 'Ducler'?"

On the great mail routes names, often fantastic, are given to the different coaches; such, for instance, as the "Caillard," the "Ducler" (the coach between Nemours and Paris), the "Grand Bureau." Every new enterprise is called the "Competition." In the days of the Lecompte company their coaches were called the "Countess."—"'Caillard' could not overtake the 'Countess'; but 'Grand Bureau' caught up with her finely," you will hear the men say. If you see a postilion pressing his horses and refusing a glass of wine, question the conductor and he will tell you, snuffing the air while his eye gazes far into space, "The 'Competition' is ahead."—"We can't get in sight of her," cries the postilion; "the vixen! she wouldn't stop to let her passengers dine."—"The question is, has she got any?" responds the conductor. "Give it to Polignac!" All lazy and bad horses are called Polignac. Such are the jokes and the basis of conversation between postilions and conductors on the roofs of the coaches. Each profession, each calling in France has its slang.

"Have you seen the 'Ducler'?" asked Minoret.

"Monsieur Desire?" said the postilion, interrupting his master. "Hey! you must have heard us, didn't our whips tell you? we felt you were somewhere along the road."

Just then a woman dressed in her Sunday clothes,—for the bells were pealing from the clock tower and calling the inhabitants to mass,—a woman about thirty-six years of age came up to the post master.

"Well, cousin," she said, "you wouldn't believe me—Uncle is with Ursula in the Grand'Rue, and they are going to mass."

In spite of the modern poetic canons as to local color, it is quite impossible to push realism so far as to repeat the horrible blasphemy mingled with oaths which this news, apparently so unexciting, brought from the huge mouth of Minoret-Levrault; his shrill voice grew sibilant, and his face took on the appearance of what people oddly enough call a sunstroke.

"Is that true?" he asked, after the first explosion of his wrath was over.

The postilions bowed to their master as they and their horses passed him, but he seemed to neither see nor hear them. Instead of waiting for his son, Minoret-Levrault hurried up to the Grand'Rue with his cousin.

"Didn't I always tell you so?" she resumed. "When Doctor Minoret goes out of his head that demure little hypocrite will drag him into religion; whoever lays hold of the mind gets hold of the purse, and she'll have our inheritance."

"But, Madame Massin—" said the post master, dumbfounded.

"There now!" exclaimed Madame Massin, interrupting her cousin. "You are going to say, just as Massin does, that a little girl of fifteen can't invent such plans and carry them out, or make an old man of eighty-three, who has never set foot in a church except to be married, change his opinions,—now don't tell me he has such a horror of priests that he wouldn't even go with the girl to the parish church when she made her first communion. I'd like to know why, if Doctor Minoret hates priests, he has spent nearly every evening for the last fifteen years of his life with the Abbe Chaperon. The old hypocrite never fails to give Ursula twenty francs for wax tapers every time she takes the sacrament. Have you forgotten the gift Ursula made to the church in gratitude to the cure for preparing her for her first communion? She spent all her money on it, and her godfather returned it to her doubled. You men! you don't pay attention to things. When I heard that, I said to myself, 'Farewell baskets, the vintage is done!' A rich uncle doesn't behave that way to a little brat picked up in the streets without some good reason."

"Pooh, cousin; I dare say the good man is only taking her to the door of the church," replied the post master. "It is a fine day, and he is out for a walk."

"I tell you he is holding a prayer-book, and looks sanctimonious—you'll see him."

"They hide their game pretty well," said Minoret, "La Bougival told me there was never any talk of religion between the doctor and the abbe. Besides, the abbe is one of the most honest men on the face of the globe; he'd give the shirt off his back to a poor man; he is incapable of a base action, and to cheat a family out of their inheritance is—"

"Theft," said Madame Massin.

"Worse!" cried Minoret-Levrault, exasperated by the tongue of his gossiping neighbour.

"Of course I know," said Madame Massin, "that the Abbe Chaperon is an honest man; but he is capable of anything for the sake of his poor. He must have mined and undermined uncle, and the old man has just tumbled into piety. We did nothing, and here he is perverted! A man who never believed in anything, and had principles of his own! Well! we're done for. My husband is absolutely beside himself."

Madame Massin, whose sentences were so many arrows stinging her fat cousin, made him walk as fast as herself, in spite of his obesity and to the great astonishment of the church-goers, who were on their way to mass. She was determined to overtake this uncle and show him to the post master.

Nemours is commanded on the Gatinais side by a hill, at the foot of which runs the road to Montargis and the Loing. The church, on the stones of which time has cast a rich discolored mantle (it was rebuilt in the fourteenth century by the Guises, for whom Nemours was raised to a peerage-duchy), stands at the end of the little town close to a great arch which frames it. For buildings, as for men, position does everything. Shaded by a few trees, and thrown into relief by a neatly kept square, this solitary church produces a really grandiose effect. As the post master of Nemours entered the open space, he beheld his uncle with the young girl called Ursula on his arm, both carrying prayer-books and just entering the church. The old man took off his hat in the porch, and his head, which was white as a hill-top covered with snow, shone among the shadows of the portal.

"Well, Minoret, what do you say to the conversion of your uncle?" cried the tax-collector of Nemours, named Cremiere.

"What do you expect me to say?" replied the post master, offering him a pinch of snuff.

"Well answered, Pere Levrault. You can't say what you think, if it is true, as an illustrious author says it is, that a man must think his words before he speaks his thoughts," cried a young man, standing near, who played the part of Mephistopheles in the little town.

This ill-conditioned youth, named Goupil, was head clerk to Monsieur Cremiere-Dionis, the Nemours notary. Notwithstanding a past conduct that was almost debauched, Dionis had taken Goupil into his office when a career in Paris—where the clerk had wasted all the money he inherited from his father, a well-to-do farmer, who educated him for a notary—was brought to a close by his absolute pauperism. The mere sight of Goupil told an observer that he had made haste to enjoy life, and had paid dear for his enjoyments. Though very short, his chest and shoulders were developed at twenty-seven years of age like those of a man of forty. Legs small and weak, and a broad face, with a cloudy complexion like the sky before a storm, surmounted by a bald forehead, brought out still further the oddity of his conformation. His face seemed as though it belonged to a hunchback whose hunch was inside of him. One singularity of that pale and sour visage confirmed the impression of an invisible gobbosity; the nose, crooked and out of shape like those of many deformed persons, turned from right to left of the face instead of dividing it down the middle. The mouth, contracted at the corners, like that of a Sardinian, was always on the qui vive of irony. His hair, thin and reddish, fell straight, and showed the skull in many places. His hands, coarse and ill-joined at the wrists to arms that were far too long, were quick-fingered and seldom clean. Goupil wore boots only fit for the dust-heap, and raw silk stockings now of a russet black; his coat and trousers, all black, and threadbare and greasy with dirt, his pitiful waistcoat with half the button-moulds gone, an old silk handkerchief which served as a cravat—in short, all his clothing revealed the cynical poverty to which his passions had reduced him. This combination of disreputable signs was guarded by a pair of eyes with yellow circles round the pupils, like those of a goat, both lascivious and cowardly. No one in Nemours was more feared nor, in a way, more deferred to than Goupil. Strong in the claims made for him by his very ugliness, he had the odious style of wit peculiar to men who allow themselves all license, and he used it to gratify the bitterness of his life-long envy. He wrote the satirical couplets sung during the carnival, organized charivaris, and was himself a "little journal" of the gossip of the town. Dionis, who was clever and insincere, and for that reason timid, kept Goupil as much through fear as for his keen mind and thorough knowledge of all the interests of the town. But the master so distrusted his clerk that he himself kept the accounts, refused to let him live in his house, held him at arm's length, and never confided any secret or delicate affair to his keeping. In return the clerk fawned upon the notary, hiding his resentment at this conduct, and watching Madame Dionis in the hope that he might get his revenge there. Gifted with a ready mind and quick comprehension he found work easy.

"You!" exclaimed the post master to the clerk, who stood rubbing his hands, "making game of our misfortunes already?"

As Goupil was known to have pandered to Dionis' passions for the last five years, the post master treated him cavalierly, without suspecting the hoard of ill-feeling he was piling up in Goupil's heart with every fresh insult. The clerk, convinced that money was more necessary to him than it was to others, and knowing himself superior in mind to the whole bourgeoisie of Nemours, was now counting on his intimacy with Minoret's son Desire to obtain the means of buying one or the other of three town offices,—that of clerk of the court, or the legal practice of one of the sheriffs, or that of Dionis himself. For this reason he put up with the affronts of the post master and the contempt of Madame Minoret-Levrault, and played a contemptible part towards Desire, consoling the fair victims whom that youth left behind him after each vacation,—devouring the crumbs of the loaves he had kneaded.

"If I were the nephew of a rich old fellow, he never would have given God to ME for a co-heir," retorted Goupil, with a hideous grin which exhibited his teeth—few, black, and menacing.

Just then Massin-Levrault, junior, the clerk of the court, joined his wife, bringing with him Madame Cremiere, the wife of the tax-collector of Nemours. This man, one of the hardest natures of the little town, had the physical characteristics of a Tartar: eyes small and round as sloes beneath a retreating brow, crimped hair, an oily skin, huge ears without any rim, a mouth almost without lips, and a scanty beard. He spoke like a man who was losing his voice. To exhibit him thoroughly it is enough to say that he employed his wife and eldest daughter to serve his legal notices.

Madame Cremiere was a stout woman, with a fair complexion injured by red blotches, always too tightly laced, intimate with Madame Dionis, and supposed to be educated because she read novels. Full of pretensions to wit and elegance, she was awaiting her uncle's money to "take a certain stand," decorate her salon, and receive the bourgeoisie. At present her husband denied her Carcel lamps, lithographs, and all the other trifles the notary's wife possessed. She was excessively afraid of Goupil, who caught up and retailed her "slapsus-linquies" as she called them. One day Madame Dionis chanced to ask what "Eau" she thought best for the teeth.

"Try opium," she replied.

Nearly all the collateral heirs of old Doctor Minoret were now assembled in the square; the importance of the event which brought them was so generally felt that even groups of peasants, armed with their scarlet umbrellas and dressed in those brilliant colors which make them so picturesque on Sundays and fete-days, stood by, with their eyes fixed on the frightened heirs. In all little towns which are midway between large villages and cities those who do not go to mass stand about in the square or market-place. Business is talked over. In Nemours the hour of church service was a weekly exchange, to which the owners of property scattered over a radius of some miles resorted.

"Well, how would you have prevented it?" said the post master to Goupil in reply to his remark.

"I should have made myself as important to him as the air he breathes. But from the very first you failed to get hold of him. The inheritance of a rich uncle should be watched as carefully as a pretty woman—for want of proper care they'll both escape you. If Madame Dionis were here she could tell you how true that comparison is."

"But Monsieur Bongrand has just told me there is nothing to worry about," said Massin.

"Oh! there are plenty of ways of saying that!" cried Goupil, laughing. "I would like to have heard your sly justice of the peace say it. If there is nothing to be done, if he, being intimate with your uncle, knows that all is lost, the proper thing for him to say to you is, 'Don't be worried.'"

As Goupil spoke, a satirical smile overspread his face, and gave such meaning to his words that the other heirs began to feel that Massin had let Bongrand deceive him. The tax-collector, a fat little man, as insignificant as a tax-collector should be, and as much of a cipher as a clever woman could wish, hereupon annihilated his co-heir, Massin, with the words:—"Didn't I tell you so?"

Tricky people always attribute trickiness to others. Massin therefore looked askance at Monsieur Bongrand, the justice of the peace, who was at that moment talking near the door of the church with the Marquis du Rouvre, a former client.

"If I were sure of it!" he said.

"You could neutralize the protection he is now giving to the Marquis du Rouvre, who is threatened with arrest. Don't you see how Bongrand is sprinkling him with advice?" said Goupil, slipping an idea of retaliation into Massin's mind. "But you had better go easy with your chief; he's a clever old fellow; he might use his influence with your uncle and persuade him not to leave everything to the church."

"Pooh! we sha'n't die of it," said Minoret-Levrault, opening his enormous snuff-box.

"You won't live of it, either," said Goupil, making the two women tremble. More quick-witted than their husbands, they saw the privations this loss of inheritance (so long counted on for many comforts) would be to them. "However," added Goupil, "we'll drown this little grief in floods of champagne in honor of Desire!—sha'n't we, old fellow?" he cried, tapping the stomach of the giant, and inviting himself to the feast for fear he should be left out.

CHAPTER II.
THE RICH UNCLE

Before proceeding further, persons of an exact turn of mind may like to read a species of family inventory, so as to understand the degrees of relationship which connected the old man thus suddenly converted to religion with these three heads of families or their wives. This cross-breeding of families in the remote provinces might be made the subject of many instructive reflections.

There are but three or four houses of the lesser nobility in Nemours; among them, at the period of which we write, that of the family of Portenduere was the most important. These exclusives visited none but nobles who possessed lands or chateaus in the neighbourhood; of the latter we may mention the d'Aiglemonts, owners of the beautiful estate of Saint-Lange, and the Marquis du Rouvre, whose property, crippled by mortgages, was closely watched by the bourgeoisie. The nobles of the town had no money. Madame de Portenduere's sole possessions were a farm which brought a rental of forty-seven hundred francs, and her town house.

In opposition to this very insignificant Faubourg St. Germain was a group of a dozen rich families, those of retired millers, or former merchants; in short a miniature bourgeoisie; below which, again, lived and moved the retail shopkeepers, the proletaries and the peasantry. The bourgeoisie presented (like that of the Swiss cantons and of other small countries) the curious spectacle of the ramifications of certain autochthonous families, old-fashioned and unpolished perhaps, but who rule a whole region and pervade it, until nearly all its inhabitants are cousins. Under Louis XI., an epoch at which the commons first made real names of their surnames (some of which are united with those of feudalism) the bourgeoisie of Nemours was made up of Minorets, Massins, Levraults and Cremieres. Under Louis XIII. these four families had already produced the Massin-Cremieres, the Levrault-Massins, the Massin-Minorets, the Minoret-Minorets, the Cremiere-Levraults, the Levrault-Minoret-Massins, Massin-Levraults, Minoret-Massins, Massin-Massins, and Cremiere-Massins,—all these varied with juniors and diversified with the names of eldest sons, as for instance, Cremiere-Francois, Levrault-Jacques, Jean-Minoret—enough to drive a Pere Anselme of the People frantic,—if the people should ever want a genealogist.

The variations of this family kaleidoscope of four branches was now so complicated by births and marriages that the genealogical tree of the bourgeoisie of Nemours would have puzzled the Benedictines of the Almanach of Gotha, in spite of the atomic science with which they arrange those zigzags of German alliances. For a long time the Minorets occupied the tanneries, the Cremieres kept the mills, the Massins were in trade, and the Levraults continued farmers. Fortunately for the neighbourhood these four stocks threw out suckers instead of depending only on their tap-roots; they scattered cuttings by the expatriation of sons who sought their fortune elsewhere; for instance, there are Minorets who are cutlers at Melun; Levraults at Montargis; Massins at Orleans; and Cremieres of some importance in Paris. Divers are the destinies of these bees from the parent hive. Rich Massins employ, of course, the poor working Massins—just as Austria and Prussia take the German princes into their service. It may happen that a public office is managed by a Minoret millionaire and guarded by a Minoret sentinel. Full of the same blood and called by the same name (for sole likeness), these four roots had ceaselessly woven a human network of which each thread was delicate or strong, fine or coarse, as the case might be. The same blood was in the head and in the feet and in the heart, in the working hands, in the weakly lungs, in the forehead big with genius.

The chiefs of the clan were faithful to the little town, where the ties of family were relaxed or tightened according to the events which happened under this curious cognomenism. In whatever part of France you may be, you will find the same thing under changed names, but without the poetic charm which feudalism gave to it, and which Walter Scott's genius reproduced so faithfully. Let us look a little higher and examine humanity as it appears in history. All the noble families of the eleventh century, most of them (except the royal race of Capet) extinct to-day, will be found to have contributed to the birth of the Rohans, Montmorencys, Beauffremonts, and Mortemarts of our time,—in fact they will all be found in the blood of the last gentleman who is indeed a gentleman. In other words, every bourgeois is cousin to a bourgeois, and every noble is cousin to a noble. A splendid page of biblical genealogy shows that in one thousand years three families, Shem, Ham, and Japhet, peopled the globe. One family may become a nation; unfortunately, a nation may become one family. To prove this we need only search back through our ancestors and see their accumulation, which time increases into a retrograde geometric progression, which multiplies of itself; reminding us of the calculation of the wise man who, being told to choose a reward from the king of Persia for inventing chess, asked for one ear of wheat for the first move on the board, the reward to be doubled for each succeeding move; when it was found that the kingdom was not large enough to pay it. The net-work of the nobility, hemmed in by the net-work of the bourgeoisie,—the antagonism of two protected races, one protected by fixed institutions, the other by the active patience of labor and the shrewdness of commerce,—produced the revolution of 1789. The two races almost reunited are to-day face to face with collaterals without a heritage. What are they to do? Our political future is big with the answer.

The family of the man who under Louis XV. was simply called Minoret was so numerous that one of the five children (the Minoret whose entrance into the parish church caused such interest) went to Paris to seek his fortune, and seldom returned to his native town, until he came to receive his share of the inheritance of his grandfather. After suffering many things, like all young men of firm will who struggle for a place in the brilliant world of Paris, this son of the Minorets reached a nobler destiny than he had, perhaps, dreamed of at the start. He devoted himself, in the first instance, to medicine, a profession which demands both talent and a cheerful nature, but the latter qualification even more than talent. Backed by Dupont de Nemours, connected by a lucky chance with the Abbe Morellet (whom Voltaire nicknamed Mords-les), and protected by the Encyclopedists, Doctor Minoret attached himself as liegeman to the famous Doctor Bordeu, the friend of Diderot, D'Alembert, Helvetius, the Baron d'Holbach and Grimm, in whose presence he felt himself a mere boy. These men, influenced by Bordeu's example, became interested in Minoret, who, about the year 1777, found himself with a very good practice among deists, encyclopedists, sensualists, materialists, or whatever you are pleased to call the rich philosophers of that period.

Though Minoret was very little of a humbug, he invented the famous balm of Lelievre, so much extolled by the "Mercure de France," the weekly organ of the Encyclopedists, in whose columns it was permanently advertised. The apothecary Lelievre, a clever man, saw a stroke of business where Minoret had only seen a new preparation for the dispensary, and he loyally shared his profits with the doctor, who was a pupil of Rouelle in chemistry as well as of Bordeu in medicine. Less than that would make a man a materialist.

The doctor married for love in 1778, during the reign of the "Nouvelle Heloise," when persons did occasionally marry for that reason. His wife was a daughter of the famous harpsichordist Valentin Mirouet, a celebrated musician, frail and delicate, whom the Revolution slew. Minoret knew Robespierre intimately, for he had once been instrumental in awarding him a gold medal for a dissertation on the following subject: "What is the origin of the opinion that covers a whole family with the shame attaching to the public punishment of a guilty member of it? Is that opinion more harmful than useful? If yes, in what way can the harm be warded off." The Royal Academy of Arts and Sciences at Metz, to which Minoret belonged, must possess this dissertation in the original. Though, thanks to this friendship, the Doctor's wife need have had no fear, she was so in dread of going to the scaffold that her terror increased a disposition to heart disease caused by the over-sensitiveness of her nature. In spite of all the precautions taken by the man who idolized her, Ursula unfortunately met the tumbril of victims among whom was Madame Roland, and the shock caused her death.

Minoret, who in tenderness to his wife had refused her nothing, and had given her a life of luxury, found himself after her death almost a poor man. Robespierre gave him an appointment as surgeon-in-charge of a hospital.

Though the name of Minoret obtained during the lively debates to which mesmerism gave rise a certain celebrity which occasionally recalled him to the minds of his relatives, still the Revolution was so great a destroyer of family relations that in 1813 Nemours knew little of Doctor Minoret, who was induced to think of returning there to die, like the hare to its form, by a circumstance that was wholly accidental.

Who has not felt in traveling through France, where the eye is often wearied by the monotony of plains, the charming sensation of coming suddenly, when the eye is prepared for a barren landscape, upon a fresh cool valley, watered by a river, with a little town sheltering beneath a cliff like a swarm of bees in the hollow of an old willow? Wakened by the "hu! hu!" of the postilion as he walks beside his horses, we shake off sleep and admire, like a dream within a dream, the beautiful scene which is to the traveler what a noble passage in a book is to a reader,—a brilliant thought of Nature. Such is the sensation caused by a first sight of Nemours as we approach it from Burgundy. We see it encircled with bare rocks, gray, black, white, fantastic in shape like those we find in the forest of Fontainebleau; from them spring scattered trees, clearly defined against the sky, which give to this particular rock formation the dilapidated look of a crumbling wall. Here ends the long wooded hill which creeps from Nemours to Bouron, skirting the road. At the bottom of this irregular amphitheater lie meadow-lands through which flows the Loing, forming sheets of water with many falls. This delightful landscape, which continues the whole way to Montargis, is like an opera scene, for its effects really seem to have been studied.

One morning Doctor Minoret, who had been summoned into Burgundy by a rich patient, was returning in all haste to Paris. Not having mentioned at the last relay the route he intended to take, he was brought without his knowledge through Nemours, and beheld once more, on waking from a nap, the scenery in which his childhood had been passed. He had lately lost many of his old friends. The votary of the Encyclopedists had witnessed the conversion of La Harpe; he had buried Lebrun-Pindare and Marie-Joseph de Chenier, and Morellet, and Madame Helvetius. He assisted at the quasi-fall of Voltaire when assailed by Geoffroy, the continuator of Freton. For some time past he had thought of retiring, and so, when his post chaise stopped at the head of the Grand'Rue of Nemours, his heart prompted him to inquire for his family. Minoret-Levrault, the post master, came forward himself to see the doctor, who discovered him to be the son of his eldest brother. The nephew presented the doctor to his wife, the only daughter of the late

Levrault-Cremiere, who had died twelve years earlier, leaving him the post business and the finest inn in Nemours.

"Well, nephew," said the doctor, "have I any other relatives?"

"My aunt Minoret, your sister, married a Massin-Massin—"

"Yes, I know, the bailiff of Saint-Lange."

"She died a widow leaving an only daughter, who has lately married a Cremiere-Cremiere, a fine young fellow, still without a place."

"Ah! she is my own niece. Now, as my brother, the sailor, died a bachelor, and Captain Minoret was killed at Monte-Legino, and here I am, that ends the paternal line. Have I any relations on the maternal side? My mother was a Jean-Massin-Levrault."

"Of the Jean-Massin-Levrault's there's only one left," answered Minoret-Levrault, "namely, Jean-Massin, who married Monsieur Cremiere-Levrault-Dionis, a purveyor of forage, who perished on the scaffold. His wife died of despair and without a penny, leaving one daughter, married to a Levrault-Minoret, a farmer at Montereau, who is doing well; their daughter has just married a Massin-Levrault, notary's clerk at Montargis, where his father is a locksmith."

"So I've plenty of heirs," said the doctor gayly, immediately proposing to take a walk through Nemours accompanied by his nephew.

The Loing runs through the town in a waving line, banked by terraced gardens and neat houses, the aspect of which makes one fancy that happiness must abide there sooner than elsewhere. When the doctor turned into the Rue des Bourgeois, Minoret-Levrault pointed out the property of Levrault-Levrault, a rich iron merchant in Paris who, he said, had just died.

"The place is for sale, uncle, and a very pretty house it is; there's a charming garden running down to the river."

"Let us go in," said the doctor, seeing, at the farther end of a small paved courtyard, a house standing between the walls of the two neighbouring houses which were masked by clumps of trees and climbing-plants.

"It is built over a cellar," said the doctor, going up the steps of a high portico adorned with vases of blue and white pottery in which geraniums were growing.

Cut in two, like the majority of provincial houses, by a long passage which led from the courtyard to the garden, the house had only one room to the right, a salon lighted by four windows, two on the courtyard and two on the garden; but Levrault-Levrault had used one of these windows to make an entrance to a long greenhouse built of brick which extended from the salon towards the river, ending in a horrible Chinese pagoda.

"Good! by building a roof to that greenhouse and laying a floor," said old Minoret, "I could put my book there and make a very comfortable study of that extraordinary bit of architecture at the end."

On the other side of the passage, toward the garden, was the dining-room, decorated in imitation of black lacquer with green and gold flowers; this was separated from the kitchen by the well of the staircase. Communication with the kitchen was had through a little pantry built behind the staircase, the kitchen itself looking into the courtyard through windows with iron railings. There were two chambers on the next floor, and above them, attic rooms sheathed in wood, which were fairly habitable. After examining the house rapidly, and observing that it was covered with trellises from top to bottom, on the side of the courtyard as well as on that to the garden,—which ended in a terrace overlooking the river and adorned with pottery vases,—the doctor remarked:—

"Levrault-Levrault must have spend a good deal of money here."

"Ho! I should think so," answered Minoret-Levrault. "He liked flowers— nonsense! 'What do they bring in?' says my wife. You saw inside there how an artist came from Paris to paint flowers in fresco in the corridor. He put those enormous mirrors everywhere. The ceilings were all re-made with cornices which cost six francs a foot. The dining-room floor is in marquetry—perfect folly! The house won't sell for a penny the more."

"Well, nephew, buy it for me: let me know what you do about it; here's my address. The rest I leave to my notary. Who lives opposite?" he asked, as they left the house.

"Emigres," answered the post master, "named Portenduere."

The house once bought, the illustrious doctor, instead of living there, wrote to his nephew to let it. The Folie-Levraught was therefore occupied by the notary of Nemours, who about that time sold his practice to Dionis, his head-clerk, and died two years later, leaving the house on the doctor's hands, just at the time when the fate of Napoleon was being decided in the neighbourhood. The doctor's heirs, at first misled, had by this time decided that his thought of returning to his native place was merely a rich man's fancy, and that probably he had some tie in Paris which would keep him there and cheat them of their hoped-for inheritance. However, Minoret-Levrault's wife seized the occasion to write him a letter. The old man replied that as soon as peace was signed, the roads cleared of soldiers, and safe communications established, he meant to go and live at Nemours. He did, in fact, put in an appearance with two of his clients, the architect of his hospital and an upholsterer, who took charge of the repairs, the indoor arrangements, and the transportation of the furniture. Madame Minoret-Levrault proposed the cook of the late notary as caretaker, and the woman was accepted.

When the heirs heard that their uncle and great-uncle Minoret was really coming to live in Nemours, they were seized (in spite of the political events which were just then weighing so heavily on Brie and on the Gatinais) with a devouring curiosity, which was not surprising. Was he rich? Economical or spendthrift? Would he leave a fine fortune or nothing? Was his property in annuities? In the end they found out what follows, but only by taking infinite pains and employing much subterraneous spying.

After the death of his wife, Ursula Mirouet, and between the years 1789 and 1813, the doctor (who had been appointed consulting physician to the Emperor in 1805) must have made a good deal of money; but no one knew how much. He lived simply, without other extravagancies than a carriage by the year and a sumptuous apartment. He received no guests, and dined out almost every day. His housekeeper, furious at not being allowed to go with him to Nemours, told Zelie Levrault, the post master's wife, that she knew the doctor had fourteen thousand francs a year on the "grand-livre." Now, after twenty years' exercise of a profession which his position as head of a hospital, physician to the Emperor, and member of the Institute, rendered lucrative, these fourteen thousand francs a year showed only one hundred and sixty thousand francs laid by. To have saved only eight thousand francs a year the doctor must have had either many vices or many virtues to gratify. But neither his housekeeper nor Zelie nor any one else could discover the reason for such moderate means. Minoret, who when he left it was much regretted in the quarter of Paris where he had lived, was one of the most benevolent of men, and, like Larrey, kept his kind deeds a profound secret.

The heirs watched the arrival of their uncle's fine furniture and large library with complacency, and looked forward to his own coming, he being now an officer of the Legion of honor, and lately appointed by the king a chevalier of the order of Saint-Michel—perhaps on account of his retirement, which left a vacancy for some favorite. But when the architect and painter and upholsterer had arranged everything in the most comfortable manner, the doctor did not come. Madame Minoret-Levrault, who kept an eye on the upholsterer and architect as if her own property was concerned, found out, through the indiscretion of a young man sent to arrange the books, that the doctor was taking care of a little orphan named Ursula. The news flew like wild-fire through the town. At last, however, towards the middle of the month of January, 1815, the old man actually arrived, installing himself quietly, almost slyly, with a little girl about ten months old, and a nurse.

"The child can't be his daughter," said the terrified heirs; "he is seventy-one years old."

"Whoever she is," remarked Madame Massin, "she'll give us plenty of tintouin" (a word peculiar to Nemours, meaning uneasiness, anxiety, or more literally, tingling in the ears).

The doctor received his great-niece on the mother's side somewhat coldly; her husband had just bought the place of clerk of the court, and the pair began at once to tell him of their difficulties. Neither Massin nor his wife were rich. Massin's father, a locksmith at Montargis, had been obliged to compromise with his creditors, and was now, at sixty-seven years of age, working like a young man, and had nothing to leave behind him. Madame Massin's father, Levrault-Minoret, had just died at Montereau after the battle, in despair at seeing his farm burned, his fields ruined, his cattle slaughtered.

"We'll get nothing out of your great-uncle," said Massin to his wife, now pregnant with her second child, after the interview.

The doctor, however, gave them privately ten thousand francs, with which Massin, who was a great friend of the notary and of the sheriff, began the business of money-lending, and carried matters so briskly with the peasantry that by the time of which we are now writing Goupil knew him to hold at least eighty thousand francs on their property.

As to his other niece, the doctor obtained for her husband, through his influence in Paris, the collectorship of Nemours, and became his bondsman. Though Minoret-Levrault needed no assistance, Zelie, his wife, being jealous of the uncle's liberality to his two nieces, took her ten-year old son to see him, and talked of the expense he would be to them at a school in Paris, where, she said, education costs so much. The doctor obtained a half-scholarship for his great-nephew at the school of Louis-le-Grand, where Desire was put into the fourth class.

Cremiere, Massin, and Minoret-Levrault, extremely common persons, were "rated without appeal" by the doctor within two months of his arrival in Nemours, during which time they courted, less their uncle than his property. Persons who are led by instinct have one great disadvantage against others with ideas. They are quickly found out; the suggestions of instinct are too natural, too open to the eye not to be seen at a glance; whereas, the conceptions of the mind require an equal amount of intellect to discover them. After buying the gratitude of his heirs, and thus, as it were, shutting their mouths, the wily doctor made a pretext of his occupations, his habits, and the care of the little Ursula to avoid receiving his relatives without exactly closing his doors to them. He liked to dine alone; he went to bed late and he got up late; he had returned to his native place for the very purpose of finding rest in solitude. These whims of an old man seemed to be natural, and his relatives contented themselves with paying him weekly visits on Sundays from one to four o'clock, to which, however, he tried to put a stop by saying: "Don't come and see me unless you want something."

The doctor, while not refusing to be called in consultation over serious cases, especially if the patients were indigent, would not serve as a physician in the little hospital of Nemours, and declared that he no longer practiced his profession.

"I've killed enough people," he said, laughing, to the Abbe Chaperon, who, knowing his benevolence, would often get him to attend the poor.

"He's an original!" These words, said of Doctor Minoret, were the harmless revenge of various wounded vanities; for a doctor collects about him a society of persons who have many of the characteristics of a set of heirs. Those of the bourgeoisie who thought themselves entitled to visit this distinguished physician kept up a ferment of jealousy against the few privileged friends whom he did admit to his intimacy, which had in the long run some unfortunate results.

CHAPTER III.
THE DOCTOR'S FRIENDS

Curiously enough, though it explains the old proverb that "extremes meet," the materialistic doctor and the cure of Nemours were soon friends. The old man loved backgammon, a favorite game of the priesthood, and the Abbe Chaperon played it with about as much skill as he himself. The game was the first tie between them. Then Minoret was charitable, and the abbe was the Fenelon of the Gatinais. Both had had a wide and varied education; the man of God was the only person in all Nemours who was fully capable of understanding the atheist. To be able to argue, men must first understand each other. What pleasure is there in saying sharp words to one who can't feel them? The doctor and the priest had far too much taste and had seen too much of good society not to practice its precepts; they were thus well-fitted for the little warfare so essential to conversation. They hated each other's opinions, but they valued each other's character. If such conflicts and such sympathies are not true elements of intimacy we must surely despair of society, which, especially in France, requires some form of antagonism. It is from the shock of characters, and not from the struggle of opinions, that antipathies are generated.

The Abbe Chaperon became, therefore, the doctor's chief friend. This excellent ecclesiastic, then sixty years of age, had been curate of Nemours ever since the re-establishment of Catholic worship. Out of attachment to his flock he had refused the vicariat of the diocese. If those who were indifferent to religion thought well of him for so doing, the faithful loved him the more for it. So, revered by his sheep, respected by the inhabitants at large, the abbe did good without inquiring into the religious opinions of those he benefited. His parsonage, with scarcely furniture enough for the common needs of life, was cold and shabby, like the lodging of a miser. Charity and avarice manifest themselves in the same way; charity lays up a treasure in heaven which avarice lays up on earth. The Abbe Chaperon argued with his servant over expenses even more sharply than Gobseck with his—if indeed that famous Jew kept a servant at all. The good priest often sold the buckles off his shoes and his breeches to give their value to some poor person who appealed to him at a moment when he had not a penny. When he was seen coming out of church with the straps of his breeches tied into the button-holes, devout women would redeem the buckles from the clock-maker and jeweler of the town and return them to their pastor with a lecture. He never bought himself any clothes or linen, and wore his garments till they scarcely held together. His linen, thick with darns, rubbed his skin like a hair shirt. Madame de Portenduere, and other good souls, had an agreement with his housekeeper to replace the old clothes with new ones after he went to sleep, and the abbe did not always find out the difference. He ate his food off pewter with iron forks and spoons. When he received his assistants and sub-curates on days of high solemnity (an expense obligatory on the heads of parishes) he borrowed linen and silver from his friend the atheist.

"My silver is his salvation," the doctor would say.

These noble deeds, always accompanied by spiritual encouragement, were done with a beautiful naivete. Such a life was all the more meritorious because the abbe was possessed of an erudition that was vast and varied, and of great and precious faculties. Delicacy and grace, the inseparable accompaniments of simplicity, lent charm to an elocution that was worthy of a prelate. His manners, his character, and his habits gave to his intercourse with others the most exquisite savor of all that is most spiritual, most sincere in the human mind. A lover of gayety, he was never priest in a salon. Until Doctor Minoret's arrival, the good man kept his light under a bushel without regret. Owning a rather fine library and an income of two thousand francs when he came to Nemours, he now possessed, in 1829, nothing at all, except his stipend as parish priest, nearly the whole of which he gave away during the year. The giver of excellent counsel in delicate matters or in great misfortunes, many persons who never went to church to obtain consolation went to the parsonage to get advice. One little anecdote will suffice to complete his portrait. Sometimes the peasants,—rarely, it is true, but occasionally,—unprincipled men, would tell him they were sued for debt, or would get themselves threatened fictitiously to stimulate the abbe's benevolence. They would even deceive their wives, who, believing their chattels were threatened with an execution and their cows seized, deceived in their turn the poor priest with their innocent tears. He would then manage with great difficulty to provide the seven or eight hundred francs demanded of him—with which the peasant bought himself a morsel of land. When pious persons and vestrymen denounced the fraud, begging the abbe to consult them in future before lending himself to such cupidity, he would say:—

"But suppose they had done something wrong to obtain their bit of land? Isn't it doing good when we prevent evil?"

Some persons may wish for a sketch of this figure, remarkable for the fact that science and literature had filled the heart and passed through the strong head without corrupting either. At sixty years of age the abbe's hair was white as snow, so keenly did he feel the sorrows of others, and so heavily had the events of the Revolution weighed upon him. Twice incarcerated for refusing to take the oath he had twice, as he used to say, uttered in "In manus." He was of medium height, neither stout nor thin. His face, much wrinkled and hollowed and quite colorless, attracted immediate attention by the absolute tranquillity expressed in its shape, and by the purity of its outline, which seemed to be edged with light. The face of a chaste man has an unspeakable radiance. Brown eyes with lively pupils brightened the irregular features, which were surmounted by a broad forehead. His glance wielded a power which came of a gentleness that was not devoid of strength. The arches of his brow formed caverns shaded by huge gray eyebrows which alarmed no one. As most of his teeth were gone his mouth had lost its shape and his cheeks had fallen in; but this physical destruction was not without charm; even the wrinkles, full of pleasantness, seemed to smile on others. Without being gouty his feet were tender; and he walked with so much difficulty that he wore shoes made of calf's skin all the year round. He thought the fashion of trousers unsuitable for priests, and he always appeared in stockings of coarse black yarn, knit by his housekeeper, and cloth breeches. He never went out in his cassock, but wore a brown overcoat, and still retained the three-cornered hat he had worn so courageously in times of danger. This noble and beautiful old man, whose face was glorified by the serenity of a soul above reproach, will be found to have so great an influence upon the men and things of this history, that it was proper to show the sources of his authority and power.

Minoret took three newspapers,—one liberal, one ministerial, one ultra,—a few periodicals, and certain scientific journals, the accumulation of which swelled his library. The newspapers, encyclopaedias, and books were an attraction to a retired captain of the Royal-Swedish regiment, named Monsieur de Jordy, a Voltairean nobleman and an old bachelor, who lived on sixteen hundred francs of pension and annuity combined. Having read the gazettes for several days, by favor of the abbe, Monsieur de Jordy thought it proper to call and thank the doctor in person. At this first visit the old captain, formerly a professor at the Military Academy, won the doctor's heart, who returned the call with alacrity. Monsieur de Jordy, a spare little man much troubled by his blood, though his face was very pale, attracted attention by the resemblance of his handsome brow to that of Charles XII.; above it he kept his hair cropped short, like that of the soldier-king. His blue eyes seemed to say that "Love had passed that way," so mournful were they; revealing memories about which he kept such utter silence that his old friends never detected even an allusion to his past life, nor a single exclamation drawn forth by similarity of circumstances. He hid the painful mystery of his past beneath a philosophic gayety, but when he thought himself alone his motions, stiffened by a slowness which was more a matter of choice than the result of old age, betrayed the constant presence of distressful thoughts. The Abbe Chaperon called him a Christian ignorant of his Christianity. Dressed always in blue cloth, his rather rigid demeanor and his clothes bespoke the old habits of military discipline. His sweet and harmonious voice stirred the soul. His beautiful hands and the general cut of his figure, recalling that of the Comte d'Artois, showed how charming he must have been in his youth, and made the mystery of his life still more mysterious. An observer asked involuntarily what misfortune had blighted such beauty, courage, grace, accomplishment, and all the precious qualities of the heart once united in his person. Monsieur de Jordy shuddered if Robespierre's name were uttered before him. He took much snuff, but, strange to say, he gave up the habit to please little Ursula, who at first showed a dislike to him on that account. As soon as he saw the little girl the captain fastened his eyes upon her with a look that was almost passionate. He loved her play so extravagantly and took such interest in all she did that the tie between himself and the doctor grew closer every day, though the latter never dared to say to him, "You, too, have you lost children?" There are beings, kind and patient as old Jordy, who pass through life with a bitter thought in their heart and a tender but sorrowful smile on their lips, carrying with them to the grave the secret of their lives; letting no one guess it,— through pride, through disdain, possibly through revenge; confiding in none but God, without other consolation than his.

Monsieur de Jordy, like the doctor, had come to die in Nemours, but he knew no one except the abbe, who was always at the beck and call of his parishioners, and Madame de Portenduere, who went to bed at nine o'clock. So, much against his will, he too had taken to going to bed early, in spite of the thorns that beset his pillow. It was therefore a great piece of good fortune for him (as well as for the doctor) when he encountered a man who had known the same world and spoken the same language as himself; with whom he could exchange ideas, and who went to bed late. After Monsieur de Jordy, the Abbe Chaperon, and Minoret had passed one evening together they found so much pleasure in it that the priest and soldier returned every night regularly at nine o'clock, the hour at which, little Ursula having gone to bed, the doctor was free. All three would then sit up till midnight or one o'clock.

After a time this trio became a quartette. Another man to whom life was known, and who owed to his practical training as a lawyer, the indulgence, knowledge, observation, shrewdness, and talent for conversation which the soldier, doctor, and priest owed to their practical dealings with the souls, diseases, and education of men, was added to the number. Monsieur Bongrand, the justice of peace, heard of the pleasure of these evenings and sought admittance to the doctor's society. Before becoming justice of peace at Nemours he had been for ten years a solicitor at Melun, where he conducted his own cases, according to the custom of small towns, where there are no barristers. He became a widower at forty-five years of age, but felt himself still too active to lead an idle life; he therefore sought and obtained the position of justice of peace at Nemours, which became vacant a few months before the arrival of Doctor Minoret. Monsieur Bongrand lived modestly on his salary of fifteen hundred francs, in order that he might devote his private income to his son, who was studying law in Paris under the famous Derville. He bore some resemblance to a retired chief of a civil service office; he had the peculiar face of a bureaucrat, less sallow than pallid, on which public business, vexations, and disgust leave their imprint,—a face lined by thought, and also by the continual restraints familiar to those who are trained not to speak their minds freely. It was often illumined by smiles characteristic of men who alternately believe all and believe nothing, who are accustomed to see and hear all without being startled, and to fathom the abysses which self-interest hollows in the depths of the human heart.

Below the hair, which was less white than discolored, and worn flattened to the head, was a fine, sagacious forehead, the yellow tones of which harmonized well with the scanty tufts of thin hair. His face, with the features set close together, bore some likeness to that of a fox, all the more because his nose was short and pointed. In speaking, he spluttered at the mouth, which was broad like that of most great talkers,—a habit which led Goupil to say, ill-naturedly, "An umbrella would be useful when listening to him," or, "The justice rains verdicts." His eyes looked keen behind his spectacles, but if he took the glasses off his dulled glance seemed almost vacant. Though he was naturally gay, even jovial, he was apt to give himself too important and pompous an air. He usually kept his hands in the pockets of his trousers, and only took them out to settle his eye-glasses on his nose, with a movement that was half comic, and which announced the coming of a keen observation or some victorious argument. His gestures, his loquacity, his innocent self-assertion, proclaimed the provincial lawyer. These slight defects were, however, superficial; he redeemed them by an exquisite kind-heartedness which a rigid moralist might call the indulgence natural to superiority. He looked a little like a fox, and he was thought to be very wily, but never false or dishonest. His wiliness was perspicacity; and consisted in foreseeing results and protecting himself and others from the traps set for them. He loved whist, a game known to the captain and the doctor, and which the abbe learned to play in a very short time.

This little circle of friends made for itself an oasis in Mironet's salon. The doctor of Nemours, who was not without education and knowledge of the world, and who greatly respected Minoret as an honor to the profession, came there sometimes; but his duties and also his fatigue (which obliged him to go to bed early and to be up early) prevented his being as assiduously present as the three other friends. This intercourse of five superior men, the only ones in Nemours who had sufficiently wide knowledge to understand each other, explains old Minoret's aversion to his relatives; if he were compelled to leave them his money, at least he need not admit them to his society. Whether the post master, the sheriff, and the collector understood this distinction, or whether they were reassured by the evident loyalty and benefactions of their uncle, certain it is that they ceased, to his great satisfaction, to see much of him. So, about eight months after the arrival of the doctor these four players of whist and backgammon made a solid and exclusive little world which was to each a fraternal aftermath, an unlooked for fine season, the gentle pleasures of which were the more enjoyed. This little circle of choice spirits closed round Ursula, a child whom each adopted according to his individual tendencies; the abbe thought of her soul, the judge imagined himself her guardian, the soldier intended to be her teacher, and as for Minoret, he was father, mother, and physician, all in one.

After he became acclimated old Minoret settled into certain habits of life, under fixed rules, after the manner of the provinces. On Ursula's account he received no visitors in the morning, and never gave dinners, but his friends were at liberty to come to his house at six o'clock and stay till midnight. The first-comers found the newspapers on the table and read them while awaiting the rest; or they sometimes sallied forth to meet the doctor if he were out for a walk. This tranquil life was not a mere necessity of old age, it was the wise and careful scheme of a man of the world to keep his happiness untroubled by the curiosity of his heirs and the gossip of a little town. He yielded nothing to that capricious goddess, public opinion, whose tyranny (one of the present great evils of France) was just beginning to establish its power and to make the whole nation a mere province. So, as soon as the child was weaned and could walk alone, the doctor sent away the housekeeper whom his niece, Madame Minoret-Levrault had chosen for him, having discovered that she told her patroness everything that happened in his household.

Ursula's nurse, the widow of a poor workman (who possessed no name but a baptismal one, and who came from Bougival) had lost her last child, aged six months, just as the doctor, who knew her to be a good and honest creature, engaged her as wetnurse for Ursula. Antoinette Patris (her maiden name), widow of Pierre, called Le Bougival, attached herself naturally to Ursula, as wetmaids do to their nurslings. This blind maternal affection was accompanied in this instance by household devotion. Told of the doctor's intention to send away his housekeeper, La Bougival secretly learned to cook, became neat and handy, and discovered the old man's ways. She took the utmost care of the house and furniture; in short she was indefatigable. Not only did the doctor wish to keep his private life within four walls, as the saying is, but he also had certain reasons for hiding a knowledge of his business affairs from his relatives. At the end of the second year after his arrival La Bougival was the only servant in the house; on her discretion he knew he could count, and he disguised his real purposes by the all-powerful open reason of a necessary economy. To the great satisfaction of his heirs he became a miser. Without fawning or wheedling, solely by the influence of her devotion and solicitude, La Bougival, who was forty-three years old at the time this tale begins, was the housekeeper of the doctor and his protegee, the pivot on which the whole house turned, in short, the confidential servant. She was called La Bougival from the admitted impossibility of applying to her person the name that actually belonged to her, Antoinette—for names and forms do obey the laws of harmony.

The doctor's miserliness was not mere talk; it was real, and it had an object. From the year 1817 he cut off two of his newspapers and ceased subscribing to periodicals. His annual expenses, which all Nemours could estimate, did not exceed eighteen hundred francs a year. Like most old men his wants in linen, boots, and clothing, were very few. Every six months he went to Paris, no doubt to draw and reinvest his income. In fifteen years he never said a single word to any one in relation to his affairs. His confidence in Bongrand was of slow growth; it was not until after the revolution of 1830 that he told him of his projects. Nothing further was known of the doctor's life either by the bourgeoisie at large or by his heirs. As for his political opinions, he did not meddle in public matters seeing that he paid less than a hundred francs a year in taxes, and refused, impartially, to subscribe to either royalist or liberal demands. His known horror for the priesthood, and his deism were so little obtrusive that he turned out of his house a commercial runner sent by his great-nephew Desire to ask a subscription to the "Cure Meslier" and the "Discours du General Foy." Such tolerance seemed inexplicable to the liberals of Nemours.

The doctor's three collateral heirs, Minoret-Levrault and his wife, Monsieur and Madame Massin-Levrault, junior, Monsieur and Madame Cremiere-Cremiere—whom we shall in future call simply Cremiere, Massin, and Minoret, because these distinctions among homonyms is quite unnecessary out of the Gatinais—met together as people do in little towns. The post master gave a grand dinner on his son's birthday, a ball during the carnival, another on the anniversary of his marriage, to all of which he invited the whole bourgeoisie of Nemours. The collector received his relations and friends twice a year. The clerk of the court, too poor, he said, to fling himself into such extravagance, lived in a small way in a house standing half-way down the Grand'Rue, the ground-floor of which was let to his sister, the letter-postmistress of Nemours, a situation she owed to the doctor's kind offices. Nevertheless, in the course of the year these three families did meet together frequently, in the houses of friends, in the public promenades, at the market, on their doorsteps, or, of a Sunday in the square, as on this occasion; so that one way and another they met nearly every day. For the last three years the doctor's age, his economies, and his probable wealth had led to allusions, or frank remarks, among the townspeople as to the disposition of his property, a topic which made the doctor and his heirs of deep interest to the little town. For the last six months not a day passed that friends and neighbours did not speak to the heirs, with secret envy, of the day the good man's eyes would shut and the coffers open.

"Doctor Minoret may be an able physician, on good terms with death, but none but God is eternal," said one.

"Pooh, he'll bury us all; his health is better than ours," replied an heir, hypocritically.

"Well, if you don't get the money yourselves, your children will, unless that little Ursula—"

"He won't leave it all to her."

Ursula, as Madame Massin had predicted, was the bete noire of the relations, their sword of Damocles; and Madame Cremiere's favorite saying, "Well, whoever lives will know," shows that they wished at any rate more harm to her than good.

The collector and the clerk of the court, poor in comparison with the post master, had often estimated, by way of conversation, the doctor's property. If they met their uncle walking on the banks of the canal or along the road they would look at each other piteously.

"He must have got hold of some elixir of life," said one.

"He has made a bargain with the devil," replied the other.

"He ought to give us the bulk of it; that fat Minoret doesn't need anything," said Massin.

"Ah! but Minoret has a son who'll waste his substance," answered Cremiere.

"How much do you really think the doctor has?"

"At the end of twelve years, say twelve thousand francs saved each year, that would give one hundred and forty-four thousand francs, and the interest brings in at least one hundred thousand more. But as he must, if he consults a notary in Paris, have made some good strokes of business, and we know that up to 1822 he could get seven or eight per cent from the State, he must now have at least four hundred thousand francs, without counting the capital of his fourteen thousand a year from the five per cents. If he were to die to-morrow without leaving anything to Ursula we should get at least seven or eight hundred thousand francs, besides the house and furniture."

"Well, a hundred thousand to Minoret, and three hundred thousand apiece to you and me, that would be fair."

"Ha, that would make us comfortable!"

"If he did that," said Massin, "I should sell my situation in court and buy an estate; I'd try to be judge at Fontainebleau, and get myself elected deputy."

"As for me I should buy a brokerage business," said the collector.

"Unluckily, that girl he has on his arm and the abbe have got round him. I don't believe we can do anything with him."

"Still, we know very well he will never leave anything to the Church."

CHAPTER IV.
ZELIE

The fright of the heirs at beholding their uncle on his way to mass will now be understood. The dullest persons have mind enough to foresee a danger to self-interests. Self-interest constitutes the mind of the peasant as well as that of the diplomatist, and on that ground the stupidest of men is sometimes the most powerful. So the fatal reasoning, "If that little Ursula has influence enough to drag her godfather into the pale of the Church she will certainly have enough to make him leave her his property," was now stamped in letters of fire on the brains of the most obtuse heir. The post master had forgotten about his son in his hurry to reach the square; for if the doctor were really in the church hearing mass it was a question of losing two hundred and fifty thousand francs. It must be admitted that the fears of these relations came from the strongest and most legitimate of social feelings, family interests.

"Well, Monsieur Minoret," said the mayor (formerly a miller who had now become royalist, named Levrault-Cremiere), "when the devil gets old the devil a monk would be. Your uncle, they say, is one of us."

"Better late than never, cousin," responded the post master, trying to conceal his annoyance.

"How that fellow will grin if we are defrauded! He is capable of marrying his son to that damned girl—may the devil get her!" cried Cremiere, shaking his fists at the mayor as he entered the porch.

"What's Cremiere grumbling about?" said the butcher of the town, a Levrault-Levrault the elder. "Isn't he pleased to see his uncle on the road to paradise?"

"Who would ever have believed it!" ejaculated Massin.

"Ha! one should never say, 'Fountain, I'll not drink of your water,'" remarked the notary, who, seeing the group from afar, had left his wife to go to church without him.

"Come, Monsieur Dionis," said Cremiere, taking the notary by the arm, "what do you advise me to do under the circumstances?"

"I advise you," said the notary, addressing the heirs collectively, "to go to bed and get up at your usual hour; to eat your soup before it gets cold; to put your feet in your shoes and your hats on your heads; in short, to continue your ways of life precisely as if nothing had happened."

"You are not consoling," said Massin.

In spite of his squat, dumpy figure and heavy face, Cremiere-Dionis was really as keen as a blade. In pursuit of usurious fortune he did business secretly with Massin, to whom he no doubt pointed out such peasants as were hampered in means, and such pieces of land as could be bought for a song. The two men were in a position to choose their opportunities; none that were good escaped them, and they shared the profits of mortgage-usury, which retards, though it does not prevent, the acquirement of the soil by the peasantry. So Dionis took a lively interest in the doctor's inheritance, not so much for the post master and the collector as for his friend the clerk of the court; sooner or later Massin's share in the doctor's money would swell the capital with which these secret associates worked the canton.

"We must try to find out through Monsieur Bongrand where the influence comes from," said the notary in a low voice, with a sign to Massin to keep quiet.

"What are you about, Minoret?" cried a little woman, suddenly descending upon the group in the middle of which stood the post master, as tall and round as a tower. "You don't know where Desire is and there you are, planted on your two legs, gossiping about nothing, when I thought you on horseback!—Oh, good morning, Messieurs and Mesdames."

This little woman, thin, pale, and fair, dressed in a gown of white cotton with pattern of large, chocolate-colored flowers, a cap trimmed with ribbon and frilled with lace, and wearing a small green shawl on her flat shoulders, was Minoret's wife, the terror of postilions, servants, and carters; who kept the accounts and managed the establishment "with finger and eye" as they say in those parts. Like the true housekeeper that she was, she wore no ornaments. She did not give in (to use her own expression) to gew-gaws and trumpery; she held to the solid and the substantial, and wore, even on Sundays, a black apron, in the pocket of which she jingled her household keys. Her screeching voice was agony to the drums of all ears. Her rigid glance, conflicting with the soft blue of her eyes, was in visible harmony with the thin lips of a pinched mouth and a high, projecting, and very imperious forehead. Sharp was the glance, sharper still both gesture and speech. "Zelie being obliged to have a will for two, had it for three," said Goupil, who pointed out the successive reigns of three young postilions, of neat appearance, who had been set up in life by Zelie, each after seven years' service. The malicious clerk named them Postilion I., Postilion II., Postilion III. But the little influence these young men had in the establishment, and their perfect obedience proved that Zelie was merely interested in worthy helpers.

This attempt at scandal was against probabilities. Since the birth of her son (nursed by her without any evidence of how it was possible for her to do so)

Madame Minoret had thought only of increasing the family fortune and was wholly given up to the management of their immense establishment. To steal a bale of hay or a bushel of oats or get the better of Zelie in even the most complicated accounts was a thing impossible, though she scribbled hardly better than a cat, and knew nothing of arithmetic but addition and subtraction. She never took a walk except to look at the hay, the oats, or the second crops. She sent "her man" to the mowing, and the postilions to tie the bales, telling them the quantity, within a hundred pounds, each field should bear. Though she was the soul of that great body called Minoret-Levrault and led him about by his pug nose, she was made to feel the fears which occasionally (we are told) assail all tamers of wild beasts. She therefore made it a rule to get into a rage before he did; the postilions knew very well when his wife had been quarreling with him, for his anger ricocheted on them. Madame Minoret was as clever as she was grasping; and it was a favorite remark in the whole town, "Where would Minoret-Levrault be without his wife?"

"When you know what has happened," replied the post master, "you'll be over the traces yourself."

"What is it?"

"Ursula has taken the doctor to mass."

Zelie's pupils dilated; she stood for a moment yellow with anger, then, crying out, "I'll see it before I believe it!" she rushed into the church. The service had reached the Elevation. The stillness of the worshippers enabled her to look along each row of chairs and benches as she went up the aisle beside the chapels to Ursula's place, where she saw old Minoret standing with bared head.

If you recall the heads of Barbe-Marbois, Boissy d'Anglas, Morellet, Helvetius, or Frederick the Great, you will see the exact image of Doctor Minoret, whose green old age resembled that of those celebrated personages. Their heads coined in the same mint (for each had the characteristics of a medal) showed a stern and quasi-puritan profile, cold tones, a mathematical brain, a certain narrowness about the features, shrewd eyes, grave lips, and a something that was surely aristocratic—less perhaps in sentiment than in habit, more in the ideas than in the character. All men of this stamp have high brows retreating at the summit, the sign of a tendency to materialism. You will find these leading characteristics of the head and these points of the face in all the Encyclopedists, in the orators of the Gironde, in the men of a period when religious ideas were almost dead, men who called themselves deists and were atheists. The deist is an atheist lucky in classification.

Minoret had a forehead of this description, furrowed with wrinkles, which recovered in his old age a sort of artless candor from the manner in which the silvery hair, brushed back like that of a woman when making her toilet, curled in light flakes upon the blackness of his coat. He persisted in dressing, as in his youth, in black silk stockings, shoes with gold buckles, breeches of black poult-de-soie, and a black coat, adorned with the red rosette. This head, so firmly characterized, the cold whiteness of which was softened by the yellowing tones of old age, happened to be, just then, in the full light of a window. As Madame Minoret came in sight of him the doctor's blue eyes with their reddened lids were raised to heaven; a new conviction had given them a new expression. His spectacles lay in his prayer-book and marked the place where he had ceased to pray. The tall and spare old man, his arms crossed on his breast, stood erect in an attitude which bespoke the full strength of his faculties and the unshakable assurance of his faith. He gazed at the altar humbly with a look of renewed hope, and took no notice of his nephew's wife, who planted herself almost in front of him as if to reproach him for coming back to God.

Zelie, seeing all eyes turned upon her, made haste to leave the church and returned to the square less hurriedly than she had left it. She had reckoned on the doctor's money, and possession was becoming problematical. She found the clerk of the court, the collector, and their wives in greater consternation than ever. Goupil was taking pleasure in tormenting them.

"It is not in the public square and before the whole town that we ought to talk of our affairs," said Zelie; "come home with me. You too, Monsieur Dionis," she added to the notary; "you'll not be in the way."

Thus the probable disinheritance of Massin, Cremiere, and the post master was the news of the day.

Just as the heirs and the notary were crossing the square to go to the post house the noise of the diligence rattling up to the office, which was only a few steps from the church, at the top of the Grand'Rue, made its usual racket.

"Goodness! I'm like you, Minoret; I forgot all about Desire," said Zelie. "Let us go and see him get down. He is almost a lawyer; and his interests are mixed up in this matter."

The arrival of the diligence is always an amusement, but when it comes in late some unusual event is expected. The crowd now moved towards the "Ducler."

"Here's Desire!" was the general cry.

The tyrant, and yet the life and soul of Nemours, Desire always put the town in a ferment when he came. Loved by the young men, with whom he was invariably generous, he stimulated them by his very presence. But his methods of amusement were so dreaded by older persons that more than one family was very thankful to have him complete his studies and study law in Paris. Desire Minoret, a slight youth, slender and fair like his mother, from whom he obtained his blue eyes and pale skin, smiled from the window on the crowd, and jumped lightly down to kiss his mother. A short sketch of the young fellow will show how proud Zelie felt when she saw him.

He wore very elegant boots, trousers of white English drilling held under his feet by straps of varnished leather, a rich cravat, admirably put on and still more admirably fastened, a pretty fancy waistcoat, in the pocket of said waistcoat a flat watch, the chain of which hung down; and, finally, a short frock-coat of blue cloth, and a gray hat,—but his lack of the manner-born was shown in the gilt buttons of the waistcoat and the ring worn outside of his purple kid glove. He carried a cane with a chased gold head.

"You are losing your watch," said his mother, kissing him.

"No, it is worn that way," he replied, letting his father hug him.

"Well, cousin, so we shall soon see you a lawyer?" said Massin.

"I shall take the oaths at the beginning of next term," said Desire, returning the friendly nods he was receiving on all sides.

"Now we shall have some fun," said Goupil, shaking him by the hand.

"Ha! my old wag, so here you are!" replied Desire.

"You take your law license for all license," said Goupil, affronted by being treated so cavalierly in presence of others.

"You know my luggage," cried Desire to the red-faced old conductor of the diligence; "have it taken to the house."

"The sweat is rolling off your horses," said Zelie sharply to the conductor; "you haven't common-sense to drive them in that way. You are stupider than your own beasts."

"But Monsieur Desire was in a hurry to get here to save you from anxiety," explained Cabirolle.

"But if there was no accident why risk killing the horses?" she retorted.

The greetings of friends and acquaintances, the crowding of the young men around Desire, and the relating of the incidents of the journey took enough time for the mass to be concluded and the worshippers to issue from the church. By mere chance (which manages many things) Desire saw Ursula on the porch as he passed along, and he stopped short amazed at her beauty. His action also stopped the advance of the relations who accompanied him.

In giving her arm to her godfather, Ursula was obliged to hold her prayer-book in one hand and her parasol in the other; and this she did with the innate grace which graceful women put into the awkward or difficult things of their charming craft of womanhood. If mind does truly reveal itself in all things, we may be permitted to say that Ursula's attitude and bearing suggested divine simplicity. She was dressed in a white cambric gown made like a wrapper, trimmed here and there with knots of blue ribbon. The pelerine, edged with the same ribbon run through a broad hem and tied with bows like those on the dress, showed the great beauty of her shape. Her throat, of a pure white, was charming in tone against the blue,—the right color for a fair skin. A long blue sash with floating ends defined a slender waist which seemed flexible,—a most seductive charm in women. She wore a rice-straw bonnet, modestly trimmed with ribbons like those of the gown, the strings of which were tied under her chin, setting off the whiteness of the straw and doing no despite to that of her beautiful complexion. Ursula dressed her own hair naturally (a la Berthe, as it was then called) in heavy braids of fine, fair hair, laid flat on either side of the head, each little strand reflecting the light as she walked. Her gray eyes, soft and proud at the same time, were in harmony with a finely modeled brow. A rosy tinge, suffusing her cheeks like a cloud, brightened a face which was regular without being insipid; for nature had given her, by some rare privilege, extreme purity of form combined with strength of countenance. The nobility of her life was manifest in the general expression of her person, which might have served as a model for a type of trustfulness, or of modesty. Her health, though brilliant, was not coarsely apparent; in fact, her whole air was distinguished. Beneath the little gloves of a light color it was easy to imagine her pretty hands. The arched and slender feet were delicately shod in bronzed kid boots trimmed with a brown silk fringe. Her blue sash holding at the waist a small flat watch and a blue purse with gilt tassels attracted the eyes of every woman she met.

"He has given her a new watch!" said Madame Cremiere, pinching her husband's arm.

"Heavens! is that Ursula?" cried Desire; "I didn't recognize her."

"Well, my dear uncle," said the post master, addressing the doctor and pointing to the whole population drawn up in parallel hedges to let the doctor pass, "everybody wants to see you."

"Was it the Abbe Chaperon or Mademoiselle Ursula who converted you, uncle," said Massin, bowing to the doctor and his protegee, with Jesuitical humility.

"Ursula," replied the doctor, laconically, continuing to walk on as if annoyed.

The night before, as the old man finished his game of whist with Ursula, the Nemours doctor, and Bongrand, he remarked, "I intend to go to church to-morrow."

"Then," said Bongrand, "your heirs won't get another night's rest."

The speech was superfluous, however, for a single glance sufficed the sagacious and clear-sighted doctor to read the minds of his heirs by the expression of their faces. Zelie's irruption into the church, her glance, which the doctor intercepted, this meeting of all the expectant ones in the public square, and the expression in their eyes as they turned them on Ursula, all proved to him their hatred, now freshly awakened, and their sordid fears.

"It is a feather in your cap, Mademoiselle," said Madame Cremiere, putting in her word with a humble bow,—"a miracle which will not cost you much."

"It is God's doing, madame," replied Ursula.

"God!" exclaimed Minoret-Levrault; "my father-in-law used to say he served to blanket many horses."

"Your father-in-law had the mind of a jockey," said the doctor severely.

"Come," said Minoret to his wife and son, "why don't you bow to my uncle?"

"I shouldn't be mistress of myself before that little hypocrite," cried Zelie, carrying off her son.

"I advise you, uncle, not to go to mass without a velvet cap," said Madame Massin; "the church is very damp."

"Pooh, niece," said the doctor, looking round on the assembly, "the sooner I'm put to bed the sooner you'll flourish."

He walked on quickly, drawing Ursula with him, and seemed in such a hurry that the others dropped behind.

"Why do you say such harsh things to them? it isn't right," said Ursula, shaking his arm in a coaxing way.

"I shall always hate hypocrites, as much after as before I became religious. I have done good to them all, and I asked no gratitude; but not one of my relatives sent you a flower on your birthday, which they know is the only day I celebrate."

At some distance behind the doctor and Ursula came Madame de Portenduere, dragging herself along as if overcome with trouble. She belonged to the class of old women whose dress recalls the style of the last century. They wear puce-colored gowns with flat sleeves, the cut of which can be seen in the portraits of Madame Lebrun; they all have black lace mantles and bonnets of a shape gone by, in keeping with their slow and dignified deportment; one might almost fancy that they still wore paniers under their petticoats or felt them there, as persons who have lost a leg are said to fancy that the foot is moving. They swathe their heads in old lace which declines to drape gracefully about their cheeks. Their wan and elongated faces, their haggard eyes and faded brows, are not without a certain melancholy grace, in spite of the false fronts with flattened curls to which they cling,—and yet these ruins are all subordinate to an unspeakable dignity of look and manner.

The red and wrinkled eyes of this old lady showed plainly that she had been crying during the service. She walked like a person in trouble, seemed to be expecting some one, and looked behind her from time to time. Now, the fact of Madame de Portenduere looking behind her was really as remarkable in its way as the conversion of Doctor Minoret.

"Who can Madame de Portenduere be looking for?" said Madame Massin, rejoining the other heirs, who were for the moment struck dumb by the doctor's answer.

"For the cure," said Dionis, the notary, suddenly striking his forehead as if some forgotten thought or memory had occurred to him. "I have an idea! I'll save your inheritance! Let us go and breakfast gayly with Madame Minoret."

We can well imagine the alacrity with which the heirs followed the notary to the post house. Goupil, who accompanied his friend Desire, locked arm in arm with him, whispered something in the youth's ear with an odious smile.

"What do I care?" answered the son of the house, shrugging his shoulders. "I am madly in love with Florine, the most celestial creature in the world."

"Florine! and who may she be?" demanded Goupil. "I'm too fond of you to let you make a goose of yourself wish such creatures."

"Florine is the idol of the famous Nathan; my passion is wasted, I know that. She has positively refused to marry me."

"Sometimes those girls who are fools with their bodies are wise with their heads," responded Goupil.

"If you could but see her—only once," said Desire, lackadaisically, "you wouldn't say such things."

"If I saw you throwing away your whole future for nothing better than a fancy," said Goupil, with a warmth which might even have deceived his master, "I would break your doll as Varney served Amy Robsart in 'Kenilworth.' Your wife must be a d'Aiglement or a Mademoiselle du Rouvre, and get you made a deputy. My future depends on yours, and I sha'n't let you commit any follies."

"I am rich enough to care only for happiness," replied Desire.

"What are you two plotting together?" cried Zelie, beckoning to the two friends, who were standing in the middle of the courtyard, to come into the house.

The doctor disappeared into the Rue des Bourgeois with the activity of a young man, and soon reached his own house, where strange events had lately taken place, the visible results of which now filled the minds of the whole community of Nemours. A few explanations are needed to make this history and the notary's remark to the heirs perfectly intelligible to the reader.

CHAPTER V.
URSULA

The father-in-law of Doctor Minoret, the famous harpsichordist and maker of instruments, Valentin Mirouet, also one of our most celebrated organists, died in 1785 leaving a natural son, the child of his old age, whom he acknowledged and called by his own name, but who turned out a worthless fellow. He was deprived on his death bed of the comfort of seeing this petted son. Joseph Mirouet, a singer and composer, having made his debut at the Italian opera under a feigned name, ran away with a young lady in Germany. The dying father commended the young man, who was really full of talent, to his son-in-law, proving to him, at the same time, that he had refused to marry the mother that he might not injure Madame Minoret. The doctor promised to give the unfortunate Joseph half of whatever his wife inherited from her father, whose business was purchased by the Erards. He made due search for his illegitimate brother-in-law; but Grimm informed him one day that after enlisting in a Prussian regiment Joseph had deserted and taken a false name and that all efforts to find him would be frustrated.

Joseph Mirouet, gifted by nature with a delightful voice, a fine figure, a handsome face, and being moreover a composer of great taste and much brilliancy, led for over fifteen years the Bohemian life which Hoffman has so well described. So, by the time he was forty, he was reduced to such depths of poverty that he took advantage of the events of 1806 to make himself once more a Frenchman. He settled in Hamburg, where he married the daughter of a bourgeois, a girl devoted to music, who fell in love with the singer (whose fame was ever prospective) and chose to devote her life to him. But after fifteen years of Bohemia, Joseph Mirouet was unable to bear prosperity; he was naturally a spendthrift, and though kind to his wife, he wasted her fortune in a very few years. The household must have dragged on a wretched existence before Joseph Mirouet reached the point of enlisting as a musician in a French regiment. In 1813 the surgeon-major of the regiment, by the merest chance, heard the name of Mirouet, was struck by it, and wrote to Doctor Minoret, to whom he was under obligations.

The answer was not long in coming. As a result, in 1814, before the allied occupation, Joseph Mirouet had a home in Paris, where his wife died giving birth to a little girl, whom the doctor desired should be called Ursula after his wife. The father did not long survive the mother, worn out, as she was, by hardship and poverty. When dying the unfortunate musician bequeathed his daughter to the doctor, who was already her godfather, in spite of his repugnance for what he called the mummeries of the Church. Having seen his own children die in succession either in dangerous confinements or during the first year of their lives, the doctor had awaited with anxiety the result of a last hope. When a nervous, delicate, and sickly woman begins with a miscarriage it is not unusual to see her go through a series of such pregnancies as Ursula Minoret did, in spite of the care and watchfulness and science of her husband. The poor man often blamed himself for their mutual persistence in desiring children. The last child, born after a rest of nearly two years, died in 1792, a victim of its mother's nervous condition—if we listen to physiologists, who tell us that in the inexplicable phenomenon of generation the child derives from the father by blood and from the mother in its nervous system.

Compelled to renounce the joys of a feeling all powerful within him, the doctor turned to benevolence as a substitute for his denied paternity. During his married life, thus cruelly disappointed, he had longed more especially for a fair little daughter, a flower to bring joy to the house; he therefore gladly accepted Joseph Mirouet's legacy, and gave to the orphan all the hopes of his vanished dreams. For two years he took part, as Cato for Pompey, in the most minute particulars of Ursula's life; he would not allow the nurse to suckle her or to take her up or put her to bed without him. His medical science and his experience were all put to use in her service. After going through many trials, alternations of hope and fear, and the joys and labors of a mother, he had the happiness of seeing this child of the fair German woman and the French singer a creature of vigorous health and profound sensibility.

With all the eager feelings of a mother the happy old man watched the growth of the pretty hair, first down, then silk, at last hair, fine and soft and clinging to the fingers that caressed it. He often kissed the little naked feet the toes of which, covered with a pellicle through which the blood was seen, were like rosebuds. He was passionately fond of the child. When she tried to speak, or when she fixed her beautiful blue eyes upon some object with that serious, reflective look which seems the dawn of thought, and which she ended with a laugh, he would stay by her side for hours, seeking, with Jordy's help, to understand the reasons (which most people call caprices) underlying the phenomena of this delicious phase of life, when childhood is both flower and fruit, a confused intelligence, a perpetual movement, a powerful desire.

Ursula's beauty and gentleness made her so dear to the doctor that he would have liked to change the laws of nature in her behalf. He declared to old Jordy that his teeth ached when Ursula was cutting hers. When old men love children there is no limit to their passion—they worship them. For these little beings they silence their own manias or recall a whole past in their service. Experience, patience, sympathy, the acquisitions of life, treasures laboriously amassed, all are spent upon that young life in which they live again; their intelligence does actually take the place of motherhood. Their wisdom, ever on the alert, is equal to the intuition of a mother; they remember the delicate perceptions which in their own mother were divinations, and import them into the exercise of a compassion which is carried to an extreme in their minds by a sense of the child's unutterable weakness. The slowness of their movements takes the place of maternal gentleness. In them, as in children, life is reduced to its simplest expression; if maternal sentiment makes the mother a slave, the abandonment of self allows an old man to devote himself utterly. For these reasons it is not unusual to see children in close intimacy with old persons. The old soldier, the old abbe, the old doctor, happy in the kisses and cajoleries of little Ursula, were never weary of answering her talk and playing with her. Far from making them impatient her petulances charmed them; and they gratified all her wishes, making each the ground of some little training.

The child grew up surrounded by old men, who smiled at her and made themselves mothers for her sake, all three equally attentive and provident. Thanks to this wise education, Ursula's soul developed in a sphere that suited it. This rare plant found its special soil; it breathed the elements of its true life and assimilated the sun rays that belonged to it.

"In what faith do you intend to bring up the little one?" asked the abbe of the doctor, when Ursula was six years old.

"In yours," answered Minoret.

An atheist after the manner of Monsieur Wolmar in the "Nouvelle Heloise" he did not claim the right to deprive Ursula of the benefits offered by the Catholic religion. The doctor, sitting at the moment on a bench outside the Chinese pagoda, felt the pressure of the abbe's hand on his.

"Yes, abbe, every time she talks to me of God I shall send her to her friend 'Shapron,'" he said, imitating Ursula's infant speech, "I wish to see whether religious sentiment is inborn or not. Therefore I shall do nothing either for or against the tendencies of that young soul; but in my heart I have appointed you her spiritual guardian."

"God will reward you, I hope," replied the abbe, gently joining his hands and raising them towards heaven as if he were making a brief mental prayer.

So, from the time she was six years old the little orphan lived under the religious influence of the abbe, just as she had already come under the educational training of her friend Jordy.

The captain, formerly a professor in a military academy, having a taste for grammar and for the differences among European languages, had studied the problem of a universal tongue. This learned man, patient as most old scholars are, delighted in teaching Ursula to read and write. He taught her also the French language and all she needed to know of arithmetic. The doctor's library afforded a choice of books which could be read by a child for amusement as well as instruction.

The abbe and the soldier allowed the young mind to enrich itself with the freedom and comfort which the doctor gave to the body. Ursula learned as she played. Religion was given with due reflection. Left to follow the divine training of a nature that was led into regions of purity by these judicious educators, Ursula inclined more to sentiment than to duty; she took as her rule of conduct the voice of her own conscience rather than the demands of social law. In her, nobility of feeling and action would ever be spontaneous; her judgment would confirm the impulse of her heart. She was destined to do right as a pleasure before doing it as an obligation. This distinction is the peculiar sign of Christian education. These principles, altogether different from those that are taught to men, were suitable for a woman,—the spirit and the conscience of the home, the beautifier of domestic life, the queen of her household. All three of these old preceptors followed the same method with Ursula. Instead of recoiling before the bold questions of innocence, they explained to her the reasons of things and the best means of action, taking care to give her none but correct ideas. When, apropos of a flower, a star, a blade of grass, her thoughts went straight to God, the doctor and the professor told her that the priest alone could answer her. None of them intruded on the territory of the others; the doctor took charge of her material well-being and the things of life; Jordy's department was instruction; moral and spiritual questions and the ideas appertaining to the higher life belonged to the abbe. This noble education was not, as it often is, counteracted by injudicious servants. La Bougival, having been lectured on the subject, and being, moreover, too simple in mind and character to interfere, did nothing to injure the work of these great minds. Ursula, a privileged being, grew up with good geniuses round her; and her naturally fine disposition made the task of each a sweet and easy one. Such manly tenderness, such gravity lighted by smiles, such liberty without danger, such perpetual care of soul and body made little Ursula, when nine years of age, a well-trained child and delightful to behold.

Unhappily, this paternal trinity was broken up. The old captain died the following year, leaving the abbe and the doctor to finish his work, of which, however, he had accomplished the most difficult part. Flowers will bloom of themselves if grown in a soil thus prepared. The old gentleman had laid by for ten years past one thousand francs a year, that he might leave ten thousand to his little Ursula, and keep a place in her memory during her whole life. In his will, the wording of which was very touching, he begged his legatee to spend the four or five hundred francs that came of her little capital exclusively on her dress. When the justice of the peace applied the seals to the effects of his old friend, they found in a small room, which the captain had allowed no one to enter, a quantity of toys, many of them broken, while all had been used,—toys of a past generation, reverently preserved, which Monsieur Bongrand was, according to the captain's last wishes, to burn with his own hands.

About this time it was that Ursula made her first communion. The abbe employed one whole year in duly instructing the young girl, whose mind and heart, each well developed, yet judiciously balancing one another, needed a special spiritual nourishment. The initiation into a knowledge of divine things which he gave her was such that Ursula grew into the pious and mystical young girl whose character rose above all vicissitudes, and whose heart was enabled to conquer adversity. Then began a secret struggle between the old man wedded to unbelief and the young girl full of faith,— long unsuspected by her who incited it,—the result of which had now stirred the whole town, and was destined to have great influence on Ursula's future by rousing against her the antagonism of the doctor's heirs.

During the first six months of the year 1824 Ursula spent all her mornings at the parsonage. The old doctor guessed the abbe's secret hope. He meant to make Ursula an unanswerable argument against him. The old unbeliever, loved by his godchild as though she were his own daughter, would surely believe in such artless candor; he could not fail to be persuaded by the beautiful effects of religion on the soul of a child, where love was like those trees of Eastern climes, bearing both flowers and fruit, always fragrant, always fertile. A beautiful life is more powerful than the strongest argument. It is impossible to resist the charms of certain sights. The doctor's eyes were wet, he knew not how or why, when he saw the child of his heart starting for the church, wearing a frock of white crape, and shoes of white satin; her hair bound with a fillet fastened at the side with a knot of white ribbon, and rippling upon her shoulders; her eyes lighted by the star of a first hope; hurrying, tall and beautiful, to a first union, and loving her godfather better since her soul had risen towards God. When the doctor perceived that the thought of immortality was nourishing that spirit (until then within the confines of childhood) as the sun gives life to the earth without knowing why, he felt sorry that he remained at home alone.

Sitting on the steps of his portico he kept his eyes fixed on the iron railing of the gate through which the child had disappeared, saying as she left him: "Why won't you come, godfather? how can I be happy without you?" Though shaken to his very center, the pride of the Encyclopedist did not as yet give way. He walked slowly in a direction from which he could see the procession of communicants, and distinguish his little Ursula brilliant with exaltation beneath her veil. She gave him an inspired look, which knocked, in the stony regions of his heart, on the corner closed to God. But still the old deist held firm. He said to himself: "Mummeries! if there be a maker of worlds, imagine the organizer of infinitude concerning himself with such trifles!" He laughed as he continued his walk along the heights which look down upon the road to the Gatinais, where the bells were ringing a joyous peal that told of the joy of families.

The noise of backgammon is intolerable to persons who do not know the game, which is really one of the most difficult that was ever invented. Not to annoy his godchild, the extreme delicacy of whose organs and nerves could not bear, he thought, without injury the noise and the exclamations she did not know the meaning of, the abbe, old Jordy while living, and the doctor always waited till their child was in bed before they began their favorite game. Sometimes the visitors came early when she was out for a walk, and the game would be going on when she returned; then she resigned herself with infinite grace and took her seat at the window with her work. She had a repugnance to the game, which is really in the beginning very hard and unconquerable to some minds, so that unless it be learned in youth it is almost impossible to take it up in after life.

The night of her first communion, when Ursula came into the salon where her godfather was sitting alone, she put the backgammon-board before him.

"Whose throw shall it be?" she asked.

"Ursula," said the doctor, "isn't it a sin to make fun of your godfather the day of your first communion?"

"I am not making fun of you," she said, sitting down. "I want to give you some pleasure—you who are always on the look-out for mine. When Monsieur Chaperon was pleased with me he gave me a lesson in backgammon, and he has given me so many that now I am quite strong enough to beat you—you shall not deprive yourself any longer for me. I have conquered all difficulties, and now I like the noise of the game."

Ursula won. The abbe had slipped in to enjoy his triumph. The next day Minoret, who had always refused to let Ursula learn music, sent to Paris for a piano, made arrangements at Fontainebleau for a teacher, and submitted to the annoyance that her constant practicing was to him. One of poor Jordy's predictions was fulfilled,—the girl became an excellent musician. The doctor, proud of her talent, had lately sent to Paris for a master, an old German named Schmucke, a distinguished professor who came once a week; the doctor willingly paying for an art which he had formerly declared to be useless in a household. Unbelievers do not like music—a celestial language, developed by Catholicism, which has taken the names of the seven notes from one of the church hymns; every note being the first syllable of the seven first lines in the hymn to Saint John.

The impression produced on the doctor by Ursula's first communion though keen was not lasting. The calm and sweet contentment which prayer and the exercise of resolution produced in that young soul had not their due influence upon him. Having no reasons for remorse or repentance himself, he enjoyed a serene peace. Doing his own benefactions without hope of a celestial harvest, he thought himself on a nobler plane than religious men whom he always accused for making, as he called it, terms with God.

"But," the abbe would say to him, "if all men would be so, you must admit that society would be regenerated; there would be no more misery. To be benevolent after your fashion one must needs be a great philosopher; you rise to your principles through reason, you are a social exception; whereas it suffices to be a Christian to make us benevolent in ours. With you, it is an effort; with us, it comes naturally."

"In other words, abbe, I think, and you feel,—that's the whole of it."

However, at twelve years of age, Ursula, whose quickness and natural feminine perceptions were trained by her superior education, and whose intelligence in its dawn was enlightened by a religious spirit (of all spirits the most refined), came to understand that her godfather did not believe in a future life, nor in the immortality of the soul, nor in providence, nor in God. Pressed with questions by the innocent creature, the doctor was unable to hide the fatal secret. Ursula's artless consternation made him smile, but when he saw her depressed and sad he felt how deep an affection her sadness revealed. Absolute devotion has a horror of every sort of disagreement, even in ideas which it does not share. Sometimes the doctor accepted his darling's reasonings as he would her kisses, said as they were in the sweetest of voices with the purest and most fervent feeling. Believers and unbelievers speak different languages and cannot understand each other. The young girl pleading God's cause was unreasonable with the old man, as a spoilt child sometimes maltreats its mother. The abbe rebuked her gently, telling her that God had power to humiliate proud spirits. Ursula replied that David had overcome Goliath.

This religious difference, these complaints of the child who wished to drag her godfather to God, were the only troubles of this happy life, so peaceful, yet so full, and wholly withdrawn from the inquisitive eyes of the little town. Ursula grew and developed, and became in time the modest and religiously trained young woman whom Desire admired as she left the church. The cultivation of flowers in the garden, her music, the pleasures of her godfather, and all the little cares she was able to give him (for she had eased La Bougival's labors by doing everything for him),—these things filled the hours, the days, the months of her calm life. Nevertheless, for about a year the doctor had felt uneasy about his Ursula, and watched her health with the utmost care. Sagacious and profoundly practical observer that he was, he thought he perceived some commotion in her moral being. He watched her like a mother, but seeing no one about her who was worthy of inspiring love, his uneasiness on the subject at length passed away.

At this conjuncture, one month before the day when this drama begins, the doctor's intellectual life was invaded by one of those events which plough to the very depths of a man's convictions and turn them over. But this event needs a succinct narrative of certain circumstances in his medical career, which will give, perhaps, fresh interest to the story.

CHAPTER VI.
A TREATISE ON MESMERISM

Towards the end of the eighteenth century science was sundered as widely by the apparition of Mesmer as art had been by that of Gluck. After re-discovering magnetism Mesmer came to France, where, from time immemorial, inventors have flocked to obtain recognition for their discoveries. France, thanks to her lucid language, is in some sense the clarion of the world.

"If homoeopathy gets to Paris it is saved," said Hahnemann, recently.

"Go to France," said Monsieur de Metternich to Gall, "and if they laugh at your bumps you will be famous."

Mesmer had disciples and antagonists as ardent for and against his theories as the Piccinists and the Gluckists for theirs. Scientific France was stirred to its center; a solemn conclave was opened. Before judgment was rendered, the medical faculty proscribed, in a body, Mesmer's so-called charlatanism, his tub, his conducting wires, and his theory. But let us at once admit that the German, unfortunately, compromised his splendid discovery by enormous pecuniary claims. Mesmer was defeated by the doubtfulness of facts, by universal ignorance of the part played in nature by imponderable fluids then unobserved, and by his own inability to study on all sides a science possessing a triple front. Magnetism has many applications; in Mesmer's hands it was, in its relation to the future, merely what cause is to effect. But, if the discoverer lacked genius, it is a sad thing both for France and for human reason to have to say that a science contemporaneous with civilization, cultivated by Egypt and Chaldea, by Greece and India, met in Paris in the eighteenth century the fate that Truth in the person of Galileo found in the sixteenth; and that magnetism was rejected and cast out by the combined attacks of science and religion, alarmed for their own positions. Magnetism, the favorite science of Jesus Christ and one of the divine powers which he gave to his disciples, was no better apprehended by the Church than by the disciples of Jean-Jacques, Voltaire, Locke, and Condillac. The Encyclopedists and the clergy were equally averse to the old human power which they took to be new. The miracles of the convulsionaries, suppressed by the Church and smothered by the indifference of scientific men (in spite of the precious writings of the Councilor, Carre de Montgeron) were the first summons to make experiments with those human fluids which give power to employ certain inward forces to neutralize the sufferings caused by outward agents. But to do this it was necessary to admit the existence of fluids intangible, invisible, imponderable, three negative terms in which the science of that day chose to see a definition of the void. In modern philosophy there is no void. Ten feet of void and the world crumbles away! To materialists especially the world is full, all things hang together, are linked, related, organized. "The world as the result of chance," said Diderot, "is more explicable than God. The multiplicity of causes, the incalculable number of issues presupposed by chance, explain creation. Take the Eneid and all the letters composing it; if you allow me time and space, I can, by continuing to cast the letters, arrive at last at the Eneid combination."

Those foolish persons who deify all rather than admit a God recoil before the infinite divisibility of matter which is in the nature of imponderable forces. Locke and Condillac retarded by fifty years the immense progress which natural science is now making under the great principle of unity due to Geoffroy de Saint-Hilaire. Some intelligent persons, without any system, convinced by facts conscientiously studied, still hold to Mesmer's doctrine, which recognizes the existence of a penetrative influence acting from man to man, put in motion by the will, curative by the abundance of the fluid, the working of which is in fact a duel between two forces, between an ill to be cured and the will to cure it.

The phenomena of somnambulism, hardly perceived by Mesmer, were revealed by du Puysegur and Deleuze; but the Revolution put a stop to their discoveries and played into the hands of the scientists and scoffers. Among the small number of believers were a few physicians. They were persecuted by their brethren as long as they lived. The respectable body of Parisian doctors displayed all the bitterness of religious warfare against the Mesmerists, and were as cruel in their hatred as it was possible to be in those days of Voltairean tolerance. The orthodox physician refused to consult with those who adopted the Mesmerian heresy. In 1820 these heretics were still proscribed. The miseries and sorrows of the Revolution had not quenched the scientific hatred. It is only priests, magistrates, and physicians who can hate in that way. The official robe is terrible! But ideas are even more implacable than things.

Doctor Bouvard, one of Minoret's friends, believed in the new faith, and persevered to the day of his death in studying a science to which he sacrificed the peace of his life, for he was one of the chief "betes noires" of the Parisian faculty. Minoret, a valiant supporter of the Encyclopedists, and a formidable adversary of Desion, Mesmer's assistant, whose pen had great weight in the controversy, quarreled with his old friend, and not only that, but he persecuted him. His conduct to Bouvard must have caused him the only remorse which troubled the serenity of his declining years. Since his retirement to Nemours the science of imponderable fluids (the only name suitable for magnetism, which, by the nature of its phenomena, is closely allied to light and electricity) had made immense progress, in spite of the ridicule of Parisian scientists. Phrenology and physiognomy, the departments of Gall and Lavater (which are in fact twins, for one is to the other as cause is to effect), proved to the minds of more than one physiologist the existence of an intangible fluid which is the basis of the phenomena of the human will, and from which result passions, habits, the shape of faces and of skulls. Magnetic facts, the miracles of somnambulism, those of divination and ecstasy, which open a way to the spiritual world, were fast accumulating. The strange tale of the apparitions of the farmer Martin, so clearly proved, and his interview with Louis XVIII.; a knowledge of the intercourse of Swedenborg with the departed, carefully investigated in Germany; the tales of Walter Scott on the effects of "second sight"; the extraordinary faculties of some fortune-tellers, who practice as a single science chiromancy, cartomancy, and the horoscope; the facts of catalepsy, and those of the action of certain morbid affections on the properties of the diaphragm,—all such phenomena, curious, to say the least, each emanating from the same source, were now undermining many scepticisms and leading even the most indifferent minds to the plane of experiments. Minoret, buried in Nemours, was ignorant of this movement of minds, strong in the north of Europe but still weak in France where, however, many facts called marvelous by superficial observers, were happening, but falling, alas! like stones to the bottom of the sea, in the vortex of Parisian excitements.

At the bottom of the present year the doctor's tranquillity was shaken by the following letter:—

My old comrade,—All friendship, even if lost, has rights which it is difficult to set aside. I know that you are still living, and I remember far less our enmity than our happy days in that old hovel of Saint-Julien-le-Pauvre.

At a time when I expect to soon leave the world I have it on my heart to prove to you that magnetism is about to become one of the most important of the sciences—if indeed all science is not *one*. I can overcome your incredulity by proof. Perhaps I shall owe to your curiosity the happiness of taking you once more by the hand—as in the days before Mesmer. Always yours,

Bouvard.

Stung like a lion by a gadfly the old scientist rushed to Paris and left his card on Bouvard, who lived in the Rue Ferou near Saint-Sulpice. Bouvard sent a card to his hotel on which was written "To-morrow; nine o'clock, Rue Saint-Honore, opposite the Assumption."

Minoret, who seemed to have renewed his youth, could not sleep. He went to see some of his friends among the faculty to inquire if the world were turned upside down, if the science of medicine still had a school, if the four faculties any longer existed. The doctors reassured him, declaring that the old spirit of opposition was as strong as ever, only, instead of persecuting as heretofore, the Academies of Medicine and of Sciences rang with laughter as they classed magnetic facts with the tricks of Comus and Comte and Bosco, with jugglery and prestidigitation and all that now went by the name of "amusing physics."

This assurance did not prevent old Minoret from keeping the appointment made for him by Bouvard. After an enmity of forty-four years the two antagonists met beneath a porte-cochere in the Rue Saint-Honore. Frenchmen have too many distractions of mind to hate each other long. In Paris especially, politics, literature, and science render life so vast that every man can find new worlds to conquer where all pretensions may live at ease. Hatred requires too many forces fully armed. None but public bodies can keep alive the sentiment. Robespierre and Danton would have fallen into each other's arms at the end of forty-four years. However, the two doctors each withheld his hand and did not offer it. Bouvard spoke first:—

"You seem wonderfully well."

"Yes, I am—and you?" said Minoret, feeling that the ice was now broken.

"As you see."

"Does magnetism prevent people from dying?" asked Minoret in a joking tone, but without sharpness.

"No, but it almost prevented me from living."

"Then you are not rich?" exclaimed Minoret.

"Pooh!" said Bouvard.

"But I am!" cried the other.

"It is not your money but your convictions that I want. Come," replied Bouvard.

"Oh! you obstinate fellow!" said Minoret.

The Mesmerist led his sceptic, with some precaution, up a dingy staircase to the fourth floor.

At this particular time an extraordinary man had appeared in Paris, endowed by faith with incalculable power, and controlling magnetic forces in all their applications. Not only did this great unknown (who still lives) heal from a distance the worst and most inveterate diseases, suddenly and radically, as the Savior of men did formerly, but he was also able to call forth instantaneously the most remarkable phenomena of somnambulism and conquer the most rebellious will. The countenance of this mysterious being, who claims to be responsible to God alone and to communicate, like

Swedenborg, with angels, resembles that of a lion; concentrated, irresistible energy shines in it. His features, singularly contorted, have a terrible and even blasting aspect. His voice, which comes from the depths of his being, seems charged with some magnetic fluid; it penetrates the hearer at every pore. Disgusted by the ingratitude of the public after his many cures, he has now returned to an impenetrable solitude, a voluntary nothingness. His all-powerful hand, which has restored a dying daughter to her mother, fathers to their grief-stricken children, adored mistresses to lovers frenzied with love, cured the sick given over by physicians, soothed the sufferings of the dying when life became impossible, wrung psalms of thanksgiving in synagogues, temples, and churches from the lips of priests recalled to the one God by the same miracle,—that sovereign hand, a sun of life dazzling the closed eyes of the somnambulist, has never been raised again even to save the heir-apparent of a kingdom. Wrapped in the memory of his past mercies as in a luminous shroud, he denies himself to the world and lives for heaven.

But, at the dawn of his reign, surprised by his own gift, this man, whose generosity equaled his power, allowed a few interested persons to witness his miracles. The fame of his work, which was mighty, and could easily be revived to-morrow, reached Dr. Bouvard, who was then on the verge of the grave. The persecuted mesmerist was at last enabled to witness the startling phenomena of a science he had long treasured in his heart. The sacrifices of the old man touched the heart of the mysterious stranger, who accorded him certain privileges. As Bouvard now went up the staircase he listened to the twittings of his old antagonist with malicious delight, answering only, "You shall see, you shall see!" with the emphatic little nods of a man who is sure of his facts.

The two physicians entered a suite of rooms that were more than modest. Bouvard went alone into a bedroom which adjoined the salon where he left Minoret, whose distrust was instantly awakened; but Bouvard returned at once and took him into the bedroom, where he saw the mysterious Swedenborgian, and also a woman sitting in an armchair. The woman did not rise, and seemed not to notice the entrance of the two old men.

"What! no tub?" cried Minoret, smiling.

"Nothing but the power of God," answered the Swedenborgian gravely. He seemed to Minoret to be about fifty years of age.

The three men sat down and the mysterious stranger talked of the rain and the coming fine weather, to the great astonishment of Minoret, who thought he was being hoaxed. The Swedenborgian soon began, however, to question his visitor on his scientific opinions, and seemed evidently to be taking time to examine him.

"You have come here solely from curiosity, monsieur," he said at last. "It is not my habit to prostitute a power which, according to my conviction, emanates from God; if I made a frivolous or unworthy use of it, it would be taken from me. Nevertheless, there is some hope, Monsieur Bouvard tells me, of changing the opinions of one who has opposed us, of enlightening a scientific man whose mind is candid; I have therefore determined to satisfy you. That woman whom you see there," he continued, pointing to her, "is now in a somnambulic sleep. The statements and manifestations of somnambulists declare that this state is a delightful other life, during which the inner being, freed from the trammels laid upon the exercise of our faculties by the visible world, moves in a world which we mistakenly term invisible. Sight and hearing are then exercised in a manner far more perfect than any we know of here, possibly without the help of the organs we now employ, which are the scabbard of the luminous blades called sight and hearing. To a person in that state, distance and material obstacles do not exist, or they can be traversed by a life within us for which our body is a mere receptacle, a necessary shelter, a casing. Terms fail to describe effects that have lately been rediscovered, for to-day the words imponderable, intangible, invisible have no meaning to the fluid whose action is demonstrated by magnetism. Light is ponderable by its heat, which, by penetrating bodies, increases their volume; and certainly electricity is only too tangible. We have condemned things themselves instead of blaming the imperfection of our instruments."

"She sleeps," said Minoret, examining the woman, who seemed to him to belong to an inferior class.

"Her body is for the time being in abeyance," said the Swedenborgian. "Ignorant persons suppose that condition to be sleep. But she will prove to you that there is a spiritual universe, and that the mind when there does not obey the laws of this material universe. I will send her wherever you wish to go,—a hundred miles from here or to China, as you will. She will tell you what is happening there."

"Send her to my house in Nemours, Rue des Bourgeois; that will do," said Minoret.

He took Minoret's hand, which the doctor let him take, and held it for a moment seeming to collect himself; then with his other hand he took that of the woman sitting in the arm-chair and placed the hand of the doctor in it, making a sign to the old sceptic to seat himself beside this oracle without a tripod. Minoret observed a slight tremor on the absolutely calm features of the woman when their hands were thus united by the Swedenborgian, but the action, though marvelous in its effects, was very simply done.

"Obey him," said the unknown personage, extending his hand above the head of the sleeping woman, who seemed to imbibe both light and life from him, "and remember that what you do for him will please me.—You can now speak to her," he added, addressing Minoret.

"Go to Nemours, to my house, Rue des Bourgeois," said the doctor.

"Give her time; put your hand in hers until she proves to you by what she tells you that she is where you wish her to be," said Bouvard to his old friend.

"I see a river," said the woman in a feeble voice, seeming to look within herself with deep attention, notwithstanding her closed eyelids. "I see a pretty garden—"

"Why do you enter by the river and the garden?" said Minoret.

"Because they are there."

"Who?"

"The young girl and her nurse, whom you are thinking of."

"What is the garden like?" said Minoret.

"Entering by the steps which go down to the river, there is the right, a long brick gallery, in which I see books; it ends in a singular building,—there are wooden bells, and a pattern of red eggs. To the left, the wall is covered with climbing plants, wild grapes, Virginia jessamine. In the middle is a sun-dial. There are many plants in pots. Your child is looking at the flowers. She shows them to her nurse—she is making holes in the earth with her trowel, and planting seeds. The nurse is raking the path. The young girl is pure as an angel, but the beginning of love is there, faint as the dawn—"

"Love for whom?" asked the doctor, who, until now, would have listened to no word said to him by somnambulists. He considered it all jugglery.

"You know nothing—though you have lately been uneasy about her health," answered the woman. "Her heart has followed the dictates of nature."

"A woman of the people to talk like this!" cried the doctor.

"In the state she is in all persons speak with extraordinary perception," said Bouvard.

"But who is it that Ursula loves?"

"Ursula does not know that she loves," said the woman with a shake of the head; "she is too angelic to know what love is; but her mind is occupied by him; she thinks of him; she tries to escape the thought; but she returns to it in spite of her will to abstain.—She is at the piano—"

"But who is he?"

"The son of a lady who lives opposite."

"Madame de Portenduere?"

"Portenduere, did you say?" replied the sleeper. "Perhaps so. But there's no danger; he is not in the neighbourhood."

"Have they spoken to each other?" asked the doctor.

"Never. They have looked at one another. She thinks him charming. He is, in fact, a fine man; he has a good heart. She sees him from her window; they see each other in church. But the young man no longer thinks of her."

"His name?"

"Ah! to tell you that I must read it, or hear it. He is named Savinien; she has just spoken his name; she thinks it sweet to say; she has looked in the almanac for his fete-day and marked a red dot against it,—child's play, that. Ah! she will love well, with as much strength as purity; she is not a girl to love twice; love will so dye her soul and fill it that she will reject all other sentiments."

"Where do you see that?"

"In her. She will know how to suffer; she inherits that; her father and her mother suffered much."

The last words overcame the doctor, who felt less shaken than surprised. It is proper to state that between her sentences the woman paused for several minutes, during which time her attention became more and more concentrated. She was seen to see; her forehead had a singular aspect; an inward effort appeared there; it seemed to clear or cloud by some mysterious power, the effects of which Minoret had seen in dying persons at moments when they appeared to have the gift of prophecy. Several times she made gestures which resembled those of Ursula.

"Question her," said the mysterious stranger, to Minoret, "she will tell you secrets you alone can know."

"Does Ursula love me?" asked Minoret.

"Almost as much as she loves God," was the answer. "But she is very unhappy at your unbelief. You do not believe in God; as if you could prevent his existence! His word fills the universe. You are the cause of her only sorrow.—Hear! she is playing scales; she longs to be a better musician than she is; she is provoked with herself. She is thinking, 'If I could sing, if my voice were fine, it would reach his ear when he is with his mother.'"

Doctor Minoret took out his pocket-book and noted the hour.

"Tell me what seeds she planted?"

"Mignonette, sweet-peas, balsams—"

"And what else?"

"Larkspur."

"Where is my money?"

"With your notary; but you invest it so as not to lose the interest of a single day."

"Yes, but where is the money that I keep for my monthly expenses?"

"You put it in a large book bound in red, entitled 'Pandects of Justinian, Vol. II.' between the last two leaves; the book is on the shelf of folios above the glass buffet. You have a whole row of them. Your money is in the last volume next to the salon—See! Vol. III. is before Vol. II.—but you have no money, it is all in—"

"—thousand-franc notes," said the doctor.

"I cannot see, they are folded. No, there are two notes of five hundred francs."

"You see them?"

"Yes."

"How do they look?"

"One is old and yellow, the other white and new."

This last phase of the inquiry petrified the doctor. He looked at Bouvard with a bewildered air; but Bouvard and the Swedenborgian, who were accustomed to the amazement of sceptics, were speaking together in a low voice and appeared not to notice him. Minoret begged them to allow him to return after dinner. The old philosopher wished to compose his mind and shake off this terror, so as to put this vast power to some new test, to subject it to more decisive experiments and obtain answers to certain questions, the truth of which should do away with every sort of doubt.

"Be here at nine o'clock this evening," said the stranger. "I will return to meet you."

Doctor Minoret was in so convulsed a state that he left the room without bowing, followed by Bouvard, who called to him from behind. "Well, what do you say? what do you say?"

"I think I am mad, Bouvard," answered Minoret from the steps of the porte-cochere. "If that woman tells the truth about Ursula,—and none but Ursula can know the things that sorceress has told me,—I shall say that *you are right*. I wish I had wings to fly to Nemours this minute and verify her words. But I shall hire a carriage and start at ten o'clock to-night. Ah! am I losing my senses?"

"What would you say if you knew of a life-long incurable disease healed in a moment; if you saw that great magnetizer bring sweat in torrents from an herpetic patient, or make a paralyzed woman walk?"

"Come and dine, Bouvard; stay with me till nine o'clock. I must find some decisive, undeniable test!"

"So be it, old comrade," answered the other.

The reconciled enemies dined in the Palais-Royal. After a lively conversation, which helped Minoret to evade the fever of the ideas which were ravaging his brain, Bouvard said to him:—

"If you admit in that woman the faculty of annihilating or of traversing space, if you obtain a certainty that here, in Paris, she sees and hears what is said and done in Nemours, you must admit all other magnetic facts; they are not more incredible than these. Ask her for some one proof which you know will satisfy you—for you might suppose that we obtained information to deceive you; but we cannot know, for instance, what will happen at nine o'clock in your goddaughter's bedroom. Remember, or write down, what the sleeper will see and hear, and then go home. Your little Ursula, whom I do not know, is not our accomplice, and if she tells you that she has said and done what you have written down—lower thy head, proud Hun!"

The two friends returned to the house opposite to the Assumption and found the somnambulist, who in her waking state did not recognize Doctor Minoret. The eyes of this woman closed gently before the hand of the Swedenborgian, which was stretched towards her at a little distance, and she took the attitude in which Minoret had first seen her. When her hand and that of the doctor were again joined, he asked her to tell him what was happening in his house at Nemours at that instant. "What is Ursula doing?" he said.

"She is undressed; she has just curled her hair; she is kneeling on her prie-Dieu, before an ivory crucifix fastened to a red velvet background."

"What is she saying?"

"Her evening prayers; she is commending herself to God; she implores him to save her soul from evil thoughts; she examines her conscience and recalls what she has done during the day; that she may know if she has failed to obey his commands and those of the church—poor dear little soul, she lays bare her breast!" Tears were in the sleeper's eyes. "She has done no sin, but she blames herself for thinking too much of Savinien. She stops to wonder what he is doing in Paris; she prays to God to make him happy. She speaks of you; she is praying aloud."

"Tell me her words." Minoret took his pencil and wrote, as the sleeper uttered it, the following prayer, evidently composed by the Abbe Chaperon.

"My God, if thou art content with thine handmaid, who worships

thee and prays to thee with a love that is equal to her devotion,

who strives not to wander from thy sacred paths, who would gladly

die as thy Son died to glorify thy name, who desires to live in

the shadow of thy will—O God, who knoweth the heart, open the

eyes of my godfather, lead him in the way of salvation, grant him

thy Divine grace, that he may live for thee in his last days; save

him from evil, and let me suffer in his stead. Kind Saint Ursula,

dear protectress, and you, Mother of God, queen of heaven,

archangels, and saints in Paradise, hear me! join your

intercessions to mine and have mercy upon us."

The sleeper imitated so perfectly the artless gestures and the inspired manner of his child that Doctor Minoret's eyes were filled with tears.

"Does she say more?" he asked.

"Yes."

"Repeat it."

"'My dear godfather; I wonder who plays backgammon with him in Paris.' She has blown out the light—her head is on the pillow—she turns to sleep! Ah! she is off! How pretty she looks in her little night-cap."

Minoret bowed to the great Unknown, wrung Bouvard by the hand, ran downstairs and hastened to a cab-stand which at that time was near the gates of a house since pulled down to make room for the Rue d'Alger. There he found a coachman who was willing to start immediately for Fontainebleau. The moment the price was agreed on, the old man, who seemed to have renewed his youth, jumped into the carriage and started. According to agreement, he stopped to rest the horse at Essonne, but arrived at Fontainebleau in time for the diligence to Nemours, on which he secured a seat, and dismissed his coachman. He reached home at five in the morning, and went to bed, with his life-long ideas of physiology, nature, and metaphysics in ruins about him, and slept till nine o'clock, so wearied was he with the events of his journey.

CHAPTER VII.
A TWO-FOLD CONVERSION

On rising, the doctor, sure that no one had crossed the threshold of his house since he re-entered it, proceeded (but not without extreme trepidation) to verify his facts. He was himself ignorant of any difference in the bank-notes and also of the misplacement of the Pandect volumes. The somnambulist was right. The doctor rang for La Bougival.

"Tell Ursula to come and speak to me," he said, seating himself in the center of his library.

The girl came; she ran up to him and kissed him. The doctor took her on his knee, where she sat contentedly, mingling her soft fair curls with the white hair of her old friend.

"Do you want something, godfather?"

"Yes; but promise me, on your salvation, to answer frankly, without evasion, the questions that I shall put to you."

Ursula colored to the temples.

"Oh! I'll ask nothing that you cannot speak of," he said, noticing how the bashfulness of young love clouded the hitherto childlike purity of the girl's blue eyes.

"Ask me, godfather."

"What thought was in your mind when you ended your prayers last evening, and what time was it when you said them."

"It was a quarter-past or half-past nine."

"Well, repeat your last prayer."

The girl fancied that her voice might convey her faith to the sceptic; she slid from his knee and knelt down, clasping her hands fervently; a brilliant light illumined her face as she turned it on the old man and said:—

"What I asked of God last night I asked again this morning, and I shall ask it till he vouchsafes to grant it."

Then she repeated her prayer with new and still more powerful expression. To her great astonishment her godfather took the last words from her mouth and finished the prayer.

"Good, Ursula," said the doctor, taking her again on his knee. "When you laid your head on the pillow and went to sleep did you think to yourself,

'That dear godfather; I wonder who is playing backgammon with him in Paris'?"

Ursula sprang up as if the last trumpet had sounded in her ears. She gave a cry of terror; her eyes, wide open, gazed at the old man with awful fixity.

"Who are you, godfather? From whom do you get such power?" she asked, imagining that in his desire to deny God he had made some compact with the devil.

"What seeds did you plant yesterday in the garden?"

"Mignonette, sweet-peas, balsams—"

"And the last were larkspur?"

She fell on her knees.

"Do not terrify me!" she exclaimed. "Oh you must have been here—you were here, were you not?"

"Am I not always with you?" replied the doctor, evading her question, to save the strain on the young girl's mind. "Let us go to your room."

"Your legs are trembling," she said.

"Yes, I am confounded, as it were."

"Can it be that you believe in God?" she cried, with artless joy, letting fall the tears that gathered in her eyes.

The old man looked round the simple but dainty little room he had given to his Ursula. On the floor was a plain green carpet, very inexpensive, which she herself kept exquisitely clean; the walls were hung with a gray paper strewn with roses and green leaves; at the windows, which looked to the court, were calico curtains edged with a band of some pink material; between the windows and beneath a tall mirror was a pier-table topped with marble, on which stood a Sevres vase in which she put her nosegays; opposite the chimney was a little bureau-desk of charming marquetry. The bed, of chintz, with chintz curtains lined with pink, was one of those duchess beds so common in the eighteenth century, which had a tuft of carved feathers at the top of each of the four posts, which were fluted on the sides. An old clock, inclosed in a sort of monument made of tortoise-shell inlaid with arabesques of ivory, decorated the mantelpiece, the marble shelf of which, with the candlesticks and the mirror in a frame painted in cameo on a gray ground, presented a remarkable harmony of color, tone, and style. A large wardrobe, the doors of which were inlaid with landscapes in different woods (some having a green tint which are no longer to be found for sale) contained, no doubt, her linen and her dresses. The air of the room was redolent of heaven.

The precise arrangement of everything showed a sense of order, a feeling for harmony, which would certainly have influenced any one, even a Minoret-Levrault. It was plain that the things about her were dear to Ursula, and that she loved a room which contained, as it were, her childhood and the whole of her girlish life.

Looking the room well over that he might seem to have a reason for his visit, the doctor saw at once how the windows looked into those of Madame de Portenduere. During the night he had meditated as to the course he ought to pursue with Ursula about his discovery of this dawning passion. To question her now would commit him to some course. He must either approve or disapprove of her love; in either case his position would be a false one. He therefore resolved to watch and examine into the state of things between the two young people, and learn whether it were his duty to check the inclination before it was irresistible. None but an old man could have shown such deliberate wisdom. Still panting from the discovery of the truth of these magnetic facts, he turned about and looked at all the various little things around the room; he wished to examine the almanac which was hanging at a corner of the chimney-piece.

"These ugly things are too heavy for your little hands," he said, taking up the marble candlesticks which were partly covered with leather.

He weighed them in his hand; then he looked at the almanac and took it, saying, "This is ugly too. Why do you keep such a common thing in your pretty room?"

"Oh, please let me have it, godfather."

"No, no, you shall have another to-morrow."

So saying he carried off this possible proof, shut himself up in his study, looked for Saint Savinien and found, as the somnambulist had told him, a little red dot at the 19th of October; he also saw another before his own saint's day, Saint Denis, and a third before Saint John, the abbe's patron. This little dot, no larger than a pin's head, had been seen by the sleeping woman in spite of distance and other obstacles! The old man thought till evening of these events, more momentous for him than for others. He was forced to yield to evidence. A strong wall, as it were, crumbled within him; for his life had rested on two bases,—indifference in matters of religion and a firm disbelief in magnetism. When it was proved to him that the senses—faculties purely physical, organs, the effects of which could be explained—attained to some of the attributes of the infinite, magnetism upset, or at least it seemed to him to upset, the powerful arguments of Spinoza. The finite and the infinite, two incompatible elements according to that remarkable man, were here united, the one in the other. No matter what power he gave to the divisibility and mobility of matter he could not help recognizing that it possessed qualities that were almost divine.

He was too old now to connect those phenomena to a system, and compare them with those of sleep, of vision, of light. His whole scientific belief, based on the assertions of the school of Locke and Condillac, was in ruins. Seeing his hollow ideas in pieces, his scepticism staggered. Thus the advantage in this struggle between the Catholic child and the Voltairean old man was on Ursula's side. In the dismantled fortress, above these ruins, shone a light; from the center of these ashes issued the path of prayer! Nevertheless, the obstinate old scientist fought his doubts. Though struck to the heart, he would not decide, he struggled on against God.

But he was no longer the same man; his mind showed its vacillation. He became unnaturally dreamy; he read Pascal, and Bossuet's sublime "History of Species"; he read Bonald, he read Saint-Augustine; he determined also to read the works of Swedenborg, and the late Saint-Martin, which the mysterious stranger had mentioned to him. The edifice within him was cracking on all sides; it needed but one more shake, and then, his heart being ripe for God, he was destined to fall into the celestial vineyard as fall the fruits. Often of an evening, when playing with the abbe, his goddaughter sitting by, he would put questions bearing on his opinions which seemed singular to the priest, who was ignorant of the inward workings by which God was remaking that fine conscience.

"Do you believe in apparitions?" asked the sceptic of the pastor, stopping short in the game.

"Cardan, a great philosopher of the sixteenth century said he had seen some," replied the abbe.

"I know all those that scholars have discussed, for I have just reread Plotinus. I am questioning you as a Catholic might, and I ask if you think that dead men can return to the living."

"Jesus reappeared to his disciples after his death," said the abbe. "The Church ought to have faith in the apparitions of the Savior. As for miracles, they are not lacking," he continued, smiling. "Shall I tell you the last? It took place in the eighteenth century."

"Pooh!" said the doctor.

"Yes, the blessed Marie-Alphonse of Ligouri, being very far from Rome, knew of the death of the Pope at the very moment the Holy Father expired; there were numerous witnesses of this miracle. The sainted bishop being in ecstasy, heard the last words of the sovereign pontiff and repeated them at the time to those about him. The courier who brought the announcement of the death did not arrive till thirty hours later."

"Jesuit!" exclaimed old Minoret, laughing, "I did not ask you for proofs; I asked you if you believed in apparitions."

"I think an apparition depends a good deal on who sees it," said the abbe, still fencing with his sceptic.

"My friend," said the doctor, seriously, "I am not setting a trap for you. What do you really believe about it?"

"I believe that the power of God is infinite," replied the abbe.

"When I am dead, if I am reconciled to God, I will ask Him to let me appear to you," said the doctor, smiling.

"That's exactly the agreement Cardan made with his friend," answered the priest.

"Ursula," said Minoret, "if danger ever threatens you, call me, and I will come."

"You have put into one sentence that beautiful elegy of 'Neere' by Andre Chenier," said the abbe. "Poets are sublime because they clothe both facts and feelings with ever-living images."

"Why do you speak of your death, dear godfather?" said Ursula in a grieved tone. "We Christians do not die; the grave is the cradle of our souls."

"Well," said the doctor, smiling, "we must go out of the world, and when I am no longer here you will be astonished at your fortune."

"When you are here no longer, my kind friend, my only consolation will be to consecrate my life to you."

"To me, dead?"

"Yes. All the good works that I can do will be done in your name to redeem your sins. I will pray God every day for his infinite mercy, that he may not punish eternally the errors of a day. I know he will summon among the righteous a soul so pure, so beautiful, as yours."

That answer, said with angelic candor, in a tone of absolute certainty, confounded error and converted Denis Minoret as God converted Saul. A ray of inward light overawed him; the knowledge of this tenderness, covering his years to come, brought tears to his eyes. This sudden effect of grace had something that seemed electrical about it. The abbe clasped his hands and rose, troubled, from his seat. The girl, astonished at her triumph, wept. The old man stood up as if a voice had called him, looking into space as though his eyes beheld the dawn; then he bent his knee upon his chair, clasped his hands, and lowered his eyes to the ground as one humiliated.

"My God," he said in a trembling voice, raising his head, "if any one can obtain my pardon and lead me to thee, surely it is this spotless creature. Have mercy on the repentant old age that this pure child presents to thee!"

He lifted his soul to God; mentally praying for the light of divine knowledge after the gift of divine grace; then he turned to the abbe and held out his hand.

"My dear pastor," he said, "I am become as a little child. I belong to you; I give my soul to your care."

Ursula kissed his hands and bathed them with her tears. The old man took her on his knee and called her gayly his godmother. The abbe, deeply moved, recited the "Veni Creator" in a species of religious ecstasy. The hymn served as the evening prayer of the three Christians kneeling together for the first time.

"What has happened?" asked La Bougival, amazed at the sight.

"My godfather believes in God at last!" replied Ursula.

"Ah! so much the better; he only needed that to make him perfect," cried the old woman, crossing herself with artless gravity.

"Dear doctor," said the good priest, "you will soon comprehend the grandeur of religion and the value of its practices; you will find its philosophy in human aspects far higher than that of the boldest sceptics."

The abbe, who showed a joy that was almost infantine, agreed to catechize the old man and confer with him twice a week. Thus the conversion attributed to Ursula and to a spirit of sordid calculation, was the spontaneous act of the doctor himself. The abbe, who for fourteen years had abstained from touching the wounds of that heart, though all the while deploring them, was now asked for help, as a surgeon is called to an injured man. Ever since this scene Ursula's evening prayers had been said in common with her godfather. Day after day the old man grew more conscious of the peace within him that succeeded all his conflicts. Having, as he said, God as the responsible editor of things inexplicable, his mind was at ease. His dear child told him that he might know by how far he had advanced already in God's kingdom. During the mass which we have seen him attend, he had read the prayers and applied his own intelligence to them; from the first, he had risen to the divine idea of the communion of the faithful. The old neophyte understood the eternal symbol attached to that sacred nourishment, which faith renders needful to the soul after conveying to it her own profound and radiant essence. When on leaving the church he had seemed in a hurry to get home, it was merely that he might once more thank his dear child for having led him to "enter religion,"—the beautiful expression of former days. He was holding her on his knee in the salon and kissing her forehead sacredly at the very moment when his relatives were degrading that saintly influence with their shameless fears, and casting their vulgar insults upon Ursula. His haste to return home, his assumed disdain for their company, his sharp replies as he left the church were naturally attributed by all the heirs to the hatred Ursula had excited against them in the old man's mind.

CHAPTER VIII.
THE CONFERENCE

While Ursula was playing variations on Weber's "Last Thought" to her godfather, a plot was hatching in the Minoret-Levraults' dining-room which was destined to have a lasting effect on the events of this drama. The breakfast, noisy as all provincial breakfasts are, and enlivened by excellent wines brought to Nemours by the canal either from Burgundy or Touraine, lasted more than two hours. Zelie had sent for oysters, salt-water fish, and other gastronomical delicacies to do honor to Desire's return. The dining-room, in the center of which a round table offered a most appetizing sight, was like the hall of an inn. Content with the size of her kitchens and offices, Zelie had built a pavilion for the family between the vast courtyard and a garden planted with vegetables and full of fruit-trees. Everything about the premises was solid and plain. The example of Levrault-Levrault had been a warning to the town. Zelie forbade her builder to lead her into such follies. The dining-room was, therefore, hung with varnished paper and furnished with walnut chairs and sideboards, a porcelain stove, a tall clock, and a barometer. Though the plates and dishes were of common white china, the table shone with handsome linen and abundant silverware. After Zelie had served the coffee, coming and going herself like shot in a decanter,—for she kept but one servant,—and when Desire, the budding lawyer, had been told of the event of the morning and its probably consequences, the door was closed, and the notary Dionis was called upon to speak. By the silence in the room and the looks that were cast on that authoritative face, it was easy to see the power that such men exercise over families.

"My dear children," said he, "your uncle having been born in 1746, is eighty-three years old at the present time; now, old men are given to folly, and that little—"

"Viper!" cried Madame Massin.

"Hussy!" said Zelie.

"Let us call her by her own name," said Dionis.

"Well, she's a thief," said Madame Cremiere.

"A pretty thief," remarked Desire.

"That little Ursula," went on Dionis, "has managed to get hold of his heart. I have been thinking of your interests, and I did not wait until now before making certain inquiries; now this is what I have discovered about that young—"

"Marauder," said the collector.

"Inveigler," said the clerk of the court.

"Hold your tongue, friends," said the notary, "or I'll take my hat and be off."

"Come, come, papa," cried Minoret, pouring out a little glass of rum and offering it to the notary; "here, drink this, it comes from Rome itself; and now go on."

"Ursula is, it is true, the legitimate daughter of Joseph Mirouet; but her father was the natural son of Valentin Mirouet, your uncle's father-in-law. Being therefore an illegitimate niece, any will the doctor might make in her favor could probably be contested; and if he leaves her his fortune in that way you could bring a suit against Ursula. This, however, might turn out ill for you, in case the court took the view that there was no relationship between Ursula and the doctor. Still, the suit would frighten an unprotected girl, and bring about a compromise—"

"The law is so rigid as to the rights of natural children," said the newly fledged licentiate, eager to parade his knowledge, "that by the judgment of the court of appeals dated July 7, 1817, a natural child can claim nothing from his natural grandfather, not even a maintenance. So you see the illegitimate parentage is made retrospective. The law pursues the natural child even to its legitimate descent, on the ground that benefactions done to grandchildren reach the natural son through that medium. This is shown by articles 757, 908, and 911 of the civil Code. The royal court of Paris, by a decision of the 26th of January of last year, cut off a legacy made to the legitimate child of a natural son by his grandfather, who, as grandfather, was as distant to a natural grandson as the doctor, being an uncle, is to Ursula."

"All that," said Goupil, "seems to me to relate only to the bequests made by grandfathers to natural descendants. Ursula is not a blood relation of Doctor Minoret. I remember a decision of the royal court at Colmar, rendered in 1825, just before I took my degree, which declared that after the decease of a natural child his descendants could no longer be prohibited from inheriting. Now, Ursula's father is dead."

Goupil's argument produced what journalists who report the sittings of legislative assemblies are wont to call "profound sensation."

"What does that signify?" cried Dionis. "The actual case of the bequest of an uncle to an illegitimate child may not yet have been presented for trial; but when it is, the sternness of French law against such children will be all the more firmly applied because we live in times when religion is honored. I'll answer for it that out of such a suit as I propose you could get a compromise,—especially if they see you are determined to carry Ursula to a court of appeals."

Here the joy of the heirs already fingering their gold was made manifest in smiles, shrugs, and gestures round the table, and prevented all notice of Goupil's dissent. This elation, however, was succeeded by deep silence and uneasiness when the notary uttered his next word, a terrible "But!"

As if he had pulled the string of a puppet-show, starting the little people in jerks by means of machinery, Dionis beheld all eyes turned on him and all faces rigid in one and the same pose.

"*But* no law prevents your uncle from adopting or marrying Ursula," he continued. "As for adoption, that could be contested, and you would, I think, have equity on your side. The royal courts would never trifle with questions of adoptions; you would get a hearing there. It is true the doctor is an officer of the Legion of honor, and was formerly surgeon to the ex-emperor; but, nevertheless, he would get the worst of it. Moreover, you would have due warning in case of adoption—but how about marriage? Old Minoret is shrewd enough to go to Paris and marry her after a year's domicile, and give her a million by the marriage contract. The only thing, therefore, that really puts your property in danger is your uncle's marriage with the girl."

Here the notary paused.

"There's another danger," said Goupil, with a knowing air,—"that of a will made in favor of a third person, old Bongrand for instance, who will hold the property in trust for Mademoiselle Ursula—"

"If you tease your uncle," continued Dionis, cutting short his head-clerk, "if you are not all of you very polite to Ursula, you will drive him into either a marriage or into making that private trust which Goupil speaks of,—though I don't think him capable of that; it is a dangerous thing. As for marriage, that is easy to prevent. Desire there has only got to hold out a finger to the girl; she's sure to prefer a handsome young man, cock of the walk in Nemours, to an old one."

"Mother," said Desire to Zelie's ear, as much allured by the millions as by Ursula's beauty, "If I married her we should get the whole property."

"Are you crazy?—you, who'll some day have fifty thousand francs a year and be made a deputy! As long as I live you never shall cut your throat by a foolish marriage. Seven hundred thousand francs, indeed! Why, the mayor's only daughter will have fifty thousand a year, and they have already proposed her to me—"

This reply, the first rough speech his mother had ever made to him, extinguished in Desire's breast all desire for a marriage with the beautiful Ursula; for his father and he never got the better of any decision once written in the terrible blue eyes of Zelie Minoret.

"Yes, but see here, Monsieur Dionis," cried Cremiere, whose wife had been nudging him, "if the good man took the thing seriously and married his goddaughter to Desire, giving her the reversion of all the property, good-by to our share in it; if he lives five years longer uncle may be worth a million."

"Never!" cried Zelie, "never in my life shall Desire marry the daughter of a bastard, a girl picked up in the streets out of charity. My son will represent the Minorets after the death of his uncle, and the Minorets have five hundred years of good bourgeoisie behind them. That's equal to the nobility. Don't be uneasy, any of you; Desire will marry when we find a chance to put him in the Chamber of deputies."

This lofty declaration was backed by Goupil, who said:—

"Desire, with an allowance of twenty-four thousand francs a year, will be president of a royal court or solicitor-general; either office leads to the peerage. A foolish marriage would ruin him."

The heirs were now all talking at once; but they suddenly held their tongues when Minoret rapped on the table with his fist to keep silence for the notary.

"Your uncle is a worthy man," continued Dionis. "He believes he's immortal; and, like most clever men, he'll let death overtake him before he has made a will. My advice therefore is to induce him to invest his capital in a way that will make it difficult for him to disinherit you, and I know of an opportunity, made to hand. That little Portenduere is in Saint-Pelagie, locked-up for one hundred and some odd thousand francs' worth of debt. His old mother knows he is in prison; she is crying like a Magdalen. The abbe is to dine with her; no doubt she wants to talk to him about her troubles. Well, I'll go and see your uncle to-night and persuade him to sell his five per cent consols, which are now at 118, and lend Madame de Portenduere, on the security of her farm at Bordieres and her house here, enough to pay the debts of the prodigal son. I have a right as notary to speak to him in behalf of young Portenduere; and it is quite natural that I should wish to make him change his investments; I get deeds and commissions out of the business. If I become his adviser I'll propose to him other land investments for his surplus capital; I have some excellent ones now in my office. If his fortune were once invested in landed estate or in mortgage notes in this neighbourhood, it could not take wings to itself very easily. It is easy to make difficulties between the wish to realize and the realization."

The heirs, struck with the truth of this argument (much cleverer than that of Monsieur Josse), murmured approval.

"You must be careful," said the notary in conclusion, "to keep your uncle in Nemours, where his habits are known, and where you can watch him. Find him a lover for the girl and you'll prevent his marrying her himself."

"Suppose she married the lover?" said Goupil, seized by an ambitious desire.

"That wouldn't be a bad thing; then you could figure up the loss; the old man would have to say how much he gives her," replied the notary. "But if you set Desire at her he could keep the girl dangling on till the old man died. Marriages are made and unmade."

"The shortest way," said Goupil, "if the doctor is likely to live much longer, is to marry her to some worthy young man who will get her out of your way by settling at Sens, or Montargis, or Orleans with a hundred thousand francs in hand."

Dionis, Massin, Zelie, and Goupil, the only intelligent heads in the company, exchanged four thoughtful smiles.

"He'd be a worm at the core," whispered Zelie to Massin.

"How did he get here?" returned the clerk.

"That will just suit you!" cried Desire to Goupil. "But do you think you can behave decently enough to satisfy the old man and the girl?"

"In these days," whispered Zelie again in Massin's year, "notaries look out for no interests but their own. Suppose Dionis went over to Ursula just to get the old man's business?"

"I am sure of him," said the clerk of the court, giving her a sly look out of his spiteful little eyes. He was just going to add, "because I hold something over him," but he withheld the words.

"I am quite of Dionis's opinion," he said aloud.

"So am I," cried Zelie, who now suspected the notary of collusion with the clerk.

"My wife has voted!" said the post master, sipping his brandy, though his face was already purple from digesting his meal and absorbing a notable quantity of liquids.

"And very properly," remarked the collector.

"I shall go and see the doctor after dinner," said Dionis.

"If Monsieur Dionis's advice is good," said Madame Cremiere to Madame Massin, "we had better go and call on our uncle, as we used to do, every Sunday evening, and behave exactly as Monsieur Dionis has told us."

"Yes, and be received as he received us!" cried Zelie. "Minoret and I have more than forty thousand francs a year, and yet he refused our invitations! We are quite his equals. If I don't know how to write prescriptions I know how to paddle my boat as well as he—I can tell him that!"

"As I am far from having forty thousand francs a year," said Madame Massin, rather piqued, "I don't want to lose ten thousand."

"We are his nieces; we ought to take care of him, and then besides we shall see how things are going," said Madame Cremiere; "you'll thank us some day, cousin."

"Treat Ursula kindly," said the notary, lifting his right forefinger to the level of his lips; "remember old Jordy left her his savings."

"You have managed those fools as well as Desroches, the best lawyer in Paris, could have done," said Goupil to his patron as they left the post-house.

"And now they are quarreling over my fee," replied the notary, smiling bitterly.

The heirs, after parting with Dionis and his clerk, met again in the square, with face rather flushed from their breakfast, just as vespers were over. As the notary predicted, the Abbe Chaperon had Madame de Portenduere on his arm.

"She dragged him to vespers, see!" cried Madame Massin to Madame Cremiere, pointing to Ursula and the doctor, who were leaving the church.

"Let us go and speak to him," said Madame Cremiere, approaching the old man.

The change in the faces of his relatives (produced by the conference) did not escape Doctor Minoret. He tried to guess the reason of this sudden amiability, and out of sheer curiosity encouraged Ursula to stop and speak to the two women, who were eager to greet her with exaggerated affection and forced smiles.

"Uncle, will you permit me to come and see you to-night?" said Madame Cremiere. "We feared sometimes we were in your way—but it is such a long time since our children have paid you their respects; our girls are old enough now to make dear Ursula's acquaintance."

"Ursula is a little bear, like her name," replied the doctor.

"Let us tame her," said Madame Massin. "And besides, uncle," added the good housewife, trying to hide her real motive under a mask of economy, "they tell us the dear girl has such talent for the forte that we are very anxious to hear her. Madame Cremiere and I are inclined to take her music-master for our children. If there were six or eight scholars in a class it would bring the price of his lessons within our means."

"Certainly," said the old man, "and it will be all the better for me because I want to give Ursula a singing-master."

"Well, to-night then, uncle. We will bring your great-nephew Desire to see you; he is now a lawyer."

"Yes, to-night," echoed Minoret, meaning to fathom the motives of these petty souls.

The two nieces pressed Ursula's hand, saying, with affected eagerness, "Au revoir."

"Oh, godfather, you have read my heart!" cried Ursula, giving him a grateful look.

"You are going to have a voice," he said; "and I shall give you masters of drawing and Italian also. A woman," added the doctor, looking at Ursula as he unfastened the gate of his house, "ought to be educated to the height of every position in which her marriage may place her."

Ursula grew red as a cherry; her godfather's thoughts evidently turned in the same direction as her own. Feeling that she was too near confessing to the doctor the involuntary attraction which led her to think about Savinien and to center all her ideas of affection upon him, she turned aside and sat down in front of a great cluster of climbing plants, on the dark background of which she looked at a distance like a blue and white flower.

"Now you see, godfather, that your nieces were very kind to me; yes, they were very kind," she repeated as he approached her, to change the thoughts that made him pensive.

"Poor little girl!" cried the old man.

He laid Ursula's hand upon his arm, tapping it gently, and took her to the terraces beside the river, where no one could hear them.

"Why do you say, 'Poor little girl'?"

"Don't you see how they fear you?"

"Fear me,—why?"

"My next of kin are very uneasy about my conversion. They no doubt attribute it to your influence over me; they fancy I deprive them of their inheritance to enrich you."

"But you won't do that?" said Ursula naively, looking up at him.

"Oh, divine consolation of my old age!" said the doctor, taking his godchild in his arms and kissing her on both cheeks. "It was for her and not for myself, oh God! that I besought thee just now to let me live until the day I give her to some good being who is worthy of her!—You will see comedies, my little angel, comedies which the Minorets and Cremieres and Massins will come and play here. You want to brighten and prolong my life; they are longing for my death."

"God forbids us to hate any one, but if that is—Ah! I despise them!" exclaimed Ursula.

"Dinner is ready!" called La Bougival from the portico, which, on the garden side, was at the end of the corridor.

CHAPTER IX.
A FIRST CONFIDENCE

Ursula and her godfather were sitting at dessert in the pretty dining-room decorated with Chinese designs in black and gold lacquer (the folly of Levrault-Levrault) when the justice of peace arrived. The doctor offered him (and this was a great mark of intimacy) a cup of his coffee, a mixture of Mocha with Bourbon and Martinique, roasted, ground, and made by himself in a silver apparatus called a Chaptal.

"Well," said Bongrand, pushing up his glasses and looking slyly at the old man, "the town is in commotion; your appearance in church has put your relatives beside themselves. You have left your fortune to the priests, to the poor. You have roused the families, and they are bestirring themselves. Ha! ha! I saw their first irruption into the square; they were as busy as ants who have lost their eggs."

"What did I tell you, Ursula?" cried the doctor. "At the risk of grieving you, my child, I must teach you to know the world and put you on your guard against undeserved enmity."

"I should like to say a word to you on this subject," said Bongrand, seizing the occasion to speak to his old friend of Ursula's future.

The doctor put a black velvet cap on his white head, the justice of peace wore his hat to protect him from the night air, and they walked up and down the terrace discussing the means of securing to Ursula what her godfather intended to bequeath her. Bongrand knew Dionis's opinion as to the invalidity of a will made by the doctor in favor of Ursula; for Nemours was so preoccupied with the Minoret affairs that the matter had been much discussed among the lawyers of the little town. Bongrand considered that Ursula was not a relative of Doctor Minoret, but he felt that the whole spirit of legislation was against the foisting into families of illegitimate off-shoots. The makers of the Code had foreseen only the weakness of fathers and mothers for their natural children, without considering that uncles and aunts might have a like tenderness and a desire to provide for such children. Evidently there was a gap in the law.

"In all other countries," he said, ending an explanation of the legal points which Dionis, Goupil, and Desire had just explained to the heirs, "Ursula would have nothing to fear; she is a legitimate child, and the disability of her father ought only to affect the inheritance from Valentine Mirouet, her grandfather. But in France the magistracy is unfortunately overwise and very consequential; it inquires into the spirit of the law. Some lawyers talk morality, and might try to show that this hiatus in the Code came from the simple-mindedness of the legislators, who did not foresee the case, though, none the less, they established a principle. To bring a suit would be long and expensive. Zelie would carry it to the court of appeals, and I might not be alive when the case was tried."

"The best of cases is often worthless," cried the doctor. "Here's the question the lawyers will put, 'To what degree of relationship ought the disability of natural children in matters of inheritance to extend?' and the credit of a good lawyer will lie in gaining a bad cause."

"Faith!" said Bongrand, "I dare not take upon myself to affirm that the judges wouldn't interpret the meaning of the law as increasing the protection given to marriage, the eternal base of society."

Without explaining his intentions, the doctor rejected the idea of a trust. When Bongrand suggested to him a marriage with Ursula as the surest means of securing his property to her, he exclaimed, "Poor little girl! I might live fifteen years; what a fate for her!"

"Well, what will you do, then?" asked Bongrand.

"We'll think about it—I'll see," said the old man, evidently at a loss for a reply.

Just then Ursula came to say that Monsieur Dionis wished to speak to the doctor.

"Already!" cried Minoret, looking at Bongrand. "Yes," he said to Ursula, "send him here."

"I'll bet my spectacles to a bunch of matches that he is the advance-guard of your heirs," said Bongrand. "They breakfasted together at the post house, and something is being engineered."

The notary, conducted by Ursula, came to the lower end of the garden. After the usual greetings and a few insignificant remarks, Dionis asked for a private interview; Ursula and Bongrand retired to the salon.

The distrust which superior men excite in men of business is very remarkable. The latter deny them the "lesser" powers while recognizing their possession of the "higher." It is, perhaps, a tribute to them. Seeing them always on the higher plane of human things, men of business believe them incapable of descending to the infinitely petty details which (like the dividends of finance and the microscopic facts of science) go to equalize capital and to form the worlds. They are mistaken! The man of honor and of genius sees all. Bongrand, piqued by the doctor's silence, but impelled by a sense of Ursula's interests which he thought endangered, resolved to defend her against the heirs. He was wretched at not knowing what was taking place between the old man and Dionis.

"No matter how pure and innocent Ursula may be," he thought as he looked at her, "there is a point on which young girls do make their own law and their own morality. I'll test here. The Minoret-Levraults," he began, settling his spectacles, "might possibly ask you in marriage for their son."

The poor child turned pale. She was too well trained, and had too much delicacy to listen to what Dionis was saying to her uncle; but after a moment's inward deliberation, she thought she might show herself, and then, if she was in the way, her godfather would let her know it. The Chinese pagoda which the doctor made his study had outside blinds to the glass doors; Ursula invented the excuse of shutting them. She begged Monsieur Bongrand's pardon for leaving him alone in the salon, but he smiled at her and said, "Go! go!"

Ursula went down the steps of the portico which led to the pagoda at the foot of the garden. She stood for some minutes slowly arranging the blinds and watching the sunset. The doctor and notary were at the end of the terrace, but as they turned she heard the doctor make an answer which reached the pagoda where she was.

"My heirs would be delighted to see me invest my property in real estate or mortgages; they imagine it would be safer there. I know exactly what they are saying; perhaps you come from them. Let me tell you, my good sir, that my disposition of my property is irrevocably made. My heirs will have the capital I brought here with me; I wish them to know that, and to let me alone. If any one of them attempts to interfere with what I think proper to do for that young girl (pointing to Ursula) I shall come back from the other world and torment him. So, Monsieur Savinien de Portenduere will stay in prison if they count on me to get him out. I shall not sell my property in the Funds."

Hearing this last fragment of the sentence Ursula experienced the first and only pain which so far had ever touched her. She laid her head against the blind to steady herself.

"Good God, what is the matter with her?" thought the old doctor. "She has no color; such an emotion after dinner might kill her."

He went to her with open arms, and she fell into them almost fainting.

"Adieu, Monsieur," he said to the notary, "please leave us."

He carried his child to an immense Louis XV. sofa which was in his study, looked for a phial of hartshorn among his remedies, and made her inhale it.

"Take my place," said the doctor to Bongrand, who was terrified; "I must be alone with her."

The justice of peace accompanied the notary to the gate, asking him, but without showing any eagerness, what was the matter with Ursula.

"I don't know," replied Dionis. "She was standing by the pagoda, listening to us, and just as her uncle (so-called) refused to lend some money at my request to young de Portenduere who is in prison for debt,—for he has not had, like Monsieur du Rouvre, a Monsieur Bongrand to defend him,—she turned pale and staggered. Can she love him? Is there anything between them?"

"At fifteen years of age? pooh!" replied Bongrand.

"She was born in February, 1813; she'll be sixteen in four months."

"I don't believe she ever saw him," said the judge. "No, it is only a nervous attack."

"Attack of the heart, more likely," said the notary.

Dionis was delighted with this discovery, which would prevent the marriage "in extremis" which they dreaded,—the only sure means by which the doctor could defraud his relatives. Bongrand, on the other hand, saw a private castle of his own demolished; he had long thought of marrying his son to Ursula.

"If the poor girl loves that youth it will be a misfortune for her," replied Bongrand after a pause. "Madame de Portenduere is a Breton and infatuated with her noble blood."

"Luckily—I mean for the honor of the Portendueres," replied the notary, on the point of betraying himself.

Let us do the faithful and upright Bongrand the justice to say that before he re-entered the salon he had abandoned, not without deep regret for his son, the hope he had cherished of some day calling Ursula his daughter. He meant to give his son six thousand francs a year the day he was appointed substitute, and if the doctor would give Ursula a hundred thousand francs what a pearl of a home the pair would make! His Eugene was so loyal and charming a fellow! Perhaps he had praised his Eugene too often, and that had made the doctor distrustful.

"I shall have to come down to the mayor's daughter," he thought. "But Ursula without any money is worth more than Mademoiselle Levrault-Cremiere with a million. However, the thing to be done is to manoeuvre the marriage with this little Portenduere—if she really loves him."

The doctor, after closing the door to the library and that to the garden, took his goddaughter to the window which opened upon the river.

"What ails you, my child?" he said. "Your life is my life. Without your smiles what would become of me?"

"Savinien in prison!" she said.

With these words a shower of tears fell from her eyes and she began to sob.

"Saved!" thought the doctor, who was holding her pulse with great anxiety. "Alas! she has all the sensitiveness of my poor wife," he thought, fetching a stethoscope which he put to Ursula's heart, applying his ear to it. "Ah, that's all right," he said to himself. "I did not know, my darling, that you loved any one as yet," he added, looking at her; "but think out loud to me as you think to yourself; tell me all that has passed between you."

"I do not love him, godfather; we have never spoken to each other," she answered, sobbing. "But to hear that he is in prison, and to know that you— harshly—refused to get him out—you, so good!"

"Ursula, my dear little good angel, if you do not love him why did you put that little red dot against Saint Savinien's day just as you put one before that of Saint Denis? Come, tell me everything about your little love-affair."

Ursula blushed, swallowed a few tears, and for a moment there was silence between them.

"Surely you are not afraid of your father, your friend, mother, doctor, and godfather, whose heart is now more tender than it ever has been."

"No, no, dear godfather," she said. "I will open my heart to you. Last May, Monsieur Savinien came to see his mother. Until then I had never taken notice of him. When he left home to live in Paris I was a child, and I did not see any difference between him and—all of you—except perhaps that I loved you, and never thought of loving any one else. Monsieur Savinien came by the mail-post the night before his mother's fete-day; but we did not know it. At seven the next morning, after I had said my prayers, I opened the window to air my room and I saw the windows in Monsieur Savinien's room open; and Monsieur Savinien was there, in a dressing gown, arranging his beard; in all his movements there was such grace—I mean, he seemed to me so charming. He combed his black moustache and the little tuft on his chin, and I saw his white throat—so round!—must I tell you all? I noticed that his throat and face and that beautiful black hair were all so different from yours when I watch you arranging your beard. There came—I don't know how— a sort of glow into my heart, and up into my throat, my head; it came so violently that I sat down—I couldn't stand, I trembled so. But I longed to see him again, and presently I got up; he saw me then, and, just for play, he sent me a kiss from the tips of his fingers and—"

"And?"

"And then," she continued, "I hid myself—I was ashamed, but happy—why should I be ashamed of being happy? That feeling—it dazzled my soul and gave it some power, but I don't know what—it came again each time I saw within me the same young face. I loved this feeling, violent as it was. Going to mass, some unconquerable power made me look at Monsieur Savinien with his mother on his arm; his walk, his clothes, even the tap of his boots on the pavement, seemed to me so charming. The least little thing about him—his hand with the delicate glove—acted like a spell upon me; and yet I had strength enough not to think of him during mass. When the service was over I stayed in the church to let Madame de Portenduere go first, and then I walked behind him. I couldn't tell you how these little things excited me. When I reached home, I turned round to fasten the iron gate—"

"Where was La Bougival?" asked the doctor.

"Oh, I let her go to the kitchen," said Ursula simply. "Then I saw Monsieur Savinien standing quite still and looking at me. Oh! godfather, I was so proud, for I thought I saw a look in his eyes of surprise and admiration—I don't know what I would not do to make him look at me again like that. It seemed to me I ought to think of nothing forevermore but pleasing him. That glance is now the best reward I have for any good I do. From that moment I have thought of him incessantly, in spite of myself. Monsieur Savinien went back to Paris that evening, and I have not seen him since. The street seems empty; he took my heart away with him—but he does not know it."

"Is that all?" asked the old man.

"All, dear godfather," she said, with a sigh of regret that there was not more to tell.

"My little girl," said the doctor, putting her on his knee; "you are nearly sixteen and your womanhood is beginning. You are now between your blessed childhood, which is ending, and the emotions of love, which will make your life a tumultuous one; for you have a nervous system of exquisite sensibility. What has happened to you, my child, is love," said the old man with an expression of deepest sadness,—"love in its holy simplicity; love as it ought to be; involuntary, sudden, coming like a thief who takes all—yes, all! I expected it. I have studied women; many need proofs and miracles of affection before love conquers them; but others there are, under the influence of sympathies explainable to-day by magnetic fluids, who are possessed by it in an instant. To you I can now tell all—as soon as I saw the charming woman whose name you bear, I felt that I should love her forever, solely and faithfully, without knowing whether our characters or persons suited each other. Is there a second-sight in love? What answer can I give to that, I who have seen so many unions formed under celestial auspices only to be ruptured later, giving rise to hatreds that are well-nigh eternal, to repugnances that are unconquerable. The senses sometimes harmonize while ideas are at variance; and some persons live more by their minds than by their bodies. The contrary is also true; often minds agree and persons displease. These phenomena, the varying and secret cause of many sorrows, show the wisdom of laws which give parents supreme power over the marriages of their children; for a young girl is often duped by one or other of these hallucinations. Therefore I do not blame you. The sensations you feel, the rush of sensibility which has come from its hidden source upon your heart and upon your mind, the happiness with which you think of Savinien, are all natural. But, my darling child, society demands, as our good abbe has told us, the sacrifice of many natural inclinations. The destinies of men and women differ. I was able to choose Ursula Mirouet for my wife; I could go to her and say that I loved her; but a young girl is false to herself if she asks the love of the man she loves. A woman has not the right which men have to seek the accomplishment of her hopes in open day. Modesty is to her—above all to you, my Ursula,—the insurmountable barrier which protects the secrets of her heart. Your hesitation in confiding to me these first emotions shows me you would suffer cruel torture rather than admit to Savinien—"

"Oh, yes!" she said.

"But, my child, you must do more. You must repress these feelings; you must forget them."

"Why?"

"Because, my darling, you must love only the man you marry; and, even if Monsieur Savinien de Portenduere loved you—"

"I never thought of it."

"But listen: even if he loved you, even if his mother asked me to give him your hand, I should not consent to the marriage until I had subjected him to a long and thorough probation. His conduct has been such as to make families distrust him and to put obstacles between himself and heiresses which cannot be easily overcome."

A soft smile came in place of tears on Ursula's sweet face as she said, "Then poverty is good sometimes."

The doctor could find no answer to such innocence.

"What has he done, godfather?" she asked.

"In two years, my treasure, he has incurred one hundred and twenty thousand francs of debt. He has had the folly to get himself locked up in Saint-Pelagie, the debtor's prison; an impropriety which will always be, in these days, a discredit to him. A spendthrift who is willing to plunge his poor mother into poverty and distress might cause his wife, as your poor father did, to die of despair."

"Don't you think he will do better?" she asked.

"If his mother pays his debts he will be penniless, and I don't know a worse punishment than to be a nobleman without means."

This answer made Ursula thoughtful; she dried her tears, and said:—

"If you can save him, save him, godfather; that service will give you a right to advise him; you can remonstrate—"

"Yes," said the doctor, imitating her, "and then he can come here, and the old lady will come here, and we shall see them, and—"

"I was thinking only of him," said Ursula, blushing.

"Don't think of him, my child; it would be folly," said the doctor gravely. "Madame de Portenduere, who was a Kergarouet, would never consent, even if she had to live on three hundred francs a year, to the marriage of her son, the Vicomte Savinien de Portenduere, with whom?—with Ursula Mirouet, daughter of a bandsman in a regiment, without money, and whose father—alas! I must now tell you all—was the bastard son of an organist, my father-in-law."

"O godfather! you are right; we are equal only in the sight of God. I will not think of him again—except in my prayers," she said, amid the sobs which this painful revelation excited. "Give him what you meant to give me—what can a poor girl like me want?—ah, in prison, he!—"

"Offer to God your disappointments, and perhaps he will help us."

There was silence for some minutes. When Ursula, who at first did not dare to look at her godfather, raised her eyes, her heart was deeply moved to see the tears which were rolling down his withered cheeks. The tears of old men are as terrible as those of children are natural.

"Oh what is it?" cried Ursula, flinging herself at his feet and kissing his hands. "Are you not sure of me?"

"I, who longed to gratify all your wishes, it is I who am obliged to cause the first great sorrow of your life!" he said. "I suffer as much as you. I never wept before, except when I lost my children—and, Ursula—Yes," he cried suddenly, "I will do all you desire!"

Ursula gave him, through her tears a look that was vivid as lightning. She smiled.

"Let us go into the salon, darling," said the doctor. "Try to keep the secret of all this to yourself," he added, leaving her alone for a moment in his study.

He felt himself so weak before that heavenly smile that he feared he might say a word of hope and thus mislead her.

CHAPTER X.
THE FAMILY OF PORTENDUERE

Madame de Portenduere was at this moment alone with the abbe in her frigid little salon on the ground floor, having finished the recital of her troubles to the good priest, her only friend. She held in her hand some letters which he had just returned to her after reading them; these letters had brought her troubles to a climax. Seated on her sofa beside a square table covered with the remains of a dessert, the old lady was looking at the abbe, who sat on the other side of the table, doubled up in his armchair and stroking his chin with the gesture common to valets on the stage, mathematicians, and priests,—a sign of profound meditation on a problem that was difficult to solve.

This little salon, lighted by two windows on the street and finished with a wainscot painted gray, was so damp that the lower panels showed the geometrical cracks of rotten wood when the paint no longer binds it. The red-tiled floor, polished by the old lady's one servant, required, for comfort's sake, before each seat small round mats of brown straw, on one of which the abbe was now resting his feet. The old damask curtains of light green with green flowers were drawn, and the outside blinds had been closed. Two wax candles lighted the table, leaving the rest of the room in semi-obscurity. Is it necessary to say that between the two windows was a fine pastel by Latour representing the famous Admiral de Portenduere, the rival of the Suffren, Guichen, Kergarouet and Simeuse naval heroes? On the paneled wall opposite to the fireplace were portraits of the Vicomte de Portenduere and of the mother of the old lady, a Kergarouet-Ploegat. Savinien's great-uncle was therefore the Vice-admiral de Kergarouet, and his cousin was the Comte de Portenduere, grandson of the admiral,—both of them very rich.

The Vice-admiral de Kergarouet lived in Paris and the Comte de Portenduere at the chateau of that name in Dauphine. The count represented the elder branch, and Savinien was the only scion of the younger. The count, who was over forty years of age and married to a rich wife, had three children. His fortune, increased by various legacies, amounted, it was said, to sixty thousand francs a year. As deputy from Isere he passed his winters in Paris, where he had bought the hotel de Portenduere with the indemnities he obtained under the Villele law. The vice-admiral had recently married his niece by marriage, for the sole purpose of securing his money to her.

The faults of the young viscount were therefore likely to cost him the favor of two powerful protectors. If Savinien had entered the navy, young and handsome as he was, with a famous name, and backed by the influence of an admiral and a deputy, he might, at twenty-three years of age, been a lieutenant; but his mother, unwilling that her only son should go into either naval or military service, had kept him at Nemours under the tutelage of one of the Abbe Chaperon's assistants, hoping that she could keep him near her until her death. She meant to marry him to a demoiselle d'Aiglemont with a fortune of twelve thousand francs a year; to whose hand the name of Portenduere and the farm at Bordieres enabled him to pretend. This narrow but judicious plan, which would have carried the family to a second generation, was already balked by events. The d'Aiglemonts were ruined, and one of the daughters, Helene, had disappeared, and the mystery of her disappearance was never solved.

The weariness of a life without atmosphere, without prospects, without action, without other nourishment than the love of a son for his mother, so worked upon Savinien that he burst his chains, gentle as they were, and swore that he would never live in the provinces—comprehending, rather late, that his future fate was not to be in the Rue des Bourgeois. At twenty-one years of age he left his mother's house to make acquaintance with his relations, and try his luck in Paris. The contrast between life in Paris and life in Nemours was likely to be fatal to a young man of twenty-one, free, with no one to say him nay, naturally eager for pleasure, and for whom his name and his connections opened the doors of all the salons. Quite convinced that his mother had the savings of many years in her strong-box, Savinien soon spent the six thousand francs which she had given him to see Paris. That sum did not defray his expenses for six months, and he soon owed double that sum to his hotel, his tailor, his boot maker, to the man from whom he hired his carriages and horses, to a jeweler,—in short, to all those traders and shopkeepers who contribute to the luxury of young men.

He had only just succeeded in making himself known, and had scarcely learned how to converse, how to present himself in a salon, how to wear his waistcoats and choose them and to order his coats and tie his cravat, before he found himself in debt for over thirty thousand francs, while still seeking the right phrases in which to declare his love for the sister of the Marquis de Ronquerolles, the elegant Madame de Serizy, whose youth had been at its climax during the Empire.

"How is that you all manage?" asked Savinien one day, at the end of a gay breakfast with a knot of young dandies, with whom he was intimate as the young men of the present day are intimate with each other, all aiming for the same thing and all claiming an impossible equality. "You were no richer than I and yet you get along without anxiety; you contrive to maintain yourselves, while as for me I make nothing but debts."

"We all began that way," answered Rastignac, laughing, and the laugh was echoed by Lucien de Rubempre, Maxime de Trailles, Emile Blondet, and others of the fashionable young men of the day.

"Though de Marsay was rich when he started in life he was an exception," said the host, a parvenu named Finot, ambitious of seeming intimate with these young men. "Any one but he," added Finot bowing to that personage, "would have been ruined by it."

"A true remark," said Maxime de Trailles.

"And a true idea," added Rastignac.

"My dear fellow," said de Marsay, gravely, to Savinien; "debts are the capital stock of experience. A good university education with tutors for all branches, who don't teach you anything, costs sixty thousand francs. If the education of the world does cost double, at least it teaches you to understand life, politics, men,—and sometimes women."

Blondet concluded the lesson by a paraphrase from La Fontaine: "The world sells dearly what we think it gives."

Instead of laying to heart the sensible advice which the cleverest pilots of the Parisian archipelago gave him, Savinien took it all as a joke.

"Take care, my dear fellow," said de Marsay one day. "You have a great name; if you don't obtain the fortune that name requires you'll end your days in the uniform of a cavalry-sergeant. 'We have seen the fall of nobler heads,'" he added, declaiming the line of Corneille as he took Savinien's arm. "About six years ago," he continued, "a young Comte d'Esgrignon came among us; but he did not stay two years in the paradise of the great world. Alas! he lived and moved like a rocket. He rose to the Duchesse de Maufrigneuse and fell to his native town, where he is now expiating his faults with a wheezy old father and a game of whist at two sous a point. Tell Madame de Serizy your situation, candidly, without shame; she will understand it and be very useful to you. Whereas, if you play the charade of first love with her she will pose as a Raffaelle Madonna, practice all the little games of innocence upon you, and take you journeying at enormous cost through the Land of Sentiment."

Savinien, still too young and too pure in honor, dared not confess his position as to money to Madame de Serizy. At a moment when he knew not which way to turn he had written his mother an appealing letter, to which she replied by sending him the sum of twenty thousand francs, which was all she possessed. This assistance brought him to the close of the first year. During the second, being harnessed to the chariot of Madame de Serizy, who was seriously taken with him, and who was, as the saying is, forming him, he had recourse to the dangerous expedient of borrowing. One of his friends, a deputy and the friend of his cousin the Comte de Portenduere, advised him in his distress to go to Gobseck or Gigonnet or Palma, who, if duly informed as to his mother's means, would give him an easy discount. Usury and the deceptive help of renewals enabled him to lead a happy life for nearly eighteen months. Without daring to leave Madame de Serizy the poor boy had fallen madly in love with the beautiful Comtesse de Kergarouet, a prude after the fashion of young women who are awaiting the death of an old husband and making capital of their virtue in the interests of a second marriage. Quite incapable of understanding that calculating virtue is invulnerable, Savinien paid court to Emilie de Kergarouet in all the splendor of a rich man. He never missed either ball or theater at which she was present.

"You haven't powder enough, my boy, to blow up that rock," said de Marsay, laughing.

That young king of fashion, who did, out of commiseration for the lad, endeavor to explain to him the nature of Emilie de Fontaine, merely wasted his words; the gloomy lights of misfortune and the twilight of a prison were needed to convince Savinien.

A note, imprudently given to a jeweler in collusion with the money-lenders, who did not wish to have the odium of arresting the young man, was the means of sending Savinien de Portenduere, in default of one hundred and seventeen thousand francs and without the knowledge of his friends, to the debtor's prison at Sainte-Pelagie. So soon as the fact was known Rastignac, de Marsay, and Lucien de Rubempre went to see him, and each offered him a banknote of a thousand francs when they found how really destitute he was. Everything belonging to him had been seized except the clothes and the few jewels he wore. The three young men (who brought an excellent dinner with them) discussed Savinien's situation while drinking de Marsay's wine, ostensibly to arrange for his future but really, no doubt, to judge of him.

"When a man is named Savinien de Portenduere," cried Rastignac, "and has a future peer of France for a cousin and Admiral Kergarouet for a great-uncle, and commits the enormous blunder of allowing himself to be put in Sainte-Pelagie, it is very certain that he must not stay there, my good fellow."

"Why didn't you tell me?" cried de Marsay. "You could have had my traveling-carriage, ten thousand francs, and letters of introduction for Germany. We know Gobseck and Gigonnet and the other crocodiles; we could have made them capitulate. But tell me, in the first place, what ass ever led you to drink of that cursed spring."

"Des Lupeaulx."

The three young men looked at each other with one and the same thought and suspicion, but they did not utter it.

"Explain all your resources; show us your hand," said de Marsay.

When Savinien had told of his mother and her old-fashioned ways, and the little house with three windows in the Rue des Bourgeois, without other grounds than a court for the well and a shed for the wood; when he had valued the house, built of sandstone and pointed in reddish cement, and put a price on the farm at Bordieres, the three dandies looked at each other, and all three said with a solemn air the word of the abbe in Alfred de Musset's "Marrons du feu" (which had then just appeared),—"Sad!"

"Your mother will pay if you write a clever letter," said Rastignac.

"Yes, but afterwards?" cried de Marsay.

"If you had merely been put in the fiacre," said Lucien, "the government would find you a place in diplomacy, but Saint-Pelagie isn't the antechamber of an embassy."

"You are not strong enough for Parisian life," said Rastignac.

"Let us consider the matter," said de Marsay, looking Savinien over as a jockey examines a horse. "You have fine blue eyes, well opened, a white forehead well shaped, magnificent black hair, a little moustache which suits those pale cheeks, and a slim figure; you've a foot that tells race, shoulders and chest not quite those of a porter, but solid. You are what I call an elegant male brunette. Your face is of the style Louis XII., hardly any color, well-formed nose; and you have the thing that pleases women, a something, I don't know what it is, which men take no account of themselves; it is in the air, the manner, the tone of the voice, the dart of the eye, the gesture,—in short, in a number of little things which women see and to which they attach a meaning which escapes us. You don't know your merits, my dear fellow. Take a certain tone and style and in six months you'll captivate an English-woman with a hundred thousand pounds; but you must call yourself viscount, a title which belongs to you. My charming step-mother, Lady Dudley, who has not her equal for matching two hearts, will find you some such woman in the fens of Great Britain. What you must now do is to get the payment of your debts postponed for ninety days. Why didn't you tell us about them? The money-lenders at Baden would have spared you—served you perhaps; but now, after you have once been in prison, they'll despise you. A money-lender is, like society, like the masses, down on his knees before the man who is strong enough to trick him, and pitiless to the lambs. To the eyes of some persons Sainte-Pelagie is a she-devil who burns the souls of young men. Do you want my candid advice? I shall tell you as I told that little d'Esgrignon: 'Arrange to pay your debts leisurely; keep enough to live on for three years, and marry some girl in the provinces who can bring you an income of thirty thousand francs.' In the course of three years you can surely find some virtuous heiress who is willing to call herself Madame la

Vicomtesse de Portenduere. Such is virtue,—let's drink to it. I give you a toast: 'The girl with money!'"

The young men did not leave their ex-friend till the official hour for parting. The gate was no sooner closed behind them than they said to each other: "He's not strong enough!" "He's quite crushed." "I don't believe he'll pull through it?"

The next day Savinien wrote his mother a confession in twenty-two pages. Madame de Portenduere, after weeping for one whole day, wrote first to her son, promising to get him out of prison, and then to the Comte de Portenduere and to Admiral Kergarouet.

The letters the abbe had just read and which the poor mother was holding in her hand and moistening with tears, were the answers to her appeal, which had arrived that morning, and had almost broken her heart.

Paris, September, 1829.

To Madame de Portenduere:

Madame,—You cannot doubt the interest which the admiral and I both feel in your troubles. What you ask of Monsieur de Kergarouet grieves me all the more because our house was a home to your son; we were proud of him. If Savinien had had more confidence in the admiral we could have taken him to live with us, and he would already have obtained some good situation. But, unfortunately, he told us nothing; he ran into debt of his own accord, and even involved himself for me, who knew nothing of his pecuniary position. It is all the more to be regretted because Savinien has, for the moment, tied our hands by allowing the authorities to arrest him.

If my nephew had not shown a foolish passion for me and sacrificed our relationship to the vanity of a lover, we could have sent him to travel in Germany while his affairs were being settled here. Monsieur de Kergarouet intended to get him a place in the War office; but this imprisonment for debt will paralyze such efforts. You must pay his debts; let him enter the navy; he will make his way like the true Portenduere that he is; he has the fire of the family in his beautiful black eyes, and we will all help him.

Do not be disheartened, madame; you have many friends, among whom I beg you to consider me as one of the most sincere; I send you our best wishes, with the respects of

Your very affectionate servant, Emilie de Kergarouet.

The second letter was as follows:—

Portenduere, August, 1829.

To Madame de Portenduere:

My dear aunt,—I am more annoyed than surprised at Savinien's pranks. As I am married and the father of two sons and one daughter, my fortune, already too small for my position and prospects, cannot be lessened to ransom a Portenduere from the hands of the Jews. Sell your farm, pay his debts, and come and live with us at Portenduere. You shall receive the welcome we owe you, even though our views may not be entirely in accordance with yours. You shall be made happy, and we will manage to marry Savinien, whom my wife thinks charming. This little outbreak is nothing; do not make yourself unhappy; it will never be known in this part of the country, where there are a number of rich girls who would be delighted to enter our family.

My wife joins me in assuring you of the happiness you would give us, and I beg you to accept her wishes for the realization of this plan, together with my affectionate respects.

Luc-Savinien, Comte de Portenduere.

"What letters for a Kergarouet to receive!" cried the old Breton lady, wiping her eyes.

"The admiral does not know his nephew is in prison," said the Abbe Chaperon at last; "the countess alone read your letter, and has answered it for him. But you must decide at once on some course," he added after a pause, "and this is what I have the honor to advise. Do not sell your farm. The lease is just out, having lasted twenty-four years; in a few months you can raise the rent to six thousand francs and get a premium for double that amount. Borrow what you need of some honest man,—not from the townspeople who make a business of mortgages. Your neighbour here is a most worthy man; a man of good society, who knew it as it was before the Revolution, who was once an atheist, and is now an earnest Catholic. Do not let your feelings debar you from going to his house this very evening; he will fully understand the step you take; forget for a moment that you are a Kergarouet."

"Never!" said the old mother, in a sharp voice.

"Well, then, be an amiable Kergarouet; come when he is alone. He will lend you the money at three and a half per cent, perhaps even at three per cent, and will do you this service delicately; you will be pleased with him. He can go to Paris and release Savinien himself,—for he will have to go there to sell out his funds,—and he can bring the lad back to you."

"Are you speaking of that little Minoret?"

"That little Minoret is eighty-three years old," said the abbe, smiling. "My dear lady, do have a little Christian charity; don't wound him,—he might be useful to you in other ways."

"What ways?"

"He has an angel in his house; a precious young girl—"

"Oh! that little Ursula. What of that?"

The poor abbe did not pursue the subject after these significant words, the laconic sharpness of which cut through the proposition he was about to make.

"I think Doctor Minoret is very rich," he said.

"So much the better for him."

"You have indirectly caused your son's misfortunes by refusing to give him a profession; beware for the future," said the abbe sternly. "Am I to tell Doctor Minoret that you are coming?"

"Why cannot he come to me if he knows I want him?" she replied.

"Ah, madame, if you go to him you will pay him three per cent; if he comes to you you will pay him five," said the abbe, inventing this reason to influence the old lady. "And if you are forced to sell your farm by Dionis the notary, or by Massin the clerk (who would refuse to lend you the money, knowing it was more their interest to buy), you would lose half its value. I have not the slightest influence on the Dionis, Massins, or Levraults, or any of those rich men who covet your farm and know that your son is in prison."

"They know it! oh, do they know it?" she exclaimed, throwing up her arms. "There! my poor abbe, you have let your coffee get cold! Tiennette, Tiennette!"

Tiennette, an old Breton servant sixty years of age, wearing a short gown and a Breton cap, came quickly in and took the abbe's coffee to warm it.

"Let be, Monsieur le recteur," she said, seeing that the abbe meant to drink it, "I'll just put it into the bain-marie, it won't spoil it."

"Well," said the abbe to Madame de Portenduere in his most insinuating voice, "I shall go and tell the doctor of your visit, and you will come—"

The old mother did not yield till after an hour's discussion, during which the abbe was forced to repeat his arguments at least ten times. And even then the proud Kergarouet was not vanquished until he used the words, "Savinien would go."

"It is better that I should go than he," she said.

CHAPTER XI.
SAVINIEN SAVED

The clock was striking nine when the little door made in the large door of Madame de Portenduere's house closed on the abbe, who immediately crossed the road and hastily rang the bell at the doctor's gate. He fell from Tiennette to La Bougival; the one said to him, "Why do you come so late, Monsieur l'abbe?" as the other had said, "Why do you leave Madame so early when she is in trouble?"

The abbe found a numerous company assembled in the green and brown salon; for Dionis had stopped at Massin's on his way home to re-assure the heirs by repeating their uncle's words.

"I believe Ursula has a love-affair," said he, "which will be nothing but pain and trouble to her; she seems romantic" (extreme sensibility is so called by notaries), "and, you'll see, she won't marry soon. Therefore, don't show her any distrust; be very attentive to her and very respectful to your uncle, for he is slyer than fifty Goupils," added the notary—without being aware that Goupil is a corruption of the word vulpes, a fox.

So Mesdames Massin and Cremiere with their husbands, the post master and Desire, together with the Nemours doctor and Bongrand, made an unusual and noisy party in the doctor's salon. As the abbe entered he heard the sound of the piano. Poor Ursula was just finishing a sonata of Beethoven's. With girlish mischief she had chosen that grand music, which must be studied to be understood, for the purpose of disgusting these women with the thing they coveted. The finer the music the less ignorant persons like it. So, when the door opened and the abbe's venerable head appeared they all cried out: "Ah! here's Monsieur l'abbe!" in a tone of relief, delighted to jump up and put an end to their torture.

The exclamation was echoed at the card-table, where Bongrand, the Nemours doctor, and old Minoret were victims to the presumption with which the collector, in order to propitiate his great-uncle, had proposed to take the fourth hand at whist. Ursula left the piano. The doctor rose as if to receive the abbe, but really to put an end to the game. After many compliments to their uncle on the wonderful proficiency of his goddaughter, the heirs made their bow and retired.

"Good-night, my friends," cried the doctor as the iron gate clanged.

"Ah! that's where the money goes," said Madame Cremiere to Madame Massin, as they walked on.

"God forbid that I should spend money to teach my little Aline to make such a din as that!" cried Madame Massin.

"She said it was Beethoven, who is thought to be fine musician," said the collector; "he has quite a reputation."

"Not in Nemours, I'm sure of that," said Madame Cremiere.

"I believe uncle made her play it expressly to drive us away," said Massin; "for I saw him give that little minx a wink as she opened the music-book."

"If that's the sort of charivari they like," said the post master, "they are quite right to keep it to themselves."

"Monsieur Bongrand must be fond of whist to stand such a dreadful racket," said Madame Cremiere.

"I shall never be able to play before persons who don't understand music," Ursula was saying as she sat down beside the whist-table.

"In natures richly organized," said the abbe, "sentiments can be developed only in a congenial atmosphere. Just as a priest is unable to give the blessing in presence of an evil spirit, or as a chestnut-tree dies in a clay soil, so a musician's genius has a mental eclipse when he is surrounded by ignorant persons. In all the arts we must receive from the souls who make the environment of our souls as much intensity as we convey to them. This axiom, which rules the human mind, has been made into proverbs: 'Howl with the wolves'; 'Like meets like.' But the suffering you felt, Ursula, affects delicate and tender natures only."

"And so, friends," said the doctor, "a thing which would merely give pain to most women might kill my Ursula. Ah! when I am no longer here, I charge you to see that the hedge of which Catullus spoke,—'Ut flos,' etc.,—a protecting hedge is raised between this cherished flower and the world."

"And yet those ladies flattered you, Ursula," said Monsieur Bongrand, smiling.

"Flattered her grossly," remarked the Nemours doctor.

"I have always noticed how vulgar forced flattery is," said old Minoret. "Why is that?"

"A true thought has its own delicacy," said the abbe.

"Did you dine with Madame de Portenduere?" asked Ursula, with a look of anxious curiosity.

"Yes; the poor lady is terribly distressed. It is possible she may come to see you this evening, Monsieur Minoret."

Ursula pressed her godfather's hand under the table.

"Her son," said Bongrand, "was rather too simple-minded to live in Paris without a mentor. When I heard that inquiries were being made here about the property of the old lady I feared he was discounting her death."

"Is it possible you think him capable of it?" said Ursula, with such a terrible glance at Monsieur Bongrand that he said to himself rather sadly, "Alas! yes, she loves him."

"Yes and no," said the Nemours doctor, replying to Ursula's question. "There is a great deal of good in Savinien, and that is why he is now in prison; a scamp wouldn't have got there."

"Don't let us talk about it any more," said old Minoret. "The poor mother must not be allowed to weep if there's a way to dry her tears."

The four friends rose and went out; Ursula accompanied them to the gate, saw her godfather and the abbe knock at the opposite door, and as soon as Tiennette admitted them she sat down on the outer wall with La Bougival beside her.

"Madame la vicomtesse," said the abbe, who entered first into the little salon, "Monsieur le docteur Minoret was not willing that you should have the trouble of coming to him—"

"I am too much of the old school, madame," interrupted the doctor, "not to know what a man owes to a woman of your rank, and I am very glad to be able, as Monsieur l'abbe tells me, to be of service to you."

Madame de Portenduere, who disliked the step the abbe had advised so much that she had almost decided, after he left her, to apply to the notary instead, was surprised by Minoret's attention to such a degree that she rose to receive him and signed to him to take a chair.

"Be seated, monsieur," she said with a regal air. "Our dear abbe has told you that the viscount is in prison on account of some youthful debts,—a hundred thousand francs or so. If you could lend them to him I would secure you on my farm at Bordieres."

"We will talk of that, madame, when I have brought your son back to you— if you will allow me to be your emissary in the matter."

"Very good, monsieur," she said, bowing her head and looking at the abbe as if to say, "You were right; he really is a man of good society."

"You see, madame," said the abbe, "that my friend the doctor is full of devotion to your family."

"We shall be grateful, monsieur," said Madame de Portenduere, making a visible effort; "a journey to Paris, at your age, in quest of a prodigal, is—"

"Madame, I had the honor to meet, in '65, the illustrious Admiral de Portenduere in the house of that excellent Monsieur de Malesherbes, and also in that of Monsieur le Comte de Buffon, who was anxious to question him on some curious results of his voyages. Possibly Monsieur de Portenduere, your late husband, was present. Those were the glorious days of the French navy; it bore comparison with that of Great Britain, and its officers had their full quota of courage. With what impatience we awaited in '83 and '84 the news from St. Roch. I came very near serving as surgeon in the king's service. Your great-uncle, who is still living, Admiral Kergarouet, fought his splendid battle at that time in the 'Belle-Poule.'"

"Ah! if he did but know his great-nephew is in prison!"

"He would not leave him there a day," said old Minoret, rising.

He held out his hand to take that of the old lady, which she allowed him to do; then he kissed it respectfully, bowed profoundly, and left the room; but returned immediately to say:—

"My dear abbe, may I ask you to engage a place in the diligence for me to-morrow?"

The abbe stayed behind for half an hour to sing the praises of his friend, who meant to win and had succeeded in winning the good graces of the old lady.

"He is an astonishing man for his age," she said. "He talks of going to Paris and attending to my son's affairs as if he were only twenty-five. He has certainly seen good society."

"The very best, madame; and to-day more than one son of a peer of France would be glad to marry his goddaughter with a million. Ah! if that idea should come into Savinien's head!—times are so changed that the objections would not come from your side, especially after his late conduct—"

The amazement into which the speech threw the old lady alone enabled him to finish it.

"You have lost your senses," she said at last.

"Think it over, madame; God grant that your son may conduct himself in future in a manner to win that old man's respect."

"If it were not you, Monsieur l'abbe," said Madame de Portenduere, "if it were any one else who spoke to me in that way—"

"You would not see him again," said the abbe, smiling. "Let us hope that your dear son will enlighten you as to what occurs in Paris in these days as to marriages. You will think only of Savinien's good; as you really have helped to compromise his future you will not stand in the way of his making himself another position."

"And it is you who say that to me?"

"If I did not say it to you, who would?" cried the abbe rising and making a hasty retreat.

As he left the house he saw Ursula and her godfather standing in their courtyard. The weak doctor had been so entreated by Ursula that he had just yielded to her. She wanted to go with him to Paris, and gave a thousand reasons. He called to the abbe and begged him to engage the whole coupe for him that very evening if the booking-office were still open.

The next day at half-past six o'clock the old man and the young girl reached Paris, and the doctor went at once to consult his notary. Political events were then very threatening. Monsieur Bongrand had remarked in the course of the preceding evening that a man must be a fool to keep a penny in the public funds so long as the quarrel between the press and the court was not made up. Minoret's notary now indirectly approved of this opinion. The doctor therefore took advantage of his journey to sell out his manufacturing stocks and his shares in the Funds, all of which were then at a high value, depositing the proceeds in the Bank of France. The notary also advised his client to sell the stocks left to Ursula by Monsieur de Jordy. He promised to employ an extremely clever broker to treat with Savinien's creditors; but said that in order to succeed it would be necessary for the young man to stay several days longer in prison.

"Haste in such matters always means the loss of at least fifteen per cent," said the notary. "Besides, you can't get your money under seven or eight days."

When Ursula heard that Savinien would have to say at least a week longer in jail she begged her godfather to let her go there, if only once. Old Minoret refused. The uncle and niece were staying at a hotel in the Rue Croix des Petits-Champs where the doctor had taken a very suitable apartment. Knowing the scrupulous honor and propriety of his goddaughter he made her promise not to go out while he was away; at other times he took her to see the arcades, the shops, the boulevards; but nothing seemed to amuse or interest her.

"What do you want to do?" asked the old man.

"See Saint-Pelagie," she answered obstinately.

Minoret called a hackney-coach and took her to the Rue de la Clef, where the carriage drew up before the shabby front of an old convent then transformed into a prison. The sight of those high gray walls, with every window barred, of the wicket through which none can enter without stooping (horrible lesson!), of the whole gloomy structure in a quarter full of wretchedness, where it rises amid squalid streets like a supreme misery,— this assemblage of dismal things so oppressed Ursula's heart that she burst into tears.

"Oh!" she said, "to imprison young men in this dreadful place for money! How can a debt to a money-lender have a power the king has not? *He* there!" she cried. "Where, godfather?" she added, looking from window to window.

"Ursula," said the old man, "you are making me commit great follies. This is not forgetting him as you promised."

"But," she argued, "if I must renounce him must I also cease to feel an interest in him? I can love him and not marry at all."

"Ah!" cried the doctor, "there is so much reason in your unreasonableness that I am sorry I brought you."

Three days later the worthy man had all the receipts signed, and the legal papers ready for Savinien's release. The payings, including the notaries' fees, amounted to eighty thousand francs. The doctor went himself to see Savinien released on Saturday at two o'clock. The young viscount, already informed of what had happened by his mother, thanked his liberator with sincere warmth of heart.

"You must return at once to see your mother," the old doctor said to him.

Savinien answered in a sort of confusion that he had contracted certain debts of honor while in prison, and related the visit of his friends.

"I suspected there was some personal debt," cried the doctor, smiling. "Your mother borrowed a hundred thousand francs of me, but I have paid out only eighty thousand. Here is the rest; be careful how you spend it, monsieur; consider what you have left of it as your stake on the green cloth of fortune."

During the last eight days Savinien had made many reflections on the present conditions of life. Competition in everything necessitated hard work on the part of whoever sought a fortune. Illegal methods and underhand dealing demanded more talent than open efforts in face of day. Success in society, far from giving a man position, wasted his time and required an immense deal of money. The name of Portenduere, which his mother considered all-powerful, had no power at all in Paris. His cousin the deputy, Comte de Portenduere, cut a very poor figure in the Elective Chamber in presence of the peerage and the court; and had none too much credit personally. Admiral Kergarouet existed only as the husband of his wife. Savinien admitted to himself that he had seen orators, men from the middle classes, or lesser noblemen, become influential personages. Money was the pivot, the sole means, the only mechanism of a society which Louis XVIII. had tried to create in the likeness of that of England.

On his way from the Rue de la Clef to the Rue Croix des Petits-Champs the young gentleman divulged the upshot of these meditations (which were certainly in keeping with de Marsay's advice) to the old doctor.

"I ought," he said, "to go into oblivion for three or four years and seek a career. Perhaps I could make myself a name by writing a book on statesmanship or morals, or a treatise on some of the great questions of the day. While I am looking out for a marriage with some young lady who could make me eligible to the Chamber, I will work hard in silence and in obscurity."

Studying the young fellow's face with a keen eye, the doctor saw the serious purpose of a wounded man who was anxious to vindicate himself. He therefore cordially approved of the scheme.

"My friend," he said, "if you strip off the skin of the old nobility (which is no longer worn these days) I will undertake, after you have lived for three or four years in a steady and industrious manner, to find you a superior young girl, beautiful, amiable, pious, and possessing from seven to eight hundred thousand francs, who will make you happy and of whom you will have every reason to be proud,—one whose only nobility is that of the heart!"

"Ah, doctor!" cried the young man, "there is no longer a nobility in these days,—nothing but an aristocracy."

"Go and pay your debts of honor and come back here. I shall engage the coupe of the diligence, for my niece is with me," said the old man.

That evening, at six o'clock, the three travelers started from the Rue Dauphine. Ursula had put on a veil and did not say a word. Savinien, who once, in a moment of superficial gallantry, had sent her that kiss which invaded and conquered her soul like a love-poem, had completely forgotten the young girl in the hell of his Parisian debts; moreover, his hopeless love for Emilie de Kergarouet hindered him from bestowing a thought on a few glances exchanged with a little country girl. He did not recognize her when the doctor handed her into the coach and then sat down beside her to separate her from the young viscount.

"I have some bills to give you," said the doctor to the young man. "I have brought all your papers and documents."

"I came very near not getting off," said Savinien, "for I had to order linen and clothes; the Philistines took all; I return like a true prodigal."

However interesting were the subjects of conversation between the young man and the old one, and however witty and clever were certain remarks of the viscount, the young girl continued silent till after dusk, her green veil lowered, and her hands crossed on her shawl.

"Mademoiselle does not seem to have enjoyed Paris very much," said Savinien at last, somewhat piqued.

"I am glad to return to Nemours," she answered in a trembling voice raising her veil.

Notwithstanding the dim light Savinien then recognized her by the heavy braids of her hair and the brilliancy of her blue eyes.

"I, too, leave Paris to bury myself in Nemours without regret now that I meet my charming neighbour again," he said; "I hope, Monsieur le docteur that you will receive me in your house; I love music, and I remember to have listened to Mademoiselle Ursula's piano."

"I do not know," replied the doctor gravely, "whether your mother would approve of your visits to an old man whose duty it is to care for this dear child with all the solicitude of a mother."

This reserved answer made Savinien reflect, and he then remembered the kisses so thoughtlessly wafted. Night came; the heat was great. Savinien and the doctor went to sleep first. Ursula, whose head was full of projects, did not succumb till midnight. She had taken off her straw-bonnet, and her head, covered with a little embroidered cap, dropped upon her uncle's shoulder. When they reached Bouron at dawn, Savinien awoke. He then saw Ursula in the slight disarray naturally caused by the jolting of the vehicle; her cap was rumpled and half off; the hair, unbound, had fallen each side of her face, which glowed from the heat of the night; in this situation, dreadful for women to whom dress is a necessary auxiliary, youth and beauty triumphed. The sleep of innocence is always lovely. The half-opened lips showed the pretty teeth; the shawl, unfastened, gave to view, beneath the folds of her muslin gown and without offence to her modesty, the gracefulness of her figure. The purity of the virgin spirit shone on the sleeping countenance all the more plainly because no other expression was there to interfere with it. Old Minoret, who presently woke up, placed his child's head in the corner of the carriage that she might be more at ease; and she let him do it unconsciously, so deep was her sleep after the many wakeful nights she had spent in thinking of Savinien's trouble.

"Poor little girl!" said the doctor to his neighbour, "she sleeps like the child she is."

"You must be proud of her," replied Savinien; "for she seems as good as she is beautiful."

"Ah! she is the joy of the house. I could not love her better if she were my own daughter. She will be sixteen on the 5th February. God grant that I may live long enough to marry her to a man who will make her happy. I wanted to take her to the theater in Paris, where she was for the first time, but she refused, the Abbe Chaperon had forbidden it. 'But,' I said, 'when you are married your husband will want you to go there.' 'I shall do what my husband wants,' she answered. 'If he asks me to do evil and I am weak enough to yield, he will be responsible before God—and so I shall have strength to refuse him, for his own sake.'"

As the coach entered Nemours, at five in the morning, Ursula woke up, ashamed at her rumpled condition, and confused by the look of admiration which she encountered from Savinien. During the hour it had taken the diligence to come from Bouron to Nemours the young man had fallen in love with Ursula; he had studied the pure candor of her soul, the beauty of that body, the whiteness of the skin, the delicacy of the features; he recalled the charm of the voice which had uttered but one expressive sentence, in which the poor child said all, intending to say nothing. A presentiment suddenly seemed to take hold of him; he saw in Ursula the woman the doctor had pictured to him, framed in gold by the magic words, "Seven or eight hundred thousand francs."

"In three of four years she will be twenty, and I shall be twenty-seven," he thought. "The good doctor talked of probation, work, good conduct! Sly as he is I shall make him tell me the truth."

The three neighbours parted in the street in front of their respective homes, and Savinien put a little courting into his eyes as he gave Ursula a parting glance.

Madame de Portenduere let her son sleep till midday; but the doctor and Ursula, in spite of their fatiguing journey, went to high mass. Savinien's release and his return in company with the doctor had explained the reason of the latter's absence to the newsmongers of the town and to the heirs, who were once more assembled in conventicle on the square, just as they were two weeks earlier when the doctor attended his first mass. To the great astonishment of all the groups, Madame de Portenduere, on leaving the church, stopped old Minoret, who offered her his arm and took her home. The old lady asked him to dinner that evening, also asking his niece and assuring him that the abbe would be the only other guest.

"He must have wished Ursula to see Paris," said Minoret-Levrault.

"Pest!" cried Cremiere; "he can't take a step without that girl!"

"Something must have happened to make old Portenduere accept his arm," said Massin.

"So none of you have guessed that your uncle has sold his Funds and released that little Savinien?" cried Goupil. "He refused Dionis, but he didn't refuse Madame de Portenduere—Ha, ha! you are all done for. The viscount will propose a marriage-contract instead of a mortgage, and the doctor will make the husband settle on his jewel of a girl the sum he has now paid to secure the alliance."

"It is not a bad thing to marry Ursula to Savinien," said the butcher. "The old lady gives a dinner to-day to Monsieur Minoret. Tiennette came early for a filet."

"Well, Dionis, here's a fine to-do!" said Massin, rushing up to the notary, who was entering the square.

"What is? It's all going right," returned the notary. "Your uncle has sold his Funds and Madame de Portenduere has sent for me to witness the signing of a mortgage on her property for one hundred thousand francs, lent to her by your uncle."

"Yes, but suppose the young people should marry?"

"That's as if you said Goupil was to be my successor."

"The two things are not so impossible," said Goupil.

On returning from mass Madame de Portenduere told Tiennette to inform her son that she wished to see him.

The little house had three bedrooms on the first floor. That of Madame de Portenduere and that of her late husband were separated by a large dressing-room lighted by a skylight, and connected by a little antechamber which opened on the staircase. The window of the other room, occupied by Savinien, looked, like that of his late father, on the street. The staircase went up at the back of the house, leaving room for a little study lighted by a small round window opening on the court. Madame de Portenduere's bedroom, the gloomiest in the house, also looked into the court; but the widow spent all her time in the salon on the ground floor, which communicated by a passage with the kitchen built at the end of the court, so that this salon was made to answer the double purpose of drawing-room and dining-room combined.

The bedroom of the late Monsieur de Portenduere remained as he had left it on the day of his death; there was no change except that he was absent. Madame de Portenduere had made the bed herself; laying upon it the uniform of a naval captain, his sword, cordon, orders, and hat. The gold snuff-box from which her late husband had taken snuff for the last time was on the table, with his prayer-book, his watch, and the cup from which he drank. His white hair, arranged in one curled lock and framed, hung above a crucifix and the holy water in the alcove. All the little ornaments he had worn, his journals, his furniture, his Dutch spittoon, his spy-glass hanging by the mantel, were all there. The widow had stopped the hands of the clock at the hour of his death, to which they always pointed. The room still smelt of the powder and the tobacco of the deceased. The hearth was as he left it. To her, entering there, he was again visible in the many articles which told of his daily habits. His tall cane with its gold head was where he had last placed it, with his buckskin gloves close by. On a table against the wall stood a gold vase, of coarse workmanship but worth three thousand francs, a gift from Havana, which city, at the time of the American War of Independence, he had protected from an attack by the British, bringing his convoy safe into port after an engagement with superior forces. To recompense this service the King of Spain had made him a knight of his order; the same event gave him a right to the next promotion to the rank of vice-admiral, and he also received the red ribbing. He then married his wife, who had a fortune of about two hundred thousand francs. But the Revolution hindered his promotion, and Monsieur de Portenduere emigrated.

"Where is my mother?" said Savinien to Tiennette.

"She is waiting for you in your father's room," said the old Breton woman.

Savinien could not repress a shudder. He knew his mother's rigid principles, her worship of honor, her loyalty, her faith in nobility, and he foresaw a scene. He went up to the assault with his heart beating and his face rather pale. In the dim light which filtered through the blinds he saw his mother dressed in black, and with an air of solemnity in keeping with that funereal room.

"Monsieur le vicomte," she said when she saw him, rising and taking his hand to lead him to his father's bed, "there died your father,—a man of honor; he died without reproach from his own conscience. His spirit is there. Surely he groaned in heaven when he saw his son degraded by imprisonment for debt. Under the old monarchy that stain could have been spared you by obtaining a lettre de cachet and shutting you up for a few days in a military prison.—But you are here; you stand before your father, who hears you. You know all that you did before you were sent to that ignoble prison. Will you swear to me before your father's shade, and in presence of God who sees all, that you have done no dishonorable act; that your debts are the result of youthful folly, and that your honor is untarnished? If your blameless father were there, sitting in that armchair, and asking an explanation of your conduct, could he embrace you after having heard it?"

"Yes, mother," replied the young man, with grave respect.

She opened her arms and pressed him to her heart, shedding a few tears.

"Let us forget it all, my son," she said; "it is only a little less money. I shall pray God to let us recover it. As you are indeed worthy of your name, kiss me—for I have suffered much."

"I swear, mother," he said, laying his hand upon the bed, "to give you no further unhappiness of that kind, and to do all I can to repair these first faults."

"Come and breakfast, my child," she said, turning to leave the room.

CHAPTER XII.
OBSTACLES TO YOUNG LOVE

In 1829 the old noblesse had recovered as to manners and customs something of the prestige it had irrevocably lost in politics. Moreover, the sentiment which governs parents and grandparents in all that relates to matrimonial conventions is an imperishable sentiment, closely allied to the very existence of civilized societies and springing from the spirit of family. It rules in Geneva as in Vienna and in Nemours, where, as we have seen, Zelie Minoret refused her consent to a possible marriage of her son with the daughter of a bastard. Still, all social laws have their exceptions. Savinien thought he might bend his mother's pride before the inborn nobility of Ursula. The struggle began at once. As soon as they were seated at table his mother told him of the horrible letters, as she called them, which the Kergarouets and the Portendueres had written her.

"There is no such thing as family in these days, mother," replied Savinien, "nothing but individuals! The nobles are no longer a compact body. No one asks or cares whether I am a Portenduere, or brave, or a statesmen; all they ask now-a-days is, 'What taxes does he pay?'"

"But the king?" asked the old lady.

"The king is caught between the two Chambers like a man between his wife and his mistress. So I shall have to marry some rich girl without regard to family,—the daughter of a peasant if she has a million and is sufficiently well brought-up—that is to say, if she has been taught in school."

"Oh! there's no need to talk of that," said the old lady.

Savinien frowned as he heard the words. He knew the granite will, called Breton obstinacy, that distinguished his mother, and he resolved to know at once her opinion on this delicate matter.

"So," he went on, "if I loved a young girl,—take for instance your neighbour's godchild, little Ursula,—would you oppose my marriage?"

"Yes, as long as I live," she replied; "and after my death you would be responsible for the honor and the blood of the Kergarouets and the Portendueres."

"Would you let me die of hunger and despair for the chimera of nobility, which has no reality to-day unless it has the lustre of great wealth?"

"You could serve France and put faith in God."

"Would you postpone my happiness till after your death?"

"It would be horrible if you took it then,—that is all I have to say."

"Louis XIV. came very near marrying the niece of Mazarin, a parvenu."

"Mazarin himself opposed it."

"Remember the widow Scarron."

"She was a d'Aubigne. Besides, the marriage was in secret. But I am very old, my son," she said, shaking her head. "When I am no more you can, as you say, marry whom you please."

Savinien both loved and respected his mother; but he instantly, though silently, set himself in opposition to her with an obstinacy equal to her own, resolving to have no other wife than Ursula, to whom this opposition gave, as often happens in similar circumstances, the value of a forbidden thing.

When, after vespers, the doctor, with Ursula, who was dressed in pink and white, entered the cold, stiff salon, the girl was seized with nervous trembling, as though she had entered the presence of the queen of France and had a favor to beg of her. Since her confession to the doctor this little house had assumed the proportions of a palace in her eyes, and the old lady herself the social value which a duchess of the Middle Ages might have had to the daughter of a serf. Never had Ursula measured as she did at that moment the distance which separated Vicomte de Portenduere from the daughter of a regimental musician, a former opera-singer and the natural son of an organist.

"What is the matter, my dear?" said the old lady, making the girl sit down beside her.

"Madame, I am confused by the honor you have done me—"

"My little girl," said Madame de Portenduere, in her sharpest tone. "I know how fond your uncle is of you, and I wished to be agreeable to him, for he has brought back my prodigal son."

"But, my dear mother," said Savinien cut to the heart by seeing the color fly into Ursula's face as she struggled to keep back her tears, "even if we were under no obligations to Monsieur le Chevalier Minoret, I think we should always be most grateful for the pleasure Mademoiselle has given us by accepting your invitation."

The young man pressed the doctor's hand in a significant manner, adding: "I see you wear, monsieur, the order of Saint-Michel, the oldest order in France, and one which confers nobility."

Ursula's extreme beauty, to which her almost hopeless love gave a depth which great painters have sometimes conveyed in pictures where the soul is brought into strong relief, had struck Madame de Portenduere suddenly, and made her suspect that the doctor's apparent generosity masked an ambitious scheme. She had made the speech to which Savinien replied with the intention of wounding the doctor in that which was dearest to him; and she succeeded, though the old man could hardly restrain a smile as he heard himself styled a "chevalier," amused to observe how the eagerness of a lover did not shrink from absurdity.

"The order of Saint-Michel which in former days men committed follies to obtain," he said, "has now, Monsieur le vicomte, gone the way of other privileges! It is given only to doctors and poor artists. The kings have done well to join it to that of Saint-Lazare who was, I believe, a poor devil recalled to life by a miracle. From this point of view the order of Saint-Michel and Saint-Lazare may be, for many of us, symbolic."

After this reply, at once sarcastic and dignified, silence reigned, which, as no one seemed inclined to break it, was becoming awkward, when there was a rap at the door.

"There is our dear abbe," said the old lady, who rose, leaving Ursula alone, and advancing to meet the Abbe Chaperon,—an honor she had not paid to the doctor and his niece.

The old man smiled to himself as he looked from his goddaughter to Savinien. To show offence or to complain of Madame de Portenduere's manners was a rock on which a man of small mind might have struck, but Minoret was too accomplished in the ways of the world not to avoid it. He began to talk to the viscount of the danger Charles X. was then running by confiding the affairs of the nation to the Prince de Polignac. When sufficient time had been spent on the subject to avoid all appearance of revenging himself by so doing, he handed the old lady, in an easy, jesting way, a packet of legal papers and receipted bills, together with the account of his notary.

"Has my son verified them?" she said, giving Savinien a look, to which he replied by bending his head. "Well, then the rest is my notary's business," she added, pushing away the papers and treating the affair with the disdain she wished to show for money.

To abase wealth was, according to Madame de Portenduere's ideas, to elevate the nobility and rob the bourgeoisie of their importance.

A few moments later Goupil came from his employer, Dionis, to ask for the accounts of the transaction between the doctor and Savinien.

"Why do you want them?" said the old lady.

"To put the matter in legal form; there have been no cash payments."

Ursula and Savinien, who both for the first time exchanged a glance with offensive personage, were conscious of a sensation like that of touching a toad, aggravated by a dark presentiment of evil. They both had the same indefinable and confused vision into the future, which has no name in any language, but which is capable of explanation as the action of the inward being of which the mysterious Swedenborgian had spoken to Doctor Minoret. The certainty that the venomous Goupil would in some way be fatal to them made Ursula tremble; but she controlled herself, conscious of unspeakable pleasure in seeing that Savinien shared her emotion.

"He is not handsome, that clerk of Monsieur Dionis," said Savinien, when Goupil had closed the door.

"What does it signify whether such persons are handsome or ugly?" said Madame de Portenduere.

"I don't complain of his ugliness," said the abbe, "but I do of his wickedness, which passes all bounds; he is a villain."

The doctor, in spite of his desire to be amiable, grew cold and dignified. The lovers were embarrassed. If it had not been for the kindly good-humor of the abbe, whose gentle gayety enlivened the dinner, the position of the doctor and his niece would have been almost intolerable. At dessert, seeing Ursula turn pale, he said to her:—

"If you don't feel well, dear child, we have only the street to cross."

"What is the matter, my dear?" said the old lady to the girl.

"Madame," said the doctor severely, "her soul is chilled, accustomed as she is to be met by smiles."

"A very bad education, monsieur," said Madame de Portenduere. "Is it not, Monsieur l'abbe?"

"Yes," answered Minoret, with a look at the abbe, who knew not how to reply. "I have, it is true, rendered life unbearable to an angelic spirit if she has to pass it in the world; but I trust I shall not die until I place her in security, safe from coldness, indifference, and hatred—"

"Oh, godfather—I beg of you—say no more. There is nothing the matter with me," cried Ursula, meeting Madame de Portenduere's eyes rather than give too much meaning to her words by looking at Savinien.

"I cannot know, madame," said Savinien to his mother, "whether Mademoiselle Ursula suffers, but I do know that you are torturing me."

Hearing these words, dragged from the generous young man by his mother's treatment of herself, Ursula turned pale and begged Madame de Portenduere to excuse her; then she took her uncle's arm, bowed, left the room, and returned home. Once there, she rushed to the salon and sat down to the piano, put her head in her hands, and burst into tears.

"Why don't you leave the management of your affairs to my old experience, cruel child?" cried the doctor in despair. "Nobles never think themselves under any obligations to the bourgeoisie. When we do them a service they consider that we do our duty, and that's all. Besides, the old lady saw that you looked favorably on Savinien; she is afraid he will love you."

"At any rate he is saved!" said Ursula. "But ah! to try to humiliate a man like you!"

"Wait till I return, my child," said the old man leaving her.

When the doctor re-entered Madame de Portenduere's salon he found Dionis the notary, accompanied by Monsieur Bongrand and the mayor of Nemours, witnesses required by law for the validity of deeds in all communes where there is but one notary. Minoret took Monsieur Dionis aside and said a word in his ear, after which the notary read the deeds aloud officially; from which it appeared that Madame de Portenduere gave a mortgage on all her property to secure payment of the hundred thousand francs, the interest on which was fixed at five per cent. At the reading of this last clause the abbe looked at Minoret, who answered with an approving nod. The poor priest whispered something in the old lady's ear to which she replied,—

"I will owe nothing to such persons."

"My mother leaves me the nobler part," said Savinien to the doctor; "she will repay the money and charges me to show our gratitude."

"But you will have to pay eleven thousand francs the first year to meet the interest and the legal costs," said the abbe.

"Monsieur," said Minoret to Dionis, "as Monsieur and Madame de Portenduere are not in a condition to pay those costs, add them to the amount of the mortgage and I will pay them."

Dionis made the change and the sum borrowed was fixed at one hundred and seven thousand francs. When the papers were all signed, Minoret made his fatigue an excuse to leave the house at the same time as the notary and witnesses.

"Madame," said the abbe, "why did you affront the excellent Monsieur Minoret, who saved you at least twenty-five thousand francs on those debts in Paris, and had the delicacy to give twenty thousand to your son for his debts of honor?"

"Your Minoret is sly," she said, taking a pinch of snuff. "He knows what he is about."

"My mother thinks he wishes to force me into marrying his niece by getting hold of our farm," said Savinien; "as if a Portenduere, son of a Kergarouet, could be made to marry against his will."

An hour later, Savinien presented himself at the doctor's house, where all the relatives had assembled, enticed by curiosity. The arrival of the young viscount produced a lively sensation, all the more because its effect was different on each person present. Mesdemoiselles Cremiere and Massin whispered together and looked at Ursula, who blushed. The mothers said to Desire that Goupil was right about the marriage. The eyes of all present turned towards the doctor, who did not rise to receive the young nobleman, but merely bowed his head without laying down the dice-box, for he was playing a game of backgammon with Monsieur Bongrand. The doctor's cold manner surprised every one.

"Ursula, my child," he said, "give us a little music."

While the young girl, delighted to have something to do to keep her in countenance, went to the piano and began to move the green-covered music-books, the heirs resigned themselves, with many demonstrations of pleasure, to the torture and the silence about to be inflicted on them, so eager were they to find out what was going on between their uncle and the Portendueres.

In sometimes happens that a piece of music, poor in itself, when played by a young girl under the influence of deep feeling, makes more impression than a fine overture played by a full orchestra. In all music there is, besides the thought of the composer, the soul of the performer, who, by a privilege granted to this art only, can give both meaning and poetry to passages which are in themselves of no great value. Chopin proves, for that unresponsive instrument the piano, the truth of this fact, already proved by Paganini on the violin. That fine genius is less a musician than a soul which makes itself felt, and communicates itself through all species of music, even simple chords. Ursula, by her exquisite and sensitive organization, belonged to this rare class of beings, and old Schmucke, the master, who came every Saturday and who, during Ursula's stay in Paris was with her every day, had brought his pupil's talent to its full perfection. "Rousseau's Dream," the piece now chosen by Ursula, composed by Herold in his young days, is not without a certain depth which is capable of being developed by execution. Ursula threw into it the feelings which were agitating her being, and justified the term "caprice" given by Herold to the fragment. With soft and dreamy touch her soul spoke to the young man's soul and wrapped it, as in a cloud, with ideas that were almost visible.

Sitting at the end of the piano, his elbow resting on the cover and his head on his left hand, Savinien admired Ursula, whose eyes, fixed on the paneling of the wall beyond him, seemed to be questioning another world. Many a man would have fallen deeply in love for a less reason. Genuine feelings have a magnetism of their own, and Ursula was willing to show her soul, as a coquette her dresses to be admired. Savinien entered that delightful kingdom, led by this pure heart, which, to interpret its feelings, borrowed the power of the only art that speaks to thought by thought, without the help of words, or color, or form. Candor, openness of heart have the same power over a man that childhood has; the same charm, the same irresistible seductions. Ursula was never more honest and candid than at this moment, when she was born again into a new life.

The abbe came to tear Savinien from his dream, requesting him to take a fourth hand at whist. Ursula went on playing; the heirs departed, all except Desire, who was resolved to find out the intentions of his uncle and the viscount and Ursula.

"You have as much talent as soul, mademoiselle," he said, when the young girl closed the piano and sat down beside her godfather. "Who is your master?"

"A German, living close to the Rue Dauphine on the quai Conti," said the doctor. "If he had not given Ursula a lesson every day during her stay in Paris he would have been here to-day."

"He is not only a great musician," said Ursula, "but a man of adorable simplicity of nature."

"Those lessons must cost a great deal," remarked Desire.

The players smiled ironically. When the game was over the doctor, who had hitherto seemed anxious and pensive, turned to Savinien with the air of a man who fulfills a duty.

"Monsieur," he said, "I am grateful for the feeling which leads you to make me this early visit; but your mother attributes unworthy and underhand motives to what I have done, and I should give her the right to call them true if I did not request you to refrain from coming here, in spite of the honor your visits are to me, and the pleasure I should otherwise feel in cultivating your society. Tell your mother that if I do not beg her, in my niece's name and my own, to do us the honor of dining here next Sunday it is because I am very certain that she would find herself indisposed on that day."

The old man held out his hand to the young viscount, who pressed it respectfully, saying:—

"You are quite right, monsieur."

He then withdrew; but not without a bow to Ursula, in which there was more of sadness than disappointment.

Desire left the house at the same time; but he found it impossible to exchange even a word with the young nobleman, who rushed into his own house precipitately.

CHAPTER XIII.
BETROTHAL OF HEARTS

This rupture between the Portendueres and Doctor Minoret gave talk among the heirs for a week; they did homage to the genius of Dionis, and regarded their inheritance as rescued.

So, in an age when ranks are leveled, when the mania for equality puts everybody on one footing and threatens to destroy all bulwarks, even military subordination,—that last refuge of power in France, where passions have now no other obstacles to overcome than personal antipathies, or differences of fortune,—the obstinacy of an old-fashioned Breton woman and the dignity of Doctor Minoret created a barrier between these lovers, which was to end, as such obstacles often do, not in destroying but in strengthening love. To an ardent man a woman's value is that which she costs him; Savinien foresaw a struggle, great efforts, many uncertainties, and already the young girl was rendered dearer to him; he was resolved to win her. Perhaps our feelings obey the laws of nature as to the lastingness of her creations; to a long life a long childhood.

The next morning, when they woke, Ursula and Savinien had the same thought. An intimate understanding of this kind would create love if it were not already its most precious proof. When the young girl parted her curtains just far enough to let her eyes take in Savinien's window, she saw the face of her lover above the fastening of his. When one reflects on the immense services that windows render to lovers it seems natural and right that a tax should be levied on them. Having thus protested against her godfather's harshness, Ursula dropped the curtain and opened her window to close the outer blinds, through which she could continue to see without being seen herself. Seven or eight times during the day she went up to her room, always to find the young viscount writing, tearing up what he had written, and then writing again—to her, no doubt!

The next morning when she woke La Bougival gave her the following letter:—

To Mademoiselle Ursula:

Mademoiselle,—I do not conceal from myself the distrust a young man inspires when he has placed himself in the position from which your godfather's kindness released me. I know that I must in future give greater guarantees of good conduct than other men; therefore, mademoiselle, it is with deep humility that I place myself at your feet and ask you to consider my love. This declaration is not dictated by passion; it comes from an inward certainty which involves the whole of life. A foolish infatuation for my young aunt, Madame de Kergarouet, was the cause of my going to prison; will you not regard as a proof of my sincere love the total disappearance of those wishes, of that image, now effaced from my heart by yours? No sooner did I see you, asleep and so engaging in your childlike slumber at Bouron, than you occupied my soul as a queen takes possession of her empire. I will have no other wife than you. You have every qualification I desire in her who is to bear my name. The education you have received and the dignity of your own mind, place you on the level of the highest positions. But I doubt myself too much to dare describe you to yourself; I can only love you. After listening to you yesterday I recalled certain words which seem as though written for you; suffer me to transcribe them:—

"Made to draw all hearts and charm all eyes, gentle and intelligent, spiritual yet able to reason, courteous as though she had passed her life at court, simple as the hermit who had never known the world, the fire of her soul is tempered in her eyes by sacred modesty."

I feel the value of the noble soul revealed in you by many, even the most trifling, things. This it is which gives me the courage to ask you, provided you love no one else, to let me prove to you by my conduct and my devotion that I am not unworthy of you. It concerns my very life; you cannot doubt that all my powers will be employed, not only in trying to please you, but in deserving your esteem, which is more precious to me than any other upon earth. With this hope, Ursula—if you will suffer me so to call you in my heart—Nemours will be to me a paradise, the hardest tasks will bring me joys derived through you, as life itself is derived from God. Tell me that I may call myself

Your Savinien.

Ursula kissed the letter; then, having re-read it and clasped it with passionate motions, she dressed herself eagerly to carry it to her uncle.

"Ah, my God! I nearly forgot to say my prayers!" she exclaimed, turning back to kneel on her prie-Dieu.

A few moments later she went down to the garden, where she found her godfather and made him read the letter. They both sat down on a bench under the arch of climbing plants opposite to the Chinese pagoda. Ursula awaited the old man's words, and the old man reflected long, too long for the impatient young girl. At last, the result of their secret interview appeared in the following answer, part of which the doctor undoubtedly dictated.

To Monsieur le Vicomte Savinien de Portenduere:

Monsieur,—I cannot be otherwise than greatly honored by the letter in which you offer me your hand; but, at my age, and according to the rules of my education, I have felt bound to communicate it to my godfather, who is all I have, and whom I love as a father and also as a friend. I must now tell you the painful objections which he has made to me, and which must be to you my answer.

Monsieur le vicomte, I am a poor girl, whose fortune depends entirely, not only on my godfather's good-will, but also on the doubtful success of the measures he may take to elude the schemes of his relatives against me. Though I am the legitimate daughter of Joseph Mirouet, band-master of the 45th regiment of infantry, my father himself was my godfather's natural half-brother; and therefore these relatives may, though without reason, being a suit against a young girl who would be defenceless. You see, monsieur, that the smallness of my fortune is not my greatest misfortune. I have many things to make me humble. It is for your sake, and not for my own, that I lay before you these facts, which to loving and devoted hearts are sometimes of little weight. But I beg you to consider, monsieur, that if I did not submit them to you, I might be suspected of leading your tenderness to overlook obstacles which the world, and more especially your mother, regard as insuperable.

I shall be sixteen in four months. Perhaps you will admit that we are both too young and too inexperienced to understand the miseries of a life entered upon without other fortune than that I have received from the kindness of the late Monsieur de Jordy. My godfather desires, moreover, not to marry me until I am twenty. Who knows what fate may have in store for you in four years, the finest years of your life? do not sacrifice them to a poor girl.

Having thus explained to you, monsieur, the opinions of my dear godfather, who, far from opposing my happiness, seeks to contribute to it in every way, and earnestly desires that his protection, which must soon fail me, may be replaced by a tenderness equal to his own; there remains only to tell you how touched I am by your offer and by the compliments which accompany it. The prudence which dictates my letter is that of an old man to whom life is well-known; but the gratitude I express is that of a young girl, in whose soul no other sentiment has arisen.

Therefore, monsieur, I can sign myself, in all sincerity,

Your servant, Ursula Mirouet.

Savinien made no reply. Was he trying to soften his mother? Had this letter put an end to his love? Many such questions, all insoluble, tormented poor Ursula, and, by repercussion, the doctor too, who suffered from every agitation of his darling child. Ursula went often to her chamber to look at Savinien, whom she usually found sitting pensively before his table with his eyes turned towards her window. At the end of the week, but no sooner, she received a letter from him; the delay was explained by his increasing love.

To Mademoiselle Ursula Mirouet:

Dear Ursula,—I am a Breton, and when my mind is once made up nothing can change me. Your godfather, whom may God preserve to us, is right; but does it follow that I am wrong in loving you? Therefore, all I want to know from you is whether you could love me. Tell me this, if only by a sign, and then the next four years will be the finest of my life.

A friend of mine has delivered to my great-uncle, Vice-admiral Kergarouet, a letter in which I asked his help to enter the navy. The kind old man, grieved at my misfortune, replies that even the king's favor would be thwarted by the rules of the service in case I wanted a certain rank. Nevertheless, if I study three months at Toulon, the minister of war can send me to sea as master's mate; then after a cruise against the Algerines, with whom we are now at war, I can go through an examination and become a midshipman. Moreover, if I distinguish myself in an expedition they are fitting out against Algiers, I shall certainly be made ensign—but how soon? that no one can tell. Only, they will make the rules as elastic as possible to have the name of Portenduere again in the navy.

I see very plainly that I can only hope to obtain you from your godfather; and your respect for him makes you still dearer to me. Before replying to the admiral, I must have an interview with the doctor; on his reply my whole future will depend. Whatever comes of it, know this, that rich or poor, the daughter of a band master or the daughter of a king, you are the woman whom the voice of my heart points out to me. Dear Ursula, we live in times when prejudices which might once have separated us have no power to prevent our marriage. To you, then, I offer the feelings of my heart, to your uncle the guarantees which secure to him your happiness. He has not seen that I, in a few hours, came to love you more than he has loved you in fifteen years.

Until this evening. Savinien.

"Here, godfather," said Ursula, holding the letter out to him with a proud gesture.

"Ah, my child!" cried the doctor when he had read it, "I am happier than even you. He repairs all his faults by this resolution."

After dinner Savinien presented himself, and found the doctor walking with Ursula by the balustrade of the terrace overlooking the river. The viscount had received his clothes from Paris, and had not missed heightening his natural advantages by a careful toilet, as elegant as though he were striving to please the proud and beautiful Comtesse de Kergarouet. Seeing him approach her from the portico, the poor girl clung to her uncle's arm as though she were saving herself from a fall over a precipice, and the doctor heard the beating of her heart, which made him shudder.

"Leave us, my child," he said to the girl, who went to the pagoda and sat upon the steps, after allowing Savinien to take her hand and kiss it respectfully.

"Monsieur, will you give this dear hand to a naval captain?" he said to the doctor in a low voice.

"No," said Minoret, smiling; "we might have to wait too long, but—I will give her to a lieutenant."

Tears of joy filled the young man's eyes as he pressed the doctor's hand affectionately.

"I am about to leave," he said, "to study hard and try to learn in six months what the pupils of the Naval School take six years to acquire."

"You are going?" said Ursula, springing towards them from the pavilion.

"Yes, mademoiselle, to deserve you. Therefore the more eager I am to go, the more I prove to you my affection."

"This is the 3rd of October," she said, looking at him with infinite tenderness; "do not go till after the 19th."

"Yes," said the old man, "we will celebrate Saint-Savinien's day."

"Good-by, then," cried the young man. "I must spend this week in Paris, to take the preliminary steps, buy books and mathematical instruments, and try to conciliate the minister and get the best terms that I can for myself."

Ursula and her godfather accompanied Savinien to the gate. Soon after he entered his mother's house they saw him come out again, followed by Tiennette carrying his valise.

"If you are rich," said Ursula to her uncle, "why do you make him serve in the navy?"

"Presently it will be I who incurred his debts," said the doctor, smiling. "I don't oblige him to do anything; but the uniform, my dear, and the cross of the Legion of honor, won in battle, will wipe out many stains. Before six years are over he may be in command of a ship, and that's all I ask of him."

"But he may be killed," she said, turning a pale face upon the doctor.

"Lovers, like drunkards, have a providence of their own," he said, laughing.

That night the poor child, with La Bougival's help, cut off a sufficient quantity of her long and beautiful blond hair to make a chain; and the next day she persuaded old Schmucke, the music-master, to take it to Paris and have the chain made and returned by the following Sunday. When Savinien got back he informed the doctor and Ursula that he had signed his articles and was to be at Brest on the 25th. The doctor asked him to dinner on the 18th, and he passed nearly two whole days in the old man's house. Notwithstanding much sage advice and many resolutions, the lovers could not help betraying their secret understanding to the watchful eyes of the abbe, Monsieur Bongrand, the Nemours doctor, and La Bougival.

"Children," said the old man, "you are risking your happiness by not keeping it to yourselves."

On the fete-day, after mass, during which several glances had been exchanged, Savinien, watched by Ursula, crossed the road and entered the little garden where the pair were practically alone; for the kind old man, by way of indulgence, was reading his newspapers in the pagoda.

"Dear Ursula," said Savinien; "will you make a gift greater than my mother could make me even if—"

"I know what you wish to ask me," she said, interrupting him. "See, here is my answer," she added, taking from the pocket of her apron the box containing the chain made of her hair, and offering it to him with a nervous tremor which testified to her illimitable happiness. "Wear it," she said, "for love of me. May it shield you from all dangers by reminding you that my life depends on yours."

"Naughty little thing! she is giving him a chain of her hair," said the doctor to himself. "How did she manage to get it? what a pity to cut those beautiful fair tresses; she will be giving him my life's blood next."

"You will not blame me if I ask you to give me, now that I am leaving you, a formal promise to have no other husband than me," said Savinien, kissing the chain and looking at Ursula with tears in his eyes.

"Have I not said so too often—I who went to see the walls of Sainte-Pelagie when you were behind them?—" she replied, blushing. "I repeat it, Savinien; I shall never love any one but you, and I will be yours alone."

Seeing that Ursula was half-hidden by the creepers, the young man could not deny himself the happiness of pressing her to his heart and kissing her forehead; but she gave a feeble cry and dropped upon the bench, and when Savinien sat beside her, entreating pardon, he saw the doctor standing before them.

"My friend," said the old man, "Ursula is a born sensitive; too rough a word might kill her. For her sake you must moderate the enthusiasm of your love—Ah! if you had loved her for sixteen years as I have, you would have been satisfied with her word of promise," he added, to revenge himself for the last sentence in Savinien's second letter.

Two days later the young man departed. In spite of the letters which he wrote regularly to Ursula, she fell a prey to an illness without apparent cause. Like a fine fruit with a worm at the core, a single thought gnawed her heart. She lost both appetite and color. The first time her godfather asked her what she felt, she replied:—

"I want to see the ocean."

"It is difficult to take you to a sea-port in the depth of winter," answered the old man.

"Shall I really go?" she said.

If the wind was high, Ursula was inwardly convulsed, certain, in spite of the learned assurances of the doctor and the abbe, that Savinien was being tossed about in a whirlwind. Monsieur Bongrand made her happy for days with the gift of an engraving representing a midshipman in uniform. She read the newspapers, imagining that they would give news of the cruiser on which her lover sailed. She devoured Cooper's sea-tales and learned to use sea-terms. Such proofs of concentration of feeling, often assumed by other women, were so genuine in Ursula that she saw in dreams the coming of Savinien's letters, and never failed to announce them, relating the dream as a forerunner.

"Now," she said to the doctor the fourth time that this happened, "I am easy; wherever Savinien may be, if he is wounded I shall know it instantly."

The old doctor thought over this remark so anxiously that the abbe and Monsieur Bongrand were troubled by the sorrowful expression of his face.

"What pains you?" they said, when Ursula had left them.

"Will she live?" replied the doctor. "Can so tender and delicate a flower endure the trials of the heart?"

Nevertheless, the "little dreamer," as the abbe called her, was working hard. She understood the importance of a fine education to a woman of the world, and all the time she did not give to her singing and to the study of harmony and composition she spent in reading the books chosen for her by the abbe from her godfather's rich library. And yet while leading this busy life she suffered, though without complaint. Sometimes she would sit for hours looking at Savinien's window. On Sundays she would leave the church behind Madame de Portenduere and watch her tenderly; for, in spite of the old lady's harshness, she loved her as Savinien's mother. Her piety increased; she went to mass every morning, for she firmly believed that her dreams were the gift of God.

At last her godfather, frightened by the effects produced by this nostalgia of love, promised on her birthday to take her to Toulon to see the departure of the fleet for Algiers. Savinien's ship formed part of it, but he was not to be informed beforehand of their intention. The abbe and Monsieur Bongrand kept secret the object of this journey, said to be for Ursula's health, which disturbed and greatly puzzled the relations. After beholding Savinien in his naval uniform, and going on board the fine flag-ship of the admiral, to whom the minister had given young Portenduere a special recommendation, Ursula, at her lover's entreaty, went with her godfather to Nice, and along the shores of the Mediterranean to Genoa, where she heard of the safe arrival of the fleet at Algiers and the landing of the troops. The doctor would have liked to continue the journey through Italy, as much to distract Ursula's mind as to finish, in some sense, her education, by enlarging her ideas through comparison with other manners and customs and countries, and by the fascination of a land where the masterpieces of art can still be seen, and where so many civilizations have left their brilliant traces. But the tidings of the opposition by the throne to the newly elected Chamber of 1830 obliged the doctor to return to France, bringing back his treasure in a flourishing state of health and possessed of a charming little model of the ship on which Savinien was serving.

The elections of 1830 united into an active body the various Minoret relations,—Desire and Goupil having formed a committee in Nemours by whose efforts a liberal candidate was put in nomination at Fontainebleau. Massin, as collector of taxes, exercised an enormous influence over the country electors. Five of the post master's farmers were electors. Dionis represented eleven votes. After a few meetings at the notary's, Cremiere, Massin, the post master, and their adherents took a habit of assembling there. By the time the doctor returned, Dionis's office and salon were the camp of his heirs. The justice of peace and the mayor, who had formed an alliance, backed by the nobility in the neighbouring castles, to resist the liberals of Nemours, now worsted in their efforts, were more closely united than ever by their defeat.

By the time Bongrand and the Abbe Chaperon were able to tell the doctor by word of mouth the result of the antagonism, which was defined for the first time, between the two classes in Nemours (giving incidentally such importance to his heirs) Charles X. had left Rambouillet for Cherbourg. Desire Minoret, whose opinions were those of the Paris bar, sent for fifteen of his friends, commanded by Goupil and mounted on horses from his father's stable, who arrived in Paris on the night of the 28th. With this troop Goupil and Desire took part in the capture of the Hotel-de-Veille. Desire was decorated with the Legion of honor and appointed deputy procureur du roi at Fontainebleau. Goupil received the July cross. Dionis was elected mayor of Nemours, and the city council was composed of the post master (now assistant-mayor), Massin, Cremiere, and all the adherents of the family faction. Bongrand retained his place only through the influence of his son, procureur du roi at Melun, whose marriage with Mademoiselle Levrault was then on the tapis.

Seeing the three-per-cents quoted at forty-five, the doctor started by post for Paris, and invested five hundred and forty thousand francs in shares to bearer. The rest of his fortune which amounted to about two hundred and seventy thousand francs, standing in his own name in the same funds, gave him ostensibly an income of fifteen thousand francs a year. He made the same disposition of Ursula's little capital bequeathed to her by de Jordy, together with the accrued interest thereon, which gave her about fourteen hundred francs a year in her own right. La Bougival, who had laid by some five thousand francs of her savings, did the same by the doctor's advice, receiving in future three hundred and fifty francs a year in dividends. These judicious transactions, agreed on between the doctor and Monsieur Bongrand, were carried out in perfect secrecy, thanks to the political troubles of the time.

When quiet was again restored the doctor bought the little house which adjoined his own and pulled it down so as to build a coach-house and stables on its side. To employ a capital which would have given him a thousand francs a year on outbuildings seemed actual folly to the Minoret heirs. This folly, if it were one, was the beginning of a new era in the doctor's existence, for he now (at a period when horses and carriages were almost given away) brought back from Paris three fine horses and a caleche.

When, in the early part of November, 1830, the old man came to church on a rainy day in the new carriage, and gave his hand to Ursula to help her out, all the inhabitants flocked to the square,—as much to see the caleche and question the coachman, as to criticize the goddaughter, to whose excessive pride and ambition Massin, Cremiere, the post master, and their wives attributed this extravagant folly of the old man.

"A caleche! Hey, Massin!" cried Goupil. "Your inheritance will go at top speed now!"

"You ought to be getting good wages, Cabirolle," said the post master to the son of one of his conductors, who stood by the horses; "for it is to be supposed an old man of eighty-four won't use up many horse-shoes. What did those horses cost?"

"Four thousand francs. The caleche, though second-hand, was two thousand; but it's a fine one, the wheels are patent."

"Yes, it's a good carriage," said Cremiere; "and a man must be rich to buy that style of thing."

"Ursula means to go at a good pace," said Goupil. "She's right; she's showing you how to enjoy life. Why don't you have fine carriages and horses, papa Minoret? I wouldn't let myself be humiliated if I were you—I'd buy a carriage fit for a prince."

"Come, Cabirolle, tell us," said Massin, "is it the girl who drives our uncle into such luxury?"

"I don't know," said Cabirolle; "but she is almost mistress of the house. There are masters upon masters down from Paris. They say now she is going to study painting."

"Then I shall seize the occasion to have my portrait drawn," said Madame Cremiere.

In the provinces they always say a picture is drawn, not painted.

"The old German is not dismissed, is he?" said Madame Massin.

"He was there yesterday," replied Cabirolle.

"Now," said Goupil, "you may as well give up counting on your inheritance. Ursula is seventeen years old, and she is prettier than ever. Travel forms young people, and the little minx has got your uncle in the toils. Five or six parcels come down for her by the diligence every week, and the dressmakers and milliners come too, to try on her gowns and all the rest of it. Madame Dionis is furious. Watch for Ursula as she comes out of church and look at the little scarf she is wearing round her neck,—real cashmere, and it cost six hundred francs!"

If a thunderbolt had fallen in the midst of the heirs the effect would have been less than that of Goupil's last words; the mischief-maker stood by rubbing his hands.

The doctor's old green salon had been renovated by a Parisian upholsterer. Judged by the luxury displayed, he was sometimes accused of hoarding immense wealth, sometimes of spending his capital on Ursula. The heirs called him in turn a miser and a spendthrift, but the saying, "He's an old fool!" summed upon, on the whole, the verdict of the neighbourhood. These mistaken judgments of the little town had the one advantage of misleading the heirs, who never suspected the love between Savinien and Ursula, which was the secret reason of the doctor's expenditure. The old man took the greatest delights in accustoming his godchild to her future station in the world. Possessing an income of over fifty thousand francs a year, it gave him pleasure to adorn his idol.

In the month of February, 1832, the day when Ursula was eighteen, her eyes beheld Savinien in the uniform of an ensign as she looked from her window when she rose in the morning.

"Why didn't I know he was coming?" she said to herself.

After the taking of Algiers, Savinien had distinguished himself by an act of courage which won him the cross. The corvette on which he was serving was many months at sea without his being able to communicate with the doctor; and he did not wish to leave the service without consulting him. Desirous of retaining in the navy a name already illustrious in its service, the new government had profited by a general change of officers to make Savinien an ensign. Having obtained leave of absence for fifteen days, the new officer arrived from Toulon by the mail, in time for Ursula's fete, intending to consult the doctor at the same time.

"He has come!" cried Ursula rushing into her godfather's bedroom.

"Very good," he answered; "I can guess what brings him, and he may now stay in Nemours."

"Ah! that's my birthday present—it is all in that sentence," she said, kissing him.

On a sign, which she ran up to make from her window, Savinien came over at once; she longed to admire him, for he seemed to her so changed for the better. Military service does, in fact, give a certain grave decision to the air and carriage and gestures of a man, and an erect bearing which enables the most superficial observer to recognize a military man even in plain clothes. The habit of command produces this result. Ursula loved Savinien the better for it, and took a childlike pleasure in walking round the garden with him, taking his arm, and hearing him relate the part he played (as midshipman) in the taking of Algiers. Evidently Savinien had taken the city. The doctor, who had been watching them from his window as he dressed, soon came down. Without telling the viscount everything, he did say that, in case Madame de Portenduere consented to his marriage with Ursula, the fortune of his godchild would make his naval pay superfluous.

"Alas!" said Savinien. "It will take a great deal of time to overcome my mother's opposition. Before I left her to enter the navy she was placed between two alternatives,—either to consent to my marrying Ursula or else to see me only from time to time and to know me exposed to the dangers of the profession; and you see she chose to let me go."

"But, Savinien, we shall be together," said Ursula, taking his hand and shaking it with a sort of impatience.

To see each other and not to part,—that was the all of love to her; she saw nothing beyond it; and her pretty gesture and the petulant tone of her voice expressed such innocence that Savinien and the doctor were both moved by it. The resignation was written and despatched, and Ursula's fete received full glory from the presence of her betrothed. A few months later, towards the month of May, the home-life of the doctor's household had resumed the quite tenor of its way but with one welcome visitor the more. The attentions of the young viscount were soon interpreted in the town as those of a future husband,—all the more because his manners and those of Ursula, whether in church, or on the promenade, though dignified and reserved, betrayed the understanding of their hearts. Dionis pointed out to the heirs that the doctor had never asked Madame de Portenduere for the interest of his money, three years of which was now due.

"She'll be forced to yield, and consent to this derogatory marriage of her son," said the notary. "If such a misfortune happens it is probable that the greater part of your uncle's fortune will serve for what Basile calls 'an irresistible argument.'"

CHAPTER XIV.
URSULA AGAIN ORPHANED

The irritation of the heirs, when convinced that their uncle loved Ursula too well not to secure her happiness at their expense, became as underhand as it was bitter. Meeting in Dionis's salon (as they had done every evening since the revolution of 1830) they inveighed against the lovers, and seldom separated without discussing some way of circumventing the old man. Zelie, who had doubtless profited by the fall in the Funds, as the doctor had done, to invest some, at least, of her enormous gains, was bitterest of them all against the orphan girl and the Portendueres. One evening, when Goupil, who usually avoided the dullness of these meetings, had come in to learn something of the affairs of the town which were under discussion, Zelie's hatred was freshly excited; she had seen the doctor, Ursula, and Savinien returning in the caleche from a country drive, with an air of intimacy that told all.

"I'd give thirty thousand francs if God would call uncle to himself before the marriage of young Portenduere with that affected minx can take place," she said.

Goupil accompanied Monsieur and Madame Minoret to the middle of their great courtyard, and there said, looking round to see if they were quite alone:

"Will you give me the means of buying Dionis's practice? If you will, I will break off the marriage between Portenduere and Ursula."

"How?" asked the colossus.

"Do you think I am such a fool as to tell you my plan?" said the notary's head clerk.

"Well, my lad, separate them, and we'll see what we can do," said Zelie.

"I don't embark in any such business on a 'we'll see.' The young man is a fire-eater who might kill me; I ought to be rough-shod and as good a hand with a sword or a pistol as he is. Set me up in business, and I'll keep my word."

"Prevent the marriage and I will set you up," said the post master.

"It is nine months since you have been thinking of lending me a paltry fifteen thousand francs to buy Lecoeur's practice, and you expect me to trust you now! Nonsense; you'll lose your uncle's property, and serve you right."

"It if were only a matter of fifteen thousand francs and Lecoeur's practice, that might be managed," said Zelie; "but to give security for you in a hundred and fifty thousand is another thing."

"But I'll do my part," said Goupil, flinging a seductive look at Zelie, which encountered the imperious glance of the post mistress.

The effect was that of venom on steel.

"We can wait," said Zelie.

"The devil's own spirit is in you," thought Goupil. "If I ever catch that pair in my power," he said to himself as he left the yard, "I'll squeeze them like lemons."

By cultivating the society of the doctor, the abbe, and Monsieur Bongrand, Savinien proved the excellence of his character. The love of this young man for Ursula, so devoid of self-interest, and so persistent, interested the three friends deeply, and they now never separated the lovers in their thoughts. Soon the monotony of this patriarchal life, and the certainty of a future before them, gave to their affection a fraternal character. The doctor often left the pair alone together. He judged the young man rightly; he saw him kiss her hand on arriving, but he knew he would ask no kiss when alone with her, so deeply did the lover respect the innocence, the frankness of the young girl, whose excessive sensibility, often tried, taught him that a harsh word, a cold look, or the alternations of gentleness and roughness might kill her. The only freedom between the two took place before the eyes of the old man in the evenings.

Two years, full of secret happiness, passed thus,—without other events than the fruitless efforts made by the young man to obtain from his mother her consent to his marriage. He talked to her sometimes for hours together. She listened and made no answer to his entreaties, other than by Breton silence or a positive denial.

At nineteen years of age Ursula, elegant in appearance, a fine musician, and well brought up, had nothing more to learn; she was perfected. The fame of her beauty and grace and education spread far. The doctor was called upon to decline the overtures of Madame d'Aiglemont, who was thinking of Ursula for her eldest son. Six months later, in spite of the secrecy the doctor and Ursula maintained on this subject, Savinien heard of it. Touched by so much delicacy, he made use of the incident in another attempt to vanquish his mother's obstinacy; but she merely replied:—

"If the d'Aiglemonts choose to ally themselves ill, is that any reason why we should do so?"

In December, 1834, the kind and now truly pious old doctor, then eighty-eight years old, declined visibly. When seen out of doors, his face pinched and wan and his eyes pale, all the town talked of his approaching death. "You'll soon know results," said the community to the heirs. In truth the old man's death had all the attraction of a problem. But the doctor himself did not know he was ill; he had his illusions, and neither poor Ursula nor Savinien nor Bongrand nor the abbe were willing to enlighten him as to his condition. The Nemours doctor who came to see him every day did not venture to prescribe. Old Minoret felt no pain; his lamp of life was gently going out. His mind continued firm and clear and powerful. In old men thus constituted the soul governs the body, and gives it strength to die erect. The abbe, anxious not to hasten the fatal end, released his parishioner from the duty of hearing mass in church, and allowed him to read the services at home, for the doctor faithfully attended to all his religious duties. The nearer he came to the grave the more he loved God; the lights eternal shone upon all difficulties and explained them more and more clearly to his mind. Early in the year Ursula persuaded him to sell the carriage and horses and dismiss Cabirolle. Monsieur Bongrand, whose uneasiness about Ursula's future was far from quieted by the doctor's half-confidence, boldly opened the subject one evening and showed his old friend the importance of making Ursula legally of age. Still the old man, though he had often consulted the justice of peace, would not reveal to him the secret of his provision for Ursula, though he agreed to the necessity of securing her independence by majority. The more Monsieur Bongrand persisted in his efforts to discover the means selected by his old friend to provide for his darling the more wary the doctor became.

"Why not secure the thing," said Bongrand, "why run any risks?"

"When you are between two risks," replied the doctor, "avoid the most risky."

Bongrand carried through the business of making Ursula of age so promptly that the papers were ready by the day she was twenty. That anniversary was the last pleasure of the old doctor who, seized perhaps with a presentiment of his end, gave a little ball, to which he invited all the young people in the families of Dionis, Cremiere, Minoret, and Massin. Savinien, Bongrand, the abbe and his two assistant priests, the Nemours doctor, and Mesdames Zelie Minoret, Massin, and Cremiere, together with old Schmucke, were the guests at a grand dinner which preceded the ball.

"I feel I am going," said the old man to the notary towards the close of the evening. "I beg you to come to-morrow and draw up my guardianship account with Ursula, so as not to complicate my property after my death. Thank God! I have not withdrawn one penny from my heirs,—I have disposed of nothing but my income. Messieurs Cremiere, Massin, and Minoret my nephew are members of the family council appointed for Ursula, and I wish them to be present at the rendering of my account."

These words, heard by Massin and quickly passed from one to another round the ball-room, poured balm into the minds of the three families, who had lived in perpetual alternations of hope and fear, sometimes thinking they were certain of wealth, oftener that they were disinherited.

When, about two in the morning, the guests were all gone and no one remained in the salon but Savinien, Bongrand, and the abbe, the old doctor said, pointing to Ursula, who was charming in her ball dress; "To you, my friends, I confide her! A few days more, and I shall be here no longer to protect her. Put yourselves between her and the world until she is married,— I fear for her."

The words made a painful impression. The guardian's account, rendered a day or two later in presence of the family council, showed that Doctor Minoret owed a balance to his ward of ten thousand six hundred francs from the bequest of Monsieur de Jordy, and also from a little capital of gifts made by the doctor himself to Ursula during the last fifteen years, on birthdays and other anniversaries.

This formal rendering of the account was insisted on by the justice of the peace, who feared (unhappily, with too much reason) the results of Doctor Minoret's death.

The following day the old man was seized with a weakness which compelled him to keep his bed. In spite of the reserve which always surrounded the doctor's house and kept it from observation, the news of his approaching death spread through the town, and the heirs began to run hither and thither through the streets, like the pearls of a chaplet when the string is broken. Massin called at the house to learn the truth, and was told by Ursula herself that the doctor was in bed. The Nemours doctor had remarked that whenever old Minoret took to his bed he would die; and therefore in spite of the cold, the heirs took their stand in the street, on the square, at their own doorsteps, talking of the event so long looked for, and watching for the moment when the priests should appear, bearing the sacrament, with all the paraphernalia customary in the provinces, to the dying man. Accordingly, two days later, when the Abbe Chaperon, with an assistant and the choir-boys, preceded by the sacristan bearing the cross, passed along the Grand'Rue, all the heirs joined the procession, to get an entrance to the house and see that nothing was abstracted, and lay their eager hands upon its coveted treasures at the earliest moment.

When the doctor saw, behind the clergy, the row of kneeling heirs, who instead of praying were looking at him with eyes that were brighter than the tapers, he could not restrain a smile. The abbe turned round, saw them, and continued to say the prayers slowly. The post master was the first to abandon the kneeling posture; his wife followed him. Massin, fearing that Zelie and her husband might lay hands on some ornament, joined them in the salon, where all the heirs were presently assembled one by one.

"He is too honest a man to steal extreme unction," said Cremiere; "we may be sure of his death now."

"Yes, we shall each get about twenty thousand francs a year," replied Madame Massin.

"I have an idea," said Zelie, "that for the last three years he hasn't invested anything—he grew fond of hoarding."

"Perhaps the money is in the cellar," whispered Massin to Cremiere.

"I hope we shall be able to find it," said Minoret-Levrault.

"But after what he said at the ball we can't have any doubt," cried Madame Massin.

"In any case," began Cremiere, "how shall we manage? Shall we divide; shall we go to law; or could we draw lots? We are adults, you know—"

A discussion, which soon became angry, now arose as to the method of procedure. At the end of half an hour a perfect uproar of voices, Zelie's screeching organ detaching itself from the rest, resounded in the courtyard and even in the street.

The noise reached the doctor's ears; he heard the words, "The house—the house is worth thirty thousand francs. I'll take it at that," said, or rather bellowed by Cremiere.

"Well, we'll take what it's worth," said Zelie, sharply.

"Monsieur l'abbe," said the old man to the priest, who remained beside his friend after administering the communion, "help me to die in peace. My heirs, like those of Cardinal Ximenes, are capable of pillaging the house before my death, and I have no monkey to revive me. Go and tell them I will have none of them in my house."

The priest and the doctor of the town went downstairs and repeated the message of the dying man, adding, in their indignation, strong words of their own.

"Madame Bougival," said the doctor, "close the iron gate and allow no one to enter; even the dying, it seems, can have no peace. Prepare mustard poultices and apply them to the soles of Monsieur's feet."

"Your uncle is not dead," said the abbe, "and he may live some time longer. He wishes for absolute silence, and no one beside him but his niece. What a difference between the conduct of that young girl and yours!"

"Old hypocrite!" exclaimed Cremiere. "I shall keep watch of him. It is possible he's plotting something against our interests."

The post master had already disappeared into the garden, intending to watch there and wait his chance to be admitted to the house as an assistant. He now returned to it very softly, his boots making no noise, for there were carpets on the stairs and corridors. He was able to reach the door of his uncle's room without being heard. The abbe and the doctor had left the house; La Bougival was making the poultices.

"Are we quite alone?" said the old man to his godchild.

Ursula stood on tiptoe and looked into the courtyard.

"Yes," she said; "the abbe has just closed the gate after him."

"My darling child," said the dying man, "my hours, my minutes even, are counted. I have not been a doctor for nothing; I shall not last till evening. Do not cry, my Ursula," he said, fearing to be interrupted by the child's weeping, "but listen to me carefully; it concerns your marriage to Savinien. As soon as La Bougival comes back go down to the pagoda,—here is the key,—lift the marble top of the Boule buffet and you will find a letter beneath it, sealed and addressed to you; take it and come back here, for I cannot die easy unless I see it in your hands. When I am dead do not let any one know of it immediately, but send for Monsieur de Portenduere; read the letter together; swear to me now, in his name and your own, that you will carry out my last wishes. When Savinien has obeyed me, then announce my death, but not till then. The comedy of the heirs will begin. God grant those monsters may not ill-treat you."

"Yes godfather."

The post master did not listen to the end of this scene; he slipped away on tip-toe, remembering that the lock of the study was on the library side of the door. He had been present in former days at an argument between the architect and a locksmith, the latter declaring that if the pagoda were entered by the window on the river it would be much safer to put the lock of the door opening into the library on the library side. Dazzled by his hopes, and his ears flushed with blood, Minoret sprang the lock with the point of his knife as rapidly as a burglar could have done it. He entered the study, followed the doctor's directions, took the package of papers without opening it, relocked the door, put everything in order, and went into the dining-room and sat down, waiting till La Bougival had gone upstairs with the poultice before he ventured to leave the house. He then made his escape,—all the more easily because poor Ursula lingered to see that La Bougival applied the poultice properly.

"The letter! the letter!" cried the old man, in a dying voice. "Obey me; take the key. I must see you with that letter in your hand."

The words were said with so wild a look that La Bougival exclaimed to Ursula:—

"Do what he asks at once or you will kill him."

She kissed his forehead, took the key and went down. A moment later, recalled by a cry from La Bougival, she ran back. The old man looked at her eagerly. Seeing her hands empty, he rose in his bed, tried to speak, and died with a horrible gasp, his eyes haggard with fear. The poor girl, who saw death for the first time, fell on her knees and burst into tears. La Bougival closed the old man's eyes and straightened him on the bed; then she ran to call Savinien; but the heirs, who stood at the corner of the street, like crows watching till a horse is buried before they scratch at the ground and turn it over with beak and claw, flocked in with the celerity of birds of prey.

CHAPTER XV.
THE DOCTOR'S WILL

While these events were taking place the post master had hurried home to open the mysterious package and know its contents.

To my dear Ursula Mirouet, daughter of my natural half-brother, Joseph Mirouet, and Dinah Grollman:—

My dear Angel,—The fatherly affection I bear you—and which you have so fully justified—came not only from the promise I gave your father to take his place, but also from your resemblance to my wife, Ursula Mirouet, whose grace, intelligence, frankness, and charm you constantly recall to my mind. Your position as the daughter of a natural son of my father-in-law might invalidate all testamentary bequests made by me in your favor—

"The old rascal!" cried the post master.

Had I adopted you the result might also have been a lawsuit, and I shrank from the idea of transmitting my fortune to you by marriage, for I might live years and thus interfere with your happiness, which is now delayed only by Madame de Portenduere. Having weighted these difficulties carefully, and wishing to leave you enough money to secure to you a prosperous existence—

"The scoundrel, he has thought of everything!"

—without injuring my heirs—

"The Jesuit! as if he did not owe us every penny of his money!"—I intend you to have the savings from my income which I have for the last eighteen years steadily invested, by the help of my notary, seeking to make you thereby as happy as any one can be made by riches. Without means, your education and your lofty ideas would cause you unhappiness. Besides, you ought to bring a liberal dowry to the fine young man who loves you. You will therefore find in the middle of the third volume of Pandects, folio, bound in red morocco (the last volume on the first shelf above the little table in the library, on the side of the room next the salon), three certificates of Funds in the three-per-cents, made out to bearer, each amounting to twelve thousand francs a year—

"What depths of wickedness!" screamed the post master. "Ah! God would not permit me to be so defrauded."

Take these at once, and also some uninvested savings made to this date, which you will find in the preceding volume. Remember, my darling child, that you must obey a wish that has made the happiness of my whole life; a wish that will force me to ask the intervention of God should you disobey me. But, to guard against all scruples in your dear conscience—for I well know how ready it is to torture you—you will find herewith a will in due form bequeathing these certificates to Monsieur Savinien de Portenduere. So, whether you possess them in your own name, or whether they come to you from him you love, they will be, in every sense, your legitimate property.

Your godfather, Denis Minoret.

To this letter was annexed the following paper written on a sheet of stamped paper.

This is my will: I, Denis Minoret, doctor of medicine, settled in Nemours, being of sound mind and body, as the date of this document will show, do bequeath my soul to God, imploring him to pardon my errors in view of my sincere repentance. Next, having found in Monsieur le Vicomte Savinien de Portenduere a true and honest affection for me, I bequeath to him the sum of thirty-six thousand francs a year from the Funds, at three per cent, the said bequest to take precedence of all inheritance accruing to my heirs.

Written by my own hand, at Nemours, on the 11th of January, 1831.

Denis Minoret.

Without an instant's hesitation the post master, who had locked himself into his wife's bedroom to insure being alone, looked about for the tinder-box, and received two warnings from heaven by the extinction of two matches which obstinately refused to light. The third took fire. He burned the letter and the will on the hearth and buried the vestiges of paper and sealing-wax in the ashes by way of superfluous caution. Then, allured by the thought of possessing thirty-six thousand francs a year of which his wife knew nothing, he returned at full speed to his uncle's house, spurred by the only idea, a clear-cut, simple idea, which was able to piece and penetrate his dull brain. Finding the house invaded by the three families, now masters of the place, he trembled lest he should be unable to accomplish a project to which he gave no reflection whatever, except so far as to fear the obstacles.

"What are you doing here?" he said to Massin and Cremiere. "We can't leave the house and the property to be pillaged. We are the heirs, but we can't camp here. You, Cremiere, go to Dionis at once and tell him to come and certify to the death; I can't draw up the mortuary certificate for an uncle, though I am assistant-mayor. You, Massin, go and ask old Bongrand to attach the seals. As for you, ladies," he added, turning to his wife and Mesdames Cremiere and Massin, "go and look after Ursula; then nothing can be stolen. Above all, close the iron gate and don't let any one leave the house."

The women, who felt the justice of this remark, ran to Ursula's bedroom, where they found the noble girl, so cruelly suspected, on her knees before God, her face covered with tears. Minoret, suspecting that the women would not long remain with Ursula, went at once to the library, found the volume, opened it, took the three certificates, and found in the other volume about thirty bank notes. In spite of his brutal nature the colossus felt as though a peal of bells were ringing in each ear. The blood whistled in his temples as he committed the theft; cold as the weather was, his shirt was wet on his back; his legs gave way under him and he fell into a chair in the salon as if an axe had fallen on his head.

"How the inheritance of money loosens a man's tongue! Did you hear Minoret?" said Massin to Cremiere as they hurried through the town. "'Go here, go there,' just as if he knew everything."

"Yes, for a dull beast like him he had a certain air of—"

"Stop!" said Massin, alarmed at a sudden thought. "His wife is there; they've got some plan! Do you do both errands; I'll go back."

Just as the post master fell into the chair he saw at the gate the heated face of the clerk of the court who returned to the house of death with the celerity of a weasel.

"Well, what is it now?" asked the post master, unlocking the gate for his co-heir.

"Nothing; I have come back to be present at the sealing," answered Massin, giving him a savage look.

"I wish those seals were already on, so that we could go home," said Minoret.

"We shall have to put a watcher over them," said Massin. "La Bougival is capable of anything in the interests of that minx. We'll put Goupil there."

"Goupil!" said the post master; "put a rat in the meal!"

"Well, let's consider," returned Massin. "To-night they'll watch the body; the seals can be affixed in an hour; our wives could look after them. To-morrow we'll have the funeral at twelve o'clock. But the inventory can't be made under a week."

"Let's get rid of that girl at once," said the colossus; "then we can safely leave the watchman of the town-hall to look after the house and the seals."

"Good," cried Massin. "You are the head of the Minoret family."

"Ladies," said Minoret, "be good enough to stay in the salon; we can't think of our dinner to-day; the seals must be put on at once for the security of all interests."

He took his wife apart and told her Massin's proposition about Ursula. The women, whose hearts were full of vengeance against the minx, as they called her, hailed the idea of turning her out. Bongrand arrived with his assistants to apply the seals, and was indignant when the request was made to him, by Zelie and Madame Massin, as a near friend of the deceased, to tell Ursula to leave the house.

"Go and turn her out of her father's house, her benefactor's house yourselves," he cried. "Go! you who owe your inheritance to the generosity of her soul; take her by the shoulders and fling her into the street before the eyes of the whole town! You think her capable of robbing you? Well, appoint a watcher of the seals; you have a right to do that. But I tell you at once I shall put no seals on Ursula's room; she has a right to that room, and everything in it is her own property. I shall tell her what her rights are, and tell her too to put everything that belongs to her in this house in that room— Oh! in your presence," he said, hearing a growl of dissatisfaction among the heirs.

"What do you think of that?" said the collector to the post master and the women, who seemed stupefied by the angry address of Bongrand.

"Call *him* a magistrate!" cried the post master.

Ursula meanwhile was sitting on her little sofa in a half-fainting condition, her head thrown back, her braids unfastened, while every now and then her sobs broke forth. Her eyes were dim and their lids swollen; she was, in fact, in a state of moral and physical prostration which might have softened the hardest hearts—except those of the heirs.

"Ah! Monsieur Bongrand, after my happy birthday comes death and mourning," she said, with the poetry natural to her. "You know, *you*, what he was. In twenty years he never said an impatient word to me. I believed he would live a hundred years. He has been my mother," she cried, "my good, kind mother."

These simple thoughts brought torrents of tears from her eyes, interrupted by sobs; then she fell back exhausted.

"My child," said the justice of peace, hearing the heirs on the staircase. "You have a lifetime before you in which to weep, but you have now only a moment to attend to your interests. Gather everything that belongs to you in this house and put it into your own room at once. The heirs insist on my affixing the seals."

"Ah! his heirs may take everything if they choose," cried Ursula, sitting upright under an impulse of savage indignation. "I have something here," she added, striking her breast, "which is far more precious—"

"What is it?" said the post master, who with Massin at his heels now showed his brutal face.

"The remembrances of his virtues, of his life, of his words—an image of his celestial soul," she said, her eyes and face glowing as she raised her hand with a glorious gesture.

"And a key!" cried Massin, creeping up to her like a cat and seizing a key which fell from the bosom of her dress in her sudden movement.

"Yes," she said, blushing, "that is the key of his study; he sent me there at the moment he was dying."

The two men glanced at each other with horrid smiles, and then at Monsieur Bongrand, with a meaning look of degrading suspicion. Ursula who intercepted it, rose to her feet, pale as if the blood had left her body. Her eyes sent forth the lightnings that perhaps can issue only at some cost of life, as she said in a choking voice:—

"Monsieur Bongrand, everything in this room is mine through the kindness of my godfather; they may have it all; I have nothing on me but the clothes I wear. I shall leave the house and never return to it."

She went to her godfather's room, and no entreaties could make her leave it,—the heirs, who now began to be slightly ashamed of their conduct, endeavoring to persuade her. She requested Monsieur Bongrand to engage two rooms for her at the "Vieille Poste" inn until she could find some lodging in town where she could live with La Bougival. She returned to her own room for her prayer-book, and spent the night, with the abbe, his assistant, and Savinien, in weeping and praying beside her uncle's body. Savinien came, after his mother had gone to bed, and knelt, without a word, beside his Ursula. She smiled at him sadly, and thanked him for coming faithfully to share her troubles.

"My child," said Monsieur Bongrand, bring her a large package, "one of your uncle's heirs has taken these necessary articles from your drawers, for the seals cannot be opened for several days; after that you will recover everything that belongs to you. I have, for your own sake, placed the seals on your room."

"Thank you," she replied, pressing his hand. "Look at him again,—he seems to sleep, does he not?"

The old man's face wore that flower of fleeting beauty which rests upon the features of the dead who die a painless death; light appeared to radiate from it.

"Did he give you anything secretly before he died?" whispered M. Bongrand.

"Nothing," she said; "he spoke only of a letter."

"Good! it will certainly be found," said Bongrand. "How fortunate for you that the heirs demanded the sealing."

At daybreak Ursula bade adieu to the house where her happy youth was passed; more particularly, to the modest chamber in which her love began. So dear to her was it that even in this hour of darkest grief tears of regret rolled down her face for the dear and peaceful haven. With one last glance at Savinien's windows she left the room and the house, and went to the inn accompanied by La Bougival, who carried the package, by Monsieur Bongrand, who gave her his arm, and by Savinien, her true protector.

Thus it happened that in spite of all his efforts and cautions the worst fears of the justice of peace were realized; he was now to see Ursula without means and at the mercy of her benefactor's heirs.

The next afternoon the whole town attended the doctor's funeral. When the conduct of the heirs to his adopted daughter was publicly known, a vast majority of the people thought it natural and necessary. An inheritance was involved; the good man was known to have hoarded; Ursula might think she had rights; the heirs were only defending their property; she had humbled them enough during their uncle's lifetime, for he had treated them like dogs and sent them about their business.

Desire Minoret, who was not going to do wonders in life (so said those who envied his father), came down for the funeral. Ursula was unable to be present, for she was in bed with a nervous fever, caused partly by the insults of the heirs and partly by her heavy affliction.

"Look at that hypocrite weeping," said some of the heirs, pointing to Savinien, who was deeply affected by the doctor's death.

"The question is," said Goupil, "has he any good grounds for weeping. Don't laugh too soon, my friends; the seals are not yet removed."

"Pooh!" said Minoret, who had good reason to know the truth, "you are always frightening us about nothing."

As the funeral procession left the church to proceed to the cemetery, a bitter mortification was inflicted on Goupil; he tried to take Desire's arm, but the latter withdrew it and turned away from his former comrade in presence of all Nemours.

"I won't be angry, or I couldn't get revenge," thought the notary's clerk, whose dry heart swelled in his bosom like a sponge.

Before breaking the seals and making the inventory, it took some time for the procureur du roi, who is the legal guardian of orphans, to commission

Monsieur Bongrand to act in his place. After that was done the settlement of the Minoret inheritance (nothing else being talked of in the town for ten days) began with all the legal formalities. Dionis had his pickings; Goupil enjoyed some mischief-making; and as the business was profitable the sessions were many. After the first of these sessions all parties breakfasted together; notary, clerk, heirs, and witnesses drank the best wines in the doctor's cellar.

In the provinces, and especially in little towns where every one lives in his own house, it is sometimes very difficult to find a lodging. When a man buys a business of any kind the dwelling-house is almost always included in the purchase. Monsieur Bongrand saw no other way of removing Ursula from the village inn than to buy a small house on the Grand'Rue at the corner of the bridge over the Loing. The little building had a front door opening on a corridor, and one room on the ground-floor with two windows on the street; behind this came the kitchen, with a glass door opening to an inner courtyard about thirty feet square. A small staircase, lighted on the side towards the river by small windows, led to the first floor where there were three chambers, and above these were two attic rooms. Monsieur Bongrand borrowed two thousand francs from La Bougival's savings to pay the first instalment of the price,—six thousand francs,—and obtained good terms for payment of the rest. As Ursula wished to buy her uncle's books, Bongrand knocked down the partition between two rooms on the bedroom floor, finding that their united length was the same as that of the doctor's library, and gave room for his bookshelves.

Savinien and Bongrand urged on the workmen who were cleaning, painting, and otherwise renewing the tiny place, so that before the end of March Ursula was able to leave the inn and take up her abode in the ugly house; where, however, she found a bedroom exactly like the one she had left; for it was filled with all her furniture, claimed by the justice of peace when the seals were removed. La Bougival, sleeping in the attic, could be summoned by a bell placed near the head of the young girl's bed. The room intended for the books, the salon on the ground-floor and the kitchen, though still unfurnished, had been hung with fresh papers and repainted, and only awaited the purchases which the young girl hoped to make when her godfather's effects were sold.

Though the strength of Ursula's character was well known to the abbe and Monsieur Bongrand, they both feared the sudden change from the comfort and elegancies to which her uncle had accustomed her to this barren and denuded life. As for Savinien he wept over it. He did, in fact, make private payments to the workman and to the upholsterer, so that Ursula should perceive no difference between the new chamber and the old one. But the young girl herself, whose happiness now lay in Savinien's own eyes, showed the gentlest resignation, which endeared her more and more to her two old friends, and proved to them for the hundredth time that no troubles but those of the heart could make her suffer. The grief she felt for the loss of her godfather was far too deep to let her even feel the bitterness of her change of fortune, though it added fresh obstacles to her marriage. Savinien's distress in seeing her thus reduced did her so much harm that she whispered to him, as they came from mass on the morning on the day when she first went to live in her new house:

"Love could not exist without patience; let us wait."

As soon as the form of the inventory was drawn up, Massin, advised by Goupil (who turned to him under the influence of his secret hatred to the post master), summoned Monsieur and Madame de Portenduere to pay off the mortgage which had now elapsed, together with the interest accruing thereon. The old lady was bewildered at a summons to pay one hundred and twenty-nine thousand five hundred and seventeen francs within twenty-four hours under pain of execution on her house. It was impossible for her to borrow the money. Savinien went to Fontainebleau to consult a lawyer.

"You are dealing with a bad set of people who will not compromise," was the lawyer's opinion. "They intend to sue in the matter and get your farm at Bordieres. The best way for you would be to make a voluntary sale of it and so escape costs."

This dreadful news broke down the old lady. Her son very gently pointed out to her that had she consented to his marriage in Minoret's life-time, the doctor would have left his property to Ursula's husband and they would to-day have been opulent instead of being, as they now were, in the depths of poverty. Though said without reproach, this argument annihilated the poor woman even more than the thought of her coming ejectment. When Ursula heard of this catastrophe she was stupefied with grief, having scarcely recovered from her fever, and the blow which the heirs had already dealt her. To love and be unable to succor the man she loves,—that is one of the most dreadful of all sufferings to the soul of a noble and sensitive woman.

"I wished to buy my uncle's house," she said, "now I will buy your mother's."

"Can you?" said Savinien. "You are a minor, and you cannot sell out your Funds without formalities to which the procureur du roi, now your legal guardian, would not agree. We shall not resist. The whole town will be glad to see the discomfiture of a noble family. These bourgeois are like hounds after a quarry. Fortunately, I still have ten thousand francs left, on which I can support my mother till this deplorable matter is settled. Besides, the inventory of your godfather's property is not yet finished; Monsieur Bongrand still thinks he shall find something for you. He is as much astonished as I am that you seem to be left without fortune. The doctor so often spoke both to him and to me of the future he had prepared for you that neither of us can understand this conclusion."

"Pooh!" she said; "so long as I can buy my godfather's books and furniture and prevent their being dispersed, I am content."

"But who knows the price these infamous creatures will set on anything you want?"

Nothing was talked of from Montargis to Fontainebleau but the million for which the Minoret heirs were searching. But the most minute search made in every corner of the house after the seals were removed, brought no discovery. The one hundred and twenty-nine thousand francs of the Portenduere debt, the capital of the fifteen thousand a year in the three per cents (then quoted at 76), the house, valued at forty thousand francs, and its handsome furniture, produced a total of about six hundred thousand francs, which to most persons seemed a comforting sum. But what had become of the money the doctor must have saved?

Minoret began to have gnawing anxieties. La Bougival and Savinien, who persisted in believing, as did the justice of peace, in the existence of a will, came every day at the close of each session to find out from Bongrand the results of the day's search. The latter would sometimes exclaim, before the agents and the heirs were fairly out of hearing, "I can't understand the thing!" Bongrand, Savinien, and the abbe often declared to each other that the doctor, who received no interest from the Portenduere loan, could not have kept his house as he did on fifteen thousand francs a year. This opinion, openly expressed, made the post master turn livid more than once.

"Yet they and I have rummaged everywhere," said Bongrand,—"they to find money, and I to find a will in favor of Monsieur de Portenduere. They have sifted the ashes, lifted the marbles, felt of the slippers, bored into the wood-work of the beds, emptied the mattresses, ripped up the quilts, turned his eider-down inside-out, examined every inch of paper piece by piece, searched the drawers, dug up the cellar floor—and I have urged on their devastations."

"What do you think about it?" said the abbe.

"The will has been suppressed by one of the heirs."

"But where's the property?"

"We may whistle for it!"

"Perhaps the will is hidden in the library," said Savinien.

"Yes, and for that reason I don't dissuade Ursula from buying it. If it were not for that, it would be absurd to let her put every penny of her ready money into books she will never open."

At first the whole town believed the doctor's niece had got possession of the unfound capital; but when it was known positively that fourteen hundred francs a year and her gifts constituted her whole fortune the search of the doctor's house and furniture excited a more wide-spread curiosity than before. Some said the money would be found in bank bills hidden away in the furniture, others that the old man had slipped them into his books. The sale of the effects exhibited a spectacle of the most extraordinary precautions on the part of the heirs. Dionis, who was doing duty as auctioneeer, declared, as each lot was cried out, that the heirs only sold the article (whatever it was) and not what it might contain; then, before allowing it to be taken away it was subjected to a final investigation, being thumped and sounded; and when at last it left the house the sellers followed with the looks a father might cast upon a son who was starting for India.

"Ah, mademoiselle," cried La Bougival, returning from the first session in despair, "I shall not go again. Monsieur Bongrand is right, you could never bear the sight. Everything is ticketed. All the town is coming and going just as in the street; the handsome furniture is being ruined, they even stand upon it; the whole place is such a muddle that a hen couldn't find her chicks. You'd think there had been a fire. Lots of things are in the courtyard; the closets are all open, and nothing in them. Oh! the poor dear man, it's well he died, the sight would have killed him."

Bongrand, who bought for Ursula certain articles which her uncle cherished, and which were suitable for her little house, did not appear at the sale of the library. Shrewder than the heirs, whose cupidity might have run up the price of the books had they known he was buying them for Ursula, he commissioned a dealer in old books living in Melun to buy them for him. As a result of the heir's anxiety the whole library was sold book by book. Three thousand volumes were examined, one by one, held by the two sides of the binding and shaken so that loose papers would infallibly fall out. The whole amount of the purchases on Ursula's account amounted to six thousand five hundred francs or thereabouts. The book-cases were not allowed to leave the premises until carefully examined by a cabinet-maker, brought down from Paris to search for secret drawers. When at last Monsieur Bongrand gave orders to take the books and the bookcases to Mademoiselle Mirouet's house the heirs were tortured with vague fears, not dissipated until in course of time they saw how poorly she lived.

Minoret bought up his uncle's house, the value of which his co-heirs ran up to fifty thousand francs, imagining that the post master expected to find a treasure in the walls; in fact the house was sold with a reservation on this subject. Two weeks later Minoret disposed of his post establishment, with all the coaches and horses, to the son of a rich farmer, and went to live in his uncle's house, where he spent considerable sums in repairing and refurnishing the rooms. By making this move he thoughtlessly condemned himself to live within sight of Ursula.

"I hope," he said to Dionis the day when Madame de Portenduere was summoned to pay her debt, "that we shall soon be rid of those nobles; after they are gone we'll drive out the rest."

"That old woman with fourteen quarterings," said Goupil, "won't want to witness her own disaster; she'll go and die in Brittany, where she can manage to find a wife for her son."

"No," said the notary, who had that morning drawn out a deed of sale at Bongrand's request. "Ursula has just bought the house she is living in."

"That cursed fool does everything she can to annoy me!" cried the post master imprudently.

"What does it signify to you whether she lives in Nemours or not?" asked Goupil, surprised at the annoyance which the colossus betrayed.

"Don't you know," answered Minoret, turning as red as a poppy, "that my son is fool enough to be in love with her? I'd give five hundred francs if I could get Ursula out of this town."

CHAPTER XVI.
THE TWO ADVERSARIES

Perhaps the foregoing conduct on the part of the post master will have shown already that Ursula, poor and resigned, was destined to be a thorn in the side of the rich Minoret. The bustle attending the settlement of an estate, the sale of the property, the going and coming necessitated by such unusual business, his discussions with his wife about the most trifling details, the purchase of the doctor's house, where Zelie wished to live in bourgeois style to advance her son's interests,—all this hurly-burly, contrasting with his usually tranquil life hindered the huge Minoret from thinking of his victim. But about the middle of May, a few days after his installation in the doctor's house, as he was coming home from a walk, he heard the sound of a piano, saw La Bougival sitting at a window, like a dragon guarding a treasure, and suddenly became aware of an importunate voice within him.

To explain why to a man of Minoret's nature the sight of Ursula, who had no suspicion of the theft committed upon her, now became intolerable; why the spectacle of so much fortitude under misfortune impelled him to a desire to drive the girl out of town; and how and why it was that this desire took the form of hatred and revenge, would require a whole treatise on moral philosophy. Perhaps he felt he was not the real possessor of thirty-six thousand francs a year so long as she to whom they really belonged lived near him. Perhaps he fancied some mere chance might betray his theft if the person despoiled was not got rid of. Perhaps to a nature in some sort primitive, almost uncivilized, and whose owner up to that time had never done anything illegal, the presence of Ursula awakened remorse. Possibly this remorse goaded him the more because he had received his share of the property legitimately acquired. In his own mind he no doubt attributed these stirrings of his conscience to the fact of Ursula's presence, imagining that if she were removed all his uncomfortable feelings would disappear with her. But still, after all, perhaps crime has its own doctrine of perfection. A beginning of evil demands its end; a first stab must be followed by the blow that kills. Perhaps robbery is doomed to lead to murder. Minoret had committed the crime without the slightest reflection, so rapidly had the events taken place; reflection came later. Now, if you have thoroughly possessed yourself of this man's nature and bodily presence you will understand the mighty effect produced on him by a thought. Remorse is more than a thought; it comes from a feeling which can no more be hidden than love; like love, it has its own tyranny. But, just as Minoret had committed the crime against Ursula without the slightest reflection, so he now blindly longed to drive her from Nemours when he felt himself disturbed by the sight of that wronged innocence. Being, in a sense, imbecile, he never thought of the consequences; he went from danger to danger, driven by a selfish instinct, like a wild animal which does not foresee the huntsman's skill, and relies on its own rapidity or strength. Before long the rich bourgeois, who still met in Dionis's salon, noticed a great change in the manners and behavior of the man who had hitherto been so free of care.

"I don't know what has come to Minoret, he is all *no how*," said his wife, from whom he was resolved to hide his daring deed.

Everybody explained his condition as being, neither more nor less, ennui (in fact the thought now expressed on his face did resemble ennui), caused, they said, by the sudden cessation of business and the change from an active life to one of well-to-do leisure.

While Minoret was thinking only of destroying Ursula's life in Nemours, La Bougival never let a day go by without torturing her foster child with some allusion to the fortune she ought to have had, or without comparing her miserable lot with the prospects the doctor had promised, and of which he had often spoken to her, La Bougival.

"It is not for myself I speak," she said, "but is it likely that monsieur, good and kind as he was, would have died without leaving me the merest trifle?—"

"Am I not here?" replied Ursula, forbidding La Bougival to say another word on the subject.

She could not endure to soil the dear and tender memories that surrounded that noble head—a sketch of which in black and white hung in her little salon—with thoughts of selfish interest. To her fresh and beautiful imagination that sketch sufficed to make her *see* her godfather, on whom her thoughts continually dwelt, all the more because surrounded with the things he loved and used,—his large duchess-sofa, the furniture from his study, his backgammon-table, and the piano he had chosen for her. The two old friends who still remained to her, the Abbe Chaperon and Monsieur Bongrand, the only visitors whom she received, were, in the midst of these inanimate objects representative of the past, like two living memories of her former life to which she attached her present by the love her godfather had blessed.

After a while the sadness of her thoughts, softening gradually, gave tone to the general tenor of her life and united all its parts in an indefinable harmony, expressed by the exquisite neatness, the exact symmetry of her room, the few flowers sent by Savinien, the dainty nothings of a young girl's life, the tranquillity which her quiet habits diffused about her, giving peace and composure to the little home. After breakfast and after mass she continued her studies and practiced; then she took her embroidery and sat at the window looking on the street. At four o'clock Savinien, returning from a walk (which he took in all weathers), finding the window open, would sit upon the outer casing and talk with her for half an hour. In the evening the abbe and Monsieur Bongrand came to see her, but she never allowed Savinien to accompany them. Neither did she accept Madame de Portenduere's proposition, which Savinien had induced his mother to make, that she should visit there.

Ursula and La Bougival lived, moreover, with the strictest economy; they did not spend, counting everything, more than sixty francs a month. The old nurse was indefatigable; she washed and ironed; cooked only twice a week,— mistress and maid eating their food cold on other days; for Ursula was determined to save the seven hundred francs still due on the purchase of the house. This rigid conduct, together with her modesty and her resignation to a life of poverty after the enjoyment of luxury and the fond indulgence of all her wishes, deeply impressed certain persons. Ursula won the respect of others, and no voice was raised against her. Even the heirs, once satisfied, did her justice. Savinien admired the strength of character of so young a girl. From time to time Madame de Portenduere, when they met in church, would address a few kind words to her, and twice she insisted on her coming to dinner and fetched her herself. If all this was not happiness it was at least tranquillity. But a benefit which came to Ursula through the legal care and ability of Bongrand started the smouldering persecution which up to this time had laid in Minoret's breast as a dumb desire.

As soon as the legal settlement of the doctor's estate was finished, the justice of peace, urged by Ursula, took the cause of the Portendueres in hand and promised her to get them out of their trouble. In dealing with the old lady, whose opposition to Ursula's happiness made him furious, he did not allow her to be ignorant of the fact that his devotion to her service was solely to give pleasure to Mademoiselle Mirouet. He chose one of his former clerks to act for the Portendueres at Fontainebleau, and himself put in a motion for a stay of proceedings. He intended to profit by the interval which must elapse between the stoppage of the present suit and some new step on the part of Massin to renew the lease at six thousand francs, get a premium from the present tenants and the payment in full of the rent of the current year.

At this time, when these matters had to be discussed, the former whist-parties were again organized in Madame de Portenduere's salon, between himself, the abbe, Savinien, and Ursula, whom the abbe and he escorted there and back every evening. In June, Bongrand succeeded in quashing the proceedings; whereupon the new lease was signed; he obtained a premium of thirty-two thousand francs from the farmer and a rent of six thousand a year for eighteen years. The evening of the day on which this was finally settled he went to see Zelie, whom he knew to be puzzled as to how to invest her money, and proposed to sell her the farm at Bordieres for two hundred and twenty thousand francs.

"I'd buy it at once," said Minoret, "if I were sure the Portendueres would go and live somewhere else."

"Why?" said the justice of peace.

"We want to get rid of the nobles in Nemours."

"I did hear the old lady say that if she could settle her affairs she should go and live in Brittany, as she would not have means enough left to live here. She is thinking of selling her house."

"Well, sell it to me," said Minoret.

"To you?" said Zelie. "You talk as if you were master of everything. What do you want with two houses in Nemours?"

"If I don't settle this matter of the farm with you to-night," said Bongrand, "our lease will get known, Massin will put in a fresh claim, and I shall lose this chance of liquidation which I am anxious to make. So if you don't take my offer I shall go at once to Melun, where some farmers I know are ready to buy the farm with their eyes shut."

"Why did you come to us, then?" said Zelie.

"Because you can pay me in cash, and my other clients would make me wait some time for the money. I don't want difficulties."

"Get *her* out of Nemours and I'll pay it," exclaimed Minoret.

"You understand that I cannot answer for Madame de Portenduere's actions," said Bongrand. "I can only repeat what I heard her say, but I feel certain they will not remain in Nemours."

On this assurance, enforced by a nudge from Zelie, Minoret agreed to the purchase, and furnished the funds to pay off the mortgage due to the doctor's estate. The deed of sale was immediately drawn up by Dionis. Towards the end of June Bongrand brought the balance of the purchase money to Madame de Portenduere, advising her to invest it in the Funds, where, joined to Savinien's ten thousand, it would give her, at five per cent, an income of six thousand francs. Thus, so far from losing her resources, the old lady actually gained by the transaction. But she did not leave Nemours. Minoret thought he had been tricked,—as though Bongrand had had an idea that Ursula's presence was intolerable to him; and he felt a keen resentment which embittered his hatred to his victim. Then began a secret drama which was terrible in its effects,—the struggle of two determinations; one which impelled Minoret to drive his victim from Nemours, the other which gave

Ursula the strength to bear persecution, the cause of which was for a certain length of time undiscoverable. The situation was a strange and even unnatural one, and yet it was led up to by all the preceding events, which served as a preface to what was now to occur.

Madame Minoret, to whom her husband had given a handsome silver service costing twenty thousand francs, gave a magnificent dinner every Sunday, the day on which her son, the deputy procureur, came from Fontainebleau, bringing with him certain of his friends. On these occasions Zelie sent to Paris for delicacies—obliging Dionis the notary to emulate her display. Goupil, whom the Minorets endeavored to ignore as a questionable person who might tarnish their splendor, was not invited until the end of July. The clerk, who was fully aware of this intended neglect, was forced to be respectful to Desire, who, since his entrance into office, had assumed a haughty and dignified air, even in his own family.

"You must have forgotten Esther," Goupil said to him, "as you are so much in love with Mademoiselle Mirouet."

"In the first place, Esther is dead, monsieur; and in the next I have never even thought of Ursula," said the new magistrate.

"Why, what did you tell me, papa Minoret?" cried Goupil, insolently.

Minoret, caught in a lie by a man whom he feared, would have lost countenance if it had not been for a project in his head, which was, in fact, the reason why Goupil was invited to dinner,—Minoret having remembered the proposition the clerk had once made to prevent the marriage between Savinien and Ursula. For all answer, he led Goupil hurriedly to the end of the garden.

"You'll soon be twenty-eight years old, my good fellow," said he, "and I don't see that you are on the road to fortune. I wish you well, for after all you were once my son's companion. Listen to me. If you can persuade that little Mirouet, who possesses in her own right forty thousand francs, to marry you, I will give you, as true as my name is Minoret, the means to buy a notary's practice at Orleans."

"No," said Goupil, "that's too far out of the way; but Montargis—"

"No," said Minoret; "Sens."

"Very good,—Sens," replied the hideous clerk. "There's an archbishop at Sens, and I don't object to devotion; a little hypocrisy and there you are, on the way to fortune. Besides, the girl is pious, and she'll succeed at Sens."

"It is to be fully understood," continued Minoret, "that I shall not pay the money till you marry my cousin, for whom I wish to provide, out of consideration for my deceased uncle."

"Why not for me too?" said Goupil maliciously, instantly suspecting a secret motive in Minoret's conduct. "Isn't it through information you got from me that you make twenty-four thousand a year from that land, without a single enclosure, around the Chateau du Rouvre? The fields and the mill the other side of the Loing make sixteen thousand more. Come, old fellow, do you mean to play fair with me?"

"Yes."

"If I wanted to show my teeth I could coax Massin to buy the Rouvre estate, park, gardens, preserves, and timber—"

"You'd better think twice before you do that," said Zelie, suddenly intervening.

"If I choose," said Goupil, giving her a viperish look; "Massin would buy the whole for two hundred thousand francs."

"Leave us, wife," said the colossus, taking Zelie by the arm, and shoving her away; "I understand him. We have been so very busy," he continued, returning to Goupil, "that we have had no time to think of you; but I rely on your friendship to buy the Rouvre estate for me."

"It is a very ancient marquisate," said Goupil, maliciously; "which will soon be worth in your hands fifty thousand francs a year; that means a capital of more than two millions as money is now."

"My son could then marry the daughter of a marshal of France, or the daughter of some old family whose influence would get him a fine place under the government in Paris," said Minoret, opening his huge snuff-box and offering a pinch to Goupil.

"Very good; but will you play fair?" cried Goupil, shaking his fingers.

Minoret pressed the clerk's hands replying:—

"On my word of honor."

CHAPTER XVII.
THE MALIGNITY OF PROVINCIAL MINDS

Like all crafty persons, Goupil, fortunately for Minoret, believed that the proposed marriage with Ursula was only a pretext on the part of the colossus and Zelie for making up with him, now that he was opposing them with Massin.

"It isn't he," thought Goupil, "who has invented this scheme; I know my Zelie,—she taught him his part. Bah! I'll let Massin go. In three years time I'll be deputy from Sens." Just then he saw Bongrand on his way to the opposite house for his whist, and he rushed hastily after him.

"You take a great interest in Mademoiselle Mirouet, my dear Monsieur Bongrand," he said. "I know you will not be indifferent to her future. Her relations are considering it, and there is the programme; she ought to marry a notary whose practice should be in the chief town of an arrondisement. This notary, who would of course be elected deputy in three years, should settle on a dower of a hundred thousand francs on her."

"She can do better than that," said Bongrand coldly. "Madame de Portenduere is greatly changed since her misfortunes; trouble is killing her. Savinien will have six thousand francs a year, and Ursula has a capital of forty thousand. I shall show them how to increase it a la Massin, but honestly, and in ten years they will have a little fortune.

"Savinien will do a foolish thing," said Goupil; "he can marry Mademoiselle du Rouvre whenever he likes,—an only daughter to whom the uncle and aunt intend to leave a fine property."

"Where love enters farewell prudence, as La Fontaine says—By the bye, who is your notary?" added Bongrand from curiosity.

"Suppose it were I?" answered Goupil.

"You!" exclaimed Bongrand, without hiding his disgust.

"Well, well!—Adieu, monsieur," replied Goupil, with a parting glance of gall and hatred and defiance.

"Do you wish to be the wife of a notary who will settle a hundred thousand francs on you?" cried Bongrand entering Madame de Portenduere's little salon, where Ursula was seated beside the old lady.

Ursula and Savinien trembled and looked at each other,—she smiling, he not daring to show his uneasiness.

"I am not mistress of myself," said Ursula, holding out her hand to Savinien in such a way that the old lady did not perceive the gesture.

"Well, I have refused the offer without consulting you."

"Why did you do that?" said Madame de Portenduere. "I think the position of a notary is a very good one."

"I prefer my peaceful poverty," said Ursula, "which is really wealth compared with what my station in life might have given me. Besides, my old nurse spares me a great deal of care, and I shall not exchange the present, which I like, for an unknown fate."

A few weeks later the post poured into two hearts the poison of anonymous letters,—one addressed to Madame de Portenduere, the other to Ursula. The following is the one to the old lady:—

"You love your son, you wish to marry him in a manner conformable with the name he bears; and yet you encourage his fancy for an ambitious girl without money and the daughter of a regimental band-master, by inviting her to your house. You ought to marry him to Mademoiselle du Rouvre, on whom her two uncles, the Marquis de Ronquerolles and the Chevalier du Rouvre, who are worth money, would settle a handsome sum rather than leave it to that old fool the Marquis du Rouvre, who runs through everything. Madame de Serizy, aunt of Clementine du Rouvre, who has just lost her only son in the campaign in Algiers, will no doubt adopt her niece. A person who is your well-wisher assures you that Savinien will be accepted."

The letter to Ursula was as follows:—

Dear Ursula,—There is a young man in Nemours who idolizes you. He cannot see you working at your window without emotions which prove to him that his love will last through life. This young man is gifted with an iron will and a spirit of perseverance which nothing can discourage. Receive his addresses favorably, for his intentions are pure, and he humbly asks your hand with a sincere desire to make you happy. His fortune, already suitable, is nothing to that which he will make for you when you are once his

wife. You shall be received at court as the wife of a minister and

one of the first ladies in the land.

As he sees you every day (without your being able to see him) put

a pot of La Bougival's pinks in your window and he will understand

from that that he has your permission to present himself.

Ursula burned the letter and said nothing about it to Savinien. Two days later she received another letter in the following language:—

"You do wrong, my dear Ursula, not to answer one who loves you

better than life itself. You think you will marry Savinien—you

are very much mistaken. That marriage will not take place. Madame

de Portenduere went this morning to Rouvre to ask for the hand of

Mademoiselle Clementine for her son. Savinien will yield in the

end. What objection can he make? The uncles of the young lady are

willing to guarantee their fortune to her; it amounts to over

sixty thousand francs a year."

This letter agonized Ursula's heart and afflicted her with the tortures of jealousy, a form of suffering hitherto unknown to her, but which to this fine organization, so sensitive to pain, threw a pall over the present and over the future, and even over the past. From the moment when she received this fatal paper she lay on the doctor's sofa, her eyes fixed on space, lost in a dreadful dream. In an instant the chill of death had come upon her warm young life. Alas, worse than that! it was like the awful awakening of the dead to the sense that there was no God,—the masterpiece of that strange genius called Jean Paul. Four times La Bougival called her to breakfast. When the faithful creature tried to remonstrate, Ursula waved her hand and answered in one harsh word, "Hush!" said despotically, in strange contrast to her usual gentle manner. La Bougival, watching her mistress through the glass door, saw her alternately red with a consuming fever, and blue as if a shudder of cold had succeeded that unnatural heat. This condition grew worse and worse up to four o'clock; then she rose to see if Savinien were coming, but he did not come. Jealousy and distrust tear all reserves from love. Ursula, who till then had never made one gesture by which her love could be guessed, now took her hat and shawl and rushed into the passage as if to go and meet him. But an afterthought of modesty sent her back to her little salon, where she stayed and wept. When the abbe arrived in the evening La Bougival met him at the door.

"Ah, monsieur!" she cried; "I don't know what's the matter with mademoiselle; she is—"

"I know," said the abbe sadly, stopping the words of the poor nurse.

He then told Ursula (what she had not dared to verify) that Madame de Portenduere had gone to dine at Rouvre.

"And Savinien too?" she asked.

"Yes."

Ursula was seized with a little nervous tremor which made the abbe quiver as though a whole Leyden jar had been discharged at him; he felt moreover a lasting commotion in his heart.

"So we shall not go there to-night," he said as gently as he could; "and, my child, it would be better if you did not go there again. The old lady will receive you in a way to wound your pride. Monsieur Bongrand and I, who had succeeded in bringing her to consider your marriage, have no idea from what quarter this new influence has come to change her, as it were in a moment."

"I expect the worst; nothing can surprise me now," said Ursula in a pained voice. "In such extremities it is a comfort to feel that we have done nothing to displease God."

"Submit, dear daughter, and do not seek to fathom the ways of Providence," said the abbe.

"I shall not unjustly distrust the character of Monsieur de Portenduere—"

"Why do you no longer call him Savinien?" asked the priest, who detected a slight bitterness in Ursula's tone.

"Of my dear Savinien," cried the girl, bursting into tears. "Yes, my good friend," she said, sobbing, "a voice tells me he is as noble in heart as he is in race. He has not only told me that he loves me alone, but he has proved it in a hundred delicate ways, and by restraining heroically his ardent feelings. Lately when he took the hand I held out to him, that evening when Monsieur Bongrand proposed to me a husband, it was the first time, I swear to you, that I had ever given it. He began with a jest when he blew me a kiss across the street, but since then our affection has never outwardly passed, as you well know, the narrowest limits. But I will tell you,—you who read my soul except in this one region where none but the angels see,—well, I will tell you, this love has been in me the secret spring of many seeming merits; it made me accept my poverty; it softened the bitterness of my irreparable loss, for my mourning is more perhaps in my clothes now than in my heart—Oh, was I wrong? can it be that love was stronger in me than my gratitude to my benefactor, and God has punished me for it? But how could it be otherwise? I respected in myself Savinien's future wife; yes, perhaps I was too proud, perhaps it is that pride which God has humbled. God alone, as you have often told me, should be the end and object of all our actions."

The abbe was deeply touched as he watched the tears roll down her pallid face. The higher her sense of security had been, the lower she was now to fall.

"But," she said, continuing, "if I return to my orphaned condition, I shall know how to take up its feelings. After all, could I have tied a mill-stone round the neck of him I love? What can he do here? Who am I to bind him to me? Besides, do I not love him with a friendship so divine that I can bear the loss of my own happiness and my hopes? You know I have often blamed myself for letting my hopes rest upon a grave, and for knowing they were waiting on that poor old lady's death. If Savinien is rich and happy with another I have enough to pay for my entrance to a convent, where I shall go at once. There can no more be two loves in a woman's heart than there can be two masters in heaven, and the life of a religious is attractive to me."

"He could not let his mother go alone to Rouvre," said the abbe, gently.

"Do not let us talk of that, my dear good friend," she answered. "I will write to-night and set him free. I am glad to have to close the windows of this room," she continued, telling her old friend of the anonymous letters, but declaring that she would not allow any inquiries to be made as to who her unknown lover might be.

"Why! it was an anonymous letter that first took Madame de Portenduere to Rouvre," cried the abbe. "You are annoyed for some object by evil persons."

"How can that be? Neither Savinien nor I have injured any one; and I am no longer an obstacle to the prosperity of others."

"Well, well, my child," said the abbe, quietly, "let us profit by this tempest, which has scattered our little circle, to put the library in order. The books are still in heaps. Bongrand and I want to get them in order; we wish to make a search among them. Put your trust in God, and remember also that in our good Bongrand and in me you have two devoted friends."

"That is much, very much," she said, going with him to the threshold of the door, where she stretched out her neck like a bird looking over its nest, hoping against hope to see Savinien.

Just then Minoret and Goupil, returning from a walk in the meadows, stopped as they passed, and the colossus spoke to Ursula.

"Is anything the matter, cousin; for we are still cousins, are we not? You seem changed."

Goupil looked so ardently at Ursula that she was frightened, and went back into the house without replying.

"She is cross," said Minoret to the abbe.

"Mademoiselle Mirouet is quite right not to talk to men on the threshold of her door," said the abbe; "she is too young—"

"Oh!" said Goupil. "I am told she doesn't lack lovers."

The abbe bowed hurriedly and went as fast as he could to the Rue des Bourgeois.

"Well," said Goupil to Minoret, "the thing is working. Did you notice how pale she was. Within a fortnight she'll have left the town—you'll see."

"Better have you for a friend than an enemy," cried Minoret, frightened at the atrocious grin which gave to Goupil's face the diabolical expression of the Mephistopheles of Joseph Brideau.

"I should think so!" returned Goupil. "If she doesn't marry me I'll make her die of grief."

"Do it, my boy, and I'll GIVE you the money to buy a practice in Paris. You can then marry a rich woman—"

"Poor Ursula! what makes you so bitter against her? what has she done to you?" asked the clerk in surprise.

"She annoys me," said Minoret, gruffly.

"Well, wait till Monday and you shall see how I'll rasp her," said Goupil, studying the expression of the late post master's face.

The next day La Bougival carried the following letter to Savinien.

"I don't know what the dear child has written to you," she said, "but she is almost dead this morning."

Who, reading this letter to her lover, could fail to understand the sufferings the poor girl had gone through during the night.

My dear Savinien,—Your mother wishes you to marry Mademoiselle du

Rouvre, and perhaps she is right. You are placed between a life

that is almost poverty-stricken and a life of opulence; between

the betrothed of your heart and a wife in conformity with the
demands of the world; between obedience to your mother and the
fulfilment of your own choice—for I still believe that you have
chosen me. Savinien, if you have now to make your decision I wish
you to do so in absolute freedom; I give you back the promise you
made to yourself—not to me—in a moment which can never fade from
my memory, for it was, like other days that have succeeded it, of
angelic purity and sweetness. That memory will suffice me for my
life. If you should persist in your pledge to me, a dark and
terrible idea would henceforth trouble my happiness. In the midst
of our privations—which we have hitherto accepted so gayly—you
might reflect, too late, that life would have been to you a better
thing had you now conformed to the laws of the world. If you were
a man to express that thought, it would be to me the sentence of
an agonizing death; if you did not express it, I should watch
suspiciously every cloud upon your brow.

Dear Savinien, I have preferred you to all else on earth. I was
right to do so, for my godfather, though jealous of you, used to
say to me, "Love him, my child; you will certainly belong to each
other one of these days." When I went to Paris I loved you
hopelessly, and the feeling contented me. I do not know if I can
now return to it, but I shall try. What are we, after all, at this
moment? Brother and sister. Let us stay so. Marry that happy girl
who can have the joy of giving to your name the lustre it ought to
have, and which your mother thinks I should diminish. You will not
hear of me again. The world will approve of you; I shall never
blame you—but I shall love you ever. Adieu, then!

"Wait," cried the young man. Signing to La Bougival to sit down, he
scratched off hastily the following reply:—

My dear Ursula,—Your letter cuts me to the heart, inasmuch as you

have needlessly felt such pain; and also because our hearts, for

the first time, have failed to understand each other. If you are

not my wife now, it is solely because I cannot marry without my

mother's consent. Dear, eight thousand francs a year and a pretty

cottage on the Loing, why, that's a fortune, is it not? You know

we calculated that if we kept La Bougival we could lay by half our

income every year. You allowed me that evening, in your uncle's

garden, to consider you mine; you cannot now of yourself break

those ties which are common to both of us.—Ursula, need I tell

you that I yesterday informed Monsieur du Rouvre that even if I

were free I could not receive a fortune from a young person whom I

did not know? My mother refuses to see you again; I must therefore

lose the happiness of our evenings; but surely you will not

deprive me of the brief moments I can spend at your window? This

evening, then—Nothing can separate us.

"Take this to her, my old woman; she must not be unhappy one moment longer."

That afternoon at four o'clock, returning from the walk which he always took expressly to pass before Ursula's house, Savinien found his mistress waiting for him, her face a little pallid from these sudden changes and excitements.

"It seems to me that until now I have never known what the pleasure of seeing you is," she said to him.

"You once said to me," replied Savinien, smiling,—"for I remember all your words,—'Love lives by patience; we will wait!' Dear, you have separated love from faith. Ah! this shall be the end of our quarrels; we will never have another. You have claimed to love me better than I love you, but—did I ever doubt you?" he said, offering her a bouquet of wild-flowers arranged to express his thoughts.

"You have never had any reason to doubt me," she replied; "and, besides, you don't know all," she added, in a troubled voice.

Ursula had refused to receive letters by the post. But that afternoon, without being able even to guess at the nature of the trick, she had found, a few moments before Savinien's arrival, a letter tossed on her sofa which contained the words: "Tremble! a rejected lover can become a tiger."

Withstanding Savinien's entreaties, she refused to tell him, out of prudence, the secret of her fears. The delight of seeing him again, after she had thought him lost to her, could alone have made her recover from the mortal chill of terror. The expectation of indefinite evil is torture to every one; suffering assumes the proportions of the unknown, and the unknown is the infinite of the soul. To Ursula the pain was exquisite. Something without her bounded at the slightest noise; yet she was afraid of silence, and suspected even the walls of collusion. Even her sleep was restless. Goupil, who knew nothing of her nature, delicate as that of a flower, had found, with the instinct of evil, the poison that could wither and destroy her.

The next day passed without a shock. Ursula sat playing on her piano till very late; and went to bed easier in mind and very sleepy. About midnight she was awakened by the music of a band composed of a clarinet, hautboy, flute, cornet a piston, trombone, bassoon, flageolet, and triangle. All the neighbours were at their windows. The poor girl, already frightened at seeing the people in the street, received a dreadful shock as she heard the coarse, rough voice of a man proclaiming in loud tones: "For the beautiful Ursula Mirouet, from her lover."

The next day, Sunday, the whole town had heard of it; and as Ursula entered and left the church she saw the groups of people who stood gossiping about her, and felt herself the object of their terrible curiosity. The serenade set all tongues wagging, and conjectures were rife on all sides. Ursula reached home more dead than alive, determined not to leave the house again,—the abbe having advised her to say vespers in her own room. As she entered the house she saw lying in the passage, which was floored with brick, a letter which had evidently been slipped under the door. She picked it up and read it, under the idea that it would obtain an explanation. It was as follows:—

"Resign yourself to becoming my wife, rich and idolized. I am resolved. If you are not mine living you shall be mine dead. To your refusal you may attribute not only your own misfortunes, but those which will fall on others.

"He who loves you, and whose wife you will be."

Curiously enough, at the very moment that the gentle victim of this plot was drooping like a cut flower, Mesdemoiselles Massin, Dionis, and Cremiere were envying her lot.

"She is a lucky girl," they were saying; "people talk of her, and court her, and quarrel about her. The serenade was charming; there was a cornet-a-piston."

"What's a piston?"

- 154 -

"A new musical instrument, as big as this, see!" replied Angelique Cremiere to Pamela Massin.

Early that morning Savinien had gone to Fontainebleau to endeavor to find out who had engaged the musicians of the regiment then in garrison. But as there were two men to each instrument it was impossible to find out which of them had gone to Nemours. The colonel forbade them to play for any private person in future without his permission. Savinien had an interview with the procureur du roi, Ursula's legal guardian, and explained to him the injury these scenes would do to a young girl naturally so delicate and sensitive, begging him to take some action to discover the author of such wrong.

Three nights later three violins, a flute, a guitar, and a hautboy began another serenade. This time the musicians fled towards Montargis, where there happened then to be a company of comic actors. A loud and ringing voice called out as they left: "To the daughter of the regimental bandsman Mirouet." By this means all Nemours came to know the profession of Ursula's father, a secret the old doctor had sedulously kept.

Savinien did not go to Montargis. He received in the course of the day an anonymous letter containing a prophecy:—

"You will never marry Ursula. If you wish her to live, give her up

at once to a man who loves her more than you love her. He has made

himself a musician and an artist to please her, and he would

rather see her dead than let her be your wife."

The doctor came to Ursula three times in the course of that day, for she was really in danger of death from the horror of this mysterious persecution. Feeling that some infernal hand had plunged her into the mire, the poor girl lay like a martyr; she said nothing, but lifted her eyes to heaven, and wept no more; she seemed awaiting other blows, and prayed fervently.

"I am glad I cannot go down into the salon," she said to Monsieur Bongrand and the abbe, who left her as little as possible; "*He* would come, and I am now unworthy of the looks with which *he* blessed me. Do you think *he* will suspect me?"

"If Savinien does not discover the author of these infamies he means to get the assistance of the Paris police," said Bongrand.

"Whoever it is will know I am dying," said Ursula; "and will cease to trouble me."

The abbe, Bongrand, and Savinien were lost in conjectures and suspicions. Together with Tiennette, La Bougival, and two persons on whom the abbe could rely, they kept the closest watch and were on their guard night and day for a week; but no indiscretion could betray Goupil, whose machinations were known to himself only. There were no more serenades and no more letters, and little by little the watch relaxed. Bongrand thought the author of the wrong was frightened; Savinien believed that the procureur du roi to whom he had sent the letters received by Ursula and himself and his mother, had taken steps to put an end to the persecution.

The armistice was not of long duration, however. When the doctor had checked the nervous fever from which poor Ursula was suffering, and just as she was recovering her courage, a rope-ladder was found, early one morning in July, attached to her window. The postilion of the mail-post declared that as he drove past the house in the middle of the night a small man was in the act of coming down the ladder, and though he tried to pull up, his horses, being startled, carried him down the hill so fast that he was out of Nemours before he stopped them. Some of the persons who frequented Dionis's salon attributed these manoeuvres to the Marquis du Rouvre, then much hampered in means, for Massin held his notes to a large amount. It was said that a prompt marriage of his daughter to Savinien would save Chateau du Rouvre from his creditors; and Madame de Portenduere, the gossips added, would approve of anything that would discredit and degrade Ursula and lead to this marriage of her son.

So far from this being true, the old lady was well-nigh vanquished by the sufferings of the innocent girl. The abbe was so painfully overcome by this act of infernal wickedness that he fell ill himself and was kept to the house for several days. Poor Ursula, to whom this last insult had caused a relapse, received by post a letter from the abbe, which was taken in by La Bougival on recognizing the handwriting. It was as follows:—

My child,—Leave Nemours, and thus evade the malice of your enemies. Perhaps they are seeking to endanger Savinien's life. I will tell you more when I am able to go to you.

Your devoted friend,

Chaperon.

When Savinien, who was almost maddened by these proceedings, carried this letter to the abbe, the poor priest read it and re-read it; so amazed and horror-stricken was he to see the perfection with which his own handwriting and signature were imitated. The dangerous condition into which this last atrocity threw poor Ursula sent Savinien once more to the procureur du roi with the forged letter.

"A murder is being committed by means that the law cannot touch," he said, "upon an orphan whom the Code places in your care as legal guardian. What is to be done?"

"If you can find any means of repression," said the official, "I will adopt them; but I know of none. That infamous wretch gives the best advice. Mademoiselle Mirouet must be sent to the sisters of the Adoration of the Sacred Heart. Meanwhile the commissary of police at Fontainebleau shall at my request authorize you to carry arms in your own defence. I have been myself to Rouvre, and I found Monsieur du Rouvre justly indignant at the suspicions some of the Nemours people have put upon him. Minoret, the father of my assistant, is in treaty for the purchase of the estate. Mademoiselle is to marry a rich Polish count; and Monsieur du Rouvre himself left the neighbourhood the day I saw him, to avoid arrest for debt."

Desire Minoret, when questioned by his chief, dared not tell his thought. He recognized Goupil. Goupil, he fully believed, was the only man capable of carrying a persecution to the very verge of the penal code without infringing a hair's-breadth upon it.

CHAPTER XVIII.
A TWO-FOLD VENGEANCE

Impunity, secrecy, and success increased Goupil's audacity. He made Massin, who was completely his dupe, sue the Marquis du Rouvre for his notes, so as to force him to sell the remainder of his property to Minoret. Thus prepared, he opened negotiations for a practice at Sens, and then resolved to strike a last blow to obtain Ursula. He meant to imitate certain young men in Paris who owed their wives and their fortunes to abduction. He knew that the services he had rendered to Minoret, to Massin, and to Cremiere, and the protection of Dionis and the mayor of Nemours would enable him to hush up the affair. He resolved to throw off the mask, believing Ursula too feeble in the condition to which he had reduced her to make any resistance. But before risking this last throw in the game he thought it best to have an explanation with Minoret, and he chose his opportunity at Rouvre, where he went with his patron for the first time after the deeds were signed.

Minoret had that morning received a confidential letter from his son asking him for information as to what was happening in connection with Ursula, information that he desired to obtain before going to Nemours with the procureur du roi to place her under shelter from these atrocities in the convent of the Adoration. Desire exhorted his father, in case this persecution should be the work of any of their friends, to give to whoever it might be warning and good advice; for even if the law could not punish this crime it would certainly discover the truth and hold it over the delinquent's head. Minoret had now attained a great object. Owner of the chateau du Rouvre, one of the finest estates in the Gatinais, he had also a rent-roll of some forty odd thousand francs a year from the rich domains which surrounded the park. He could well afford to snap his fingers at Goupil. Besides, he intended to live on the estate, where the sight of Ursula would no longer trouble him.

"My boy," he said to Goupil, as they walked along the terrace, "let my young cousin alone, now."

"Pooh!" said the clerk, unable to imagine what capricious conduct meant.

"Oh! I'm not ungrateful; you have enabled me to get this fine brick chateau with the stone copings (which couldn't be built now for two hundred thousand francs) and those farms and preserves and the park and gardens and woods, all for two hundred and eighty thousand francs. No, I'm not ungrateful; I'll give you ten per cent, twenty thousand francs, for your services, and you can buy a sheriff's practice in Nemours. I'll guarantee you a marriage with one of Cremiere's daughters, the eldest."

"The one who talks piston!" cried Goupil.

"She'll have thirty thousand francs," replied Minoret. "Don't you see, my dear boy, that you are cut out for a sheriff, just as I was to be a post master? People should keep to their vocation."

"Very well, then," said Goupil, falling from the pinnacle of his hopes; "here's a stamped cheque; write me an order for twenty thousand francs; I want the money in hand at once."

Minoret had eighteen thousand francs by him at that moment of which his wife knew nothing. He thought the best way to get rid of Goupil was to sign the draft. The clerk, seeing the flush of seigniorial fever on the face of the imbecile and colossal Machiavelli, threw him an "au revoir," by way of farewell, accompanied with a glance which would have made any one but an idiotic parvenu, lost in contemplation of the magnificent chateau built in the style in vogue under Louis XIII., tremble in his shoes.

"Are you not going to wait for me?" he cried, observing that Goupil was going away on foot.

"You'll find me on our path, never fear, papa Minoret," replied Goupil, athirst for vengeance and resolved to know the meaning of the zigzags of Minoret's strange conduct.

Since the day when the last vile calumny had sullied her life Ursula, a prey to one of those inexplicable maladies the seat of which is in the soul, seemed to be rapidly nearing death. She was deathly pale, speaking only at rare intervals and then in slow and feeble words; everything about her, her glance of gentle indifference, even the expression of her forehead, all revealed the presence of some consuming thought. She was thinking how the ideal wreath of chastity, with which throughout all ages the Peoples crowned their virgins, had fallen from her brow. She heard in the void and in the silence the dishonoring words, the malicious comments, the laughter of the little town. The trial was too heavy, her innocence was too delicate to allow her to survive the murderous blow. She complained no more; a sorrowful smile was on her lips; her eyes appealed to heaven, to the Sovereign of angels, against man's injustice.

When Goupil reached Nemours, Ursula had just been carried down from her chamber to the ground-floor in the arms of La Bougival and the doctor. A great event was about to take place. When Madame de Portenduere became really aware that the girl was dying like an ermine, though less injured in her honor than Clarissa Harlowe, she resolved to go to her and comfort her. The sight of her son's anguish, who during the whole preceding night had seemed beside himself, made the Breton soul of the old woman yield. Moreover, it seemed worthy of her own dignity to revive the courage of a girl so pure, and she saw in her visit a counterpoise to all the evil done by the little town. Her opinion, surely more powerful than that of the crowd, ought to carry with it, she thought, the influence of race. This step, which the abbe came to announce, made so great a change in Ursula that the doctor, who was about to ask for a consultation of Parisian doctors, recovered hope. They placed her on her uncle's sofa, and such was the character of her beauty that she lay there in her mourning garments, pale from suffering, she was more exquisitely lovely than in the happiest hours of her life. When Savinien, with his mother on his arm, entered the room she colored vividly.

"Do not rise, my child," said the old lady imperatively; "weak and ill as I am myself, I wished to come and tell you my feelings about what is happening. I respect you as the purest, the most religious and excellent girl in the Gatinais; and I think you worthy to make the happiness of a gentleman."

At first poor Ursula was unable to answer; she took the withered hands of Savinien's mother and kissed them.

"Ah, madame," she said in a faltering voice, "I should never have had the boldness to think of rising above my condition if I had not been encouraged by promises; my only claim was that of an affection without bounds; but now they have found the means to separate me from him I love,—they have made me unworthy of him. Never!" she cried, with a ring in her voice which painfully affected those about her, "never will I consent to give to any man a degraded hand, a stained reputation. I loved too well,—yes, I can admit it in my present condition,—I love a creature almost as I love God, and God—"

"Hush, my child! do not calumniate God. Come, my daughter," said the old lady, making an effort, "do not exaggerate the harm done by an infamous joke in which no one believes. I give you my word, you will live and you shall be happy."

"We shall be happy!" cried Savinien, kneeling beside Ursula and kissing her hand; "my mother has called you her daughter."

"Enough, enough," said the doctor feeling his patient's pulse; "do not kill her with joy."

At that moment Goupil, who found the street door ajar, opened that of the little salon, and showed his hideous face blazing with thoughts of vengeance which had crowded into his mind as he hurried along.

"Monsieur de Portenduere," he said, in a voice like the hissing of a viper forced from its hole.

"What do you want?" said Savinien, rising from his knees.

"I have a word to say to you."

Savinien left the room, and Goupil took him into the little courtyard.

"Swear to me by Ursula's life, by your honor as a gentleman, to do by me as if I had never told you what I am about to tell. Do this, and I will reveal to you the cause of the persecutions directed against Mademoiselle Mirouet."

"Can I put a stop to them?"

"Yes."

"Can I avenge them?"

"On their author, yes—on his tool, no."

"Why not?"

"Because—I am the tool."

Savinien turned pale.

"I have just seen Ursula—" said Goupil.

"Ursula?" said the lover, looking fixedly at the clerk.

"Mademoiselle Mirouet," continued Goupil, made respectful by Savinien's tone; "and I would undo with my blood the wrong that has been done; I repent of it. If you were to kill me, in a duel or otherwise, what good would my blood do you? can you drink it? At this moment it would poison you."

The cold reasoning of the man, together with a feeling of eager curiosity, calmed Savinien's anger. He fixed his eyes on Goupil with a look which made that moral deformity writhe.

"Who set you at this work?" said the young man.

"Will you swear?"

"What,—to do you no harm?"

"I wish that you and Mademoiselle Mirouet should not forgive me."

"She will forgive you,—I, never!"

"But at least you will forget?"

What terrible power the reason has when it is used to further self-interest. Here were two men, longing to tear one another in pieces, standing in that courtyard within two inches of each other, compelled to talk together and united by a single sentiment.

"I will forgive you, but I shall not forget."

"The agreement is off," said Goupil coldly. Savinien lost patience. He applied a blow upon the man's face which echoed through the courtyard and nearly knocked him down, making Savinien himself stagger.

"It is only what I deserve," said Goupil, "for committing such a folly. I thought you more noble than you are. You have abused the advantage I gave you. You are in my power now," he added with a look of hatred.

"You are a murderer!" said Savinien.

"No more than a dagger is a murderer."

"I beg your pardon," said Savinien.

"Are you revenged enough?" said Goupil, with ferocious irony; "will you stop here?"

"Reciprocal pardon and forgetfulness," replied Savinien.

"Give me your hand," said the clerk, holding out his own.

"It is yours," said Savinien, swallowing the shame for Ursula's sake. "Now speak; who made you do this thing?"

Goupil looked into the scales as it were; on one side was Savinien's blow, on the other his hatred against Minoret. For a second he was undecided; then a voice said to him: "You will be notary!" and he answered:—

"Pardon and forgetfulness? Yes, on both sides, monsieur—"

"Who is persecuting Ursula?" persisted Savinien.

"Minoret. He would have liked to see her buried. Why? I can't tell you that; but we might find out the reason. Don't mix me up in all this; I could do nothing to help you if the others distrusted me. Instead of annoying Ursula I will defend her; instead of serving Minoret I will try to defeat his schemes. I live only to ruin him, to destroy him—I'll crush him under foot, I'll dance on his carcass, I'll make his bones into dominoes! To-morrow, every wall in Nemours and Fontainebleau and Rouvre shall blaze with the letters, 'Minoret is a thief!' Yes, I'll burst him like a gun—There! we're allies now by the imprudence of that outbreak! If you choose I'll beg Mademoiselle Mirouet's pardon and tell her I curse the madness which impelled me to injure her. It may do her good; the abbe and the justice are both there; but Monsieur Bongrand must promise on his honor not to injure my career. I have a career now."

"Wait a minute;" said Savinien, bewildered by the revelation.

"Ursula, my child," he said, returning to the salon, "the author of all your troubles is ashamed of his work; he repents and wishes to ask your pardon in presence of these gentlemen, on condition that all be forgotten."

"What! Goupil?" cried the abbe, the justice, and the doctor, all together.

"Keep his secret," said Ursula, putting a finger on her lips.

Goupil heard the words, saw the gesture, and was touched.

"Mademoiselle," he said in a troubled voice, "I wish that all Nemours could hear me tell you that a fatal passion has bewildered my brain and led me to commit a crime punishable by the blame of honest men. What I say now I would be willing to say everywhere, deploring the harm done by such miserable tricks—which may have hastened your happiness," he added, rather maliciously, "for I see that Madame de Portenduere is with you."

"That is all very well, Goupil," said the abbe, "Mademoiselle forgives you; but you must not forget that you came near being her murderer."

"Monsieur Bongrand," said Goupil, addressing the justice of peace. "I shall negotiate to-night for Lecoeur's practice; I hope the reparation I have now made will not injure me with you, and that you will back my petition to the bar and the ministry."

Bongrand made a thoughtful inclination of his head; and Goupil left the house to negotiate on the best terms he could for the sheriff's practice. The others remained with Ursula and did their best to restore the peace and tranquillity of her mind, already much relieved by Goupil's confession.

"You see, my child, that God was not against you," said the abbe.

Minoret came home late from Rouvre. About nine o'clock he was sitting in the Chinese pagoda digesting his dinner beside his wife, with whom he was making plans for Desire's future. Desire had become very sedate since entering the magistracy; he worked hard, and it was not unlikely that he would succeed the present procureur du roi at Fontainebleau, who, they said, was to be advanced to Melun. His parents felt that they must find him a wife,—some poor girl belonging to an old and noble family; he would then make his way to the magistracy of Paris. Perhaps they could get him elected deputy from Fontainebleau, where Zelie was proposing to pass the winter after living at Rouvre for the summer season. Minoret, inwardly congratulating himself for having managed his affairs so well, no longer thought or cared about Ursula, at the very moment when the drama so heedlessly begun by him was closing down upon him in a terrible manner.

"Monsieur de Portenduere is here and wishes to speak to you," said Cabirolle.

"Show him in," answered Zelie.

The twilight shadows prevented Madame Minoret from noticing the sudden pallor of her husband, who shuddered as he heard Savinien's boots on the floor of the gallery, where the doctor's library used to be. A vague presentiment of danger ran through the robber's veins. Savinien entered and remaining standing, with his hat on his head, his cane in his hand, and both hands crossed in front of him, motionless before the husband and wife.

"I have come to ascertain, Monsieur and Madame Minoret," he said, "your reasons for tormenting in an infamous manner a young lady who, as the whole town knows, is to be my wife. Why have you endeavored to tarnish her honor? why have you wished to kill her? why did you deliver her over to Goupil's insults?—Answer!"

"How absurd you are, Monsieur Savinien," said Zelie, "to come and ask us the meaning of a thing we think inexplicable. I bother myself as little about Ursula as I do about the year one. Since Uncle Minoret died I've not thought of her more than I do of my first tooth. I've never said one word about her to Goupil, who is, moreover, a queer rogue whom I wouldn't think of consulting about even a dog. Why don't you speak up, Minoret? Are you going to let monsieur box your ears in that way and accuse you of wickedness that's beneath you? As if a man with forty-eight thousand francs a year from landed property, and a castle fit for a prince, would stoop to such things! Get up, and don't sit there like a wet rag!"

"I don't know what monsieur means," said Minoret in his squeaking voice, the trembling of which was all the more noticeable because the voice was clear. "What object could I have in persecuting the girl? I may have said to Goupil how annoyed I was at seeing her in Nemours. My son Desire fell in love with her, and I didn't want him to marry her, that's all."

"Goupil has confessed everything, Monsieur Minoret."

There was a moment's silence, but it was terrible, when all three persons examined one another. Zelie saw a nervous quiver on the heavy face of her colossus.

"Though you are only insects," said the young nobleman, "I will make you feel my vengeance. It is not from you, Monsieur Minoret, a man sixty-eight years of age, but from your son that I shall seek satisfaction for the insults offered to Mademoiselle Mirouet. The first time he sets his foot in Nemours we shall meet. He must fight me; he will do so, or be dishonored and never dare to show his face again. If he does not come to Nemours I shall go to Fontainebleau, for I will have satisfaction. It shall never be said that you were tamely allowed to dishonor a defenceless young girl—"

"But the calumnies of a Goupil—are—not—" began Minoret.

"Do you wish me to bring him face to face with you? Believe me, you had better hush up this affair; it lies between you and Goupil and me. Leave it as it is; God will decide between us and when I meet your son."

"But this sha'n't go one!" cried Zelie. "Do you suppose I'll stand by and let Desire fight you,—a sailor whose business it is to handle swords and guns? If you've got any cause of complaint against Minoret, there's Minoret; take Minoret, fight Minoret! But do you think my boy, who, by your own account, knew nothing of all this, is going to bear the brunt of it? No, my little gentleman! somebody's teeth will pin your legs first! Come, Minoret, don't stand staring there like a big canary; you are in your own house, and you allow a man to keep his hat on before your wife! I say he shall go. Now, monsieur, be off! a man's house is his castle. I don't know what you mean with your nonsense, but show me your heels, and if you dare touch Desire you'll have to answer to *me*,—you and your minx Ursula."

She rang the bell violently and called to the servants.

"Remember what I have said to you," repeated Savinien to Minoret, paying no attention to Zelie's tirade. Suspending the sword of Damocles over their heads, he left the room.

"Now, then, Minoret," said Zelie, "you will explain to me what this all means. A young man doesn't rush into a house and make an uproar like that and demand the blood of a family for nothing."

"It's some mischief of that vile Goupil," said the colossus. "I promised to help him buy a practice if he would get me the Rouvre property cheap. I gave him ten per cent on the cost, twenty thousand francs in a note, and I suppose he isn't satisfied."

"Yes, but why did he get up those serenades and the scandals against Ursula?"

"He wanted to marry her."

"A girl without a penny! the sly thing! Now Minoret, you are telling me lies, and you are too much of a fool, my son, to make me believe them. There is something under all this, and you are going to tell me what it is."

"There's nothing."

"Nothing? I tell you you lie, and I shall find it out."

"Do let me alone!"

"I'll turn the faucet of that fountain of venom, Goupil—whom you're afraid of—and we'll see who gets the best of it then."

"Just as you choose."

"I know very well it will be as I choose! and what I choose first and foremost is that no harm shall come to Desire. If anything happens to him, mark you, I'll do something that may send me to the scaffold—and you, you haven't any feeling about him—"

A quarrel thus begun between Minoret and his wife was sure not to end without a long and angry strife. So at the moment of his self-satisfaction the foolish robber found his inward struggle against himself and against Ursula revived by his own fault, and complicated with a new and terrible adversary. The next day, when he left the house early to find Goupil and try to appease him with additional money, the walls were already placarded with the words: "Minoret is a thief." All those whom he met commiserated him and asked him who was the author of the anonymous placard. Fortunately for him, everybody made allowance for his equivocal replies by reflecting on his utter stupidity; fools get more advantage from their weakness than able men from their strength. The world looks on at a great man battling against fate, and does not help him, but it supplies the capital of a grocer who may fail and lose all. Why? Because men like to feel superior in protecting an incapable, and are displeased at not feeling themselves the equal of a man of genius. A clever man would have been lost in public estimation had he stammered, as Minoret did, evasive and foolish answers with a frightened air. Zelie sent her servants to efface the vindictive words wherever they were found; but the effect of them on Minoret's conscience still remained.

The result of his interview with his assailant was soon apparent. Though Goupil had concluded his bargain with the sheriff the night before, he now impudently refused to fulfil it.

"My dear Lecoeur," he said, "I am unexpectedly enabled to buy up Monsieur Dionis's practice; I am therefore in a position to help you to sell to others. Tear up the agreement; it's only the loss of two stamps,—here are seventy centimes."

Lecoeur was too much afraid of Goupil to complain. All Nemours knew before night that Minoret had given Dionis security to enable Goupil to buy his practice. The latter wrote to Savinien denying his charges against Minoret, and telling the young nobleman that in his new position he was forbidden by the rules of the supreme court, and also by his respect for law, to fight a duel. But he warned Savinien to treat him well in future; assuring him he was a capital boxer, and would break his leg at the first offence.

The walls of Nemours were cleared of the inscription; but the quarrel between Minoret and his wife went on; and Savinien maintained a threatening silence. Ten days after these events the marriage of Mademoiselle

Massin, the elder, to the future notary was bruited about the town. Mademoiselle Massin had a dowry of eighty thousand francs and her own peculiar ugliness; Goupil had his deformities and his practice; the union therefore seemed suitable and probable. One evening, towards midnight, two unknown men seized Goupil in the street as he was leaving Massin's house, gave him a sound beating, and disappeared. The notary kept the matter a profound secret, and even contradicted an old woman who saw the scene from her window and thought that she recognized him.

These great little events were carefully studied by Bongrand, who became convinced that Goupil held some mysterious power over Minoret, and he determined to find out its cause.

CHAPTER XIX.
APPARITIONS

Though the public opinion of the little town recognized Ursula's perfect innocence, she recovered slowly. While in a state of bodily exhaustion, which left her mind and spirit free, she became the medium of phenomena the effects of which were astounding, and of a nature to challenge science, if science had been brought into contact with them.

Ten days after Madame de Portenduere's visit Ursula had a dream, with all the characteristics of a supernatural vision, as much in its moral aspects as in the, so to speak, physical circumstances. Her godfather appeared to her and made a sign that she should come with him. She dressed herself and followed him through the darkness to their former house in the Rue des Bourgeois, where she found everything precisely as it was on the day of her godfather's death. The old man wore the clothes that were on him the evening before his death. His face was pale, his movements caused no sound; nevertheless, Ursula heard his voice distinctly, though it was feeble and as if repeated by a distant echo. The doctor conducted his child as far as the Chinese pagoda, where he made her lift the marble top of the little Boule cabinet just as she had raised it on the day of his death; but instead of finding nothing there she saw the letter her godfather had told her to fetch. She opened it and read both the letter addressed to herself and the will in favor of Savinien. The writing, as she afterwards told the abbe, shone as if traced by sunbeams—"it burned my eyes," she said. When she looked at her uncle to thank him she saw the old benevolent smile upon his discolored lips. Then, in a feeble voice, but still clearly, he told her to look at Minoret, who was listening in the corridor to what he said to her; and next, slipping the lock of the library door with his knife, and taking the papers from the study. With his right hand the old man seized his goddaughter and obliged her to walk at the pace of death and follow Minoret to his own house. Ursula crossed the town, entered the post house and went into Zelie's old room, where the spectre showed her Minoret unfolding the letters, reading them and burning them.

"He could not," said Ursula, telling her dream to the abbe, "light the first two matches, but the third took fire; he burned the papers and buried their remains in the ashes. Then my godfather brought me back to our house, and I saw Minoret-Levrault slipping into the library, where he took from the third volume of Pandects three certificates of twelve thousand francs each; also, from the preceding volume, a number of banknotes. 'He is,' said my godfather, 'the cause of all the trouble which has brought you to the verge of the tomb; but God wills that you shall yet be happy. You will not die now; you will marry Savinien. If you love me, and if you love Savinien, I charge you to demand your fortune from my nephew. Swear it.'"

Resplendent as though transfigured, the spectre had so powerful an influence on Ursula's soul that she promised all her uncle asked, hoping to put an end to the nightmare. She woke suddenly and found herself standing in the middle of her bedroom, facing her godfather's portrait, which had been placed there during her illness. She went back to bed and fell asleep after much agitation, and on waking again she remembered all the particulars of this singular vision; but she dared not speak of it. Her judgment and her delicacy both shrank from revealing a dream the end and object of which was her pecuniary benefit. She attributed the vision, not unnaturally, to remarks made by La Bougival the preceding evening, when the old woman talked of the doctor's intended liberality and of her own convictions on that subject. But the dream returned, with aggravated circumstances which made it fearful to the poor girl. On the second occasion the icy hand of her godfather was laid upon her shoulder, causing her the most horrible distress, an indefinable sensation. "You must obey the dead," he said, in a sepulchral voice. "Tears," said Ursula, relating her dreams, "fell from his white, wide-open eyes."

The third time the vision came the dead man took her by the braids of her long hair and showed her the post master talking with Goupil and promising money if he would remove Ursula to Sens. Ursula then decided to relate the three dreams to the Abbe Chaperon.

"Monsieur l'abbe," she said, "do you believe that the dead reappear?"

"My child, sacred history, profane history, and modern history, have much testimony to that effect; but the Church has never made it an article of faith; and as for science, in France science laughs at the idea."

"What do *you* believe?"

"That the power of God is infinite."

"Did my godfather ever speak to you of such matters?"

"Yes, often. He had entirely changed his views of them. His conversion, as he told me at least twenty times, dated from the day when a woman in Paris heard you praying for him in Nemours, and saw the red dot you made against Saint-Savinien's day in your almanac."

Ursula uttered a piercing cry, which alarmed the priest; she remembered the scene when, on returning to Nemours, her godfather read her soul, and took away the almanac.

"If that is so," she said, "then my visions are possibly true. My godfather has appeared to me, as Jesus appeared to his disciples. He was wrapped in yellow light; he spoke to me. I beg you to say a mass for the repose of his soul and to implore the help of God that these visions may cease, for they are destroying me."

She then related the three dreams with all their details, insisting on the truth of what she said, on her own freedom of action, on the somnambulism of her inner being, which, she said, detached itself from her body at the bidding of the spectre and followed him with perfect ease. The thing that most surprised the abbe, to whom Ursula's veracity was known, was the exact description which she gave of the bedroom formerly occupied by Zelie at the post house, which Ursula had never entered and about which no one had ever spoken to her.

"By what means can these singular apparitions take place?" asked Ursula. "What did my godfather think?"

"Your godfather, my dear child, argued my hypothesis. He recognized the possibility of a spiritual world, a world of ideas. If ideas are of man's creation, if they subsist in a life of their own, they must have forms which our external senses cannot grasp, but which are perceptible to our inward senses when brought under certain conditions. Thus your godfather's ideas might so enfold you that you would clothe them with his bodily presence. Then, if Minoret really committed those actions, they too resolve themselves into ideas; for all action is the result of many ideas. Now, if ideas live and move in a spiritual world, your spirit must be able to perceive them if it penetrates that world. These phenomena are not more extraordinary than those of memory; and those of memory are quite as amazing and inexplicable as those of the perfume of plants—which are perhaps the ideas of the plants."

"How you enlarge and magnify the world!" exclaimed Ursula. "But to hear the dead speak, to see them walk, act—do you think it possible?"

"In Sweden," replied the abbe, "Swedenborg has proved by evidence that he communicated with the dead. But come with me into the library and you shall read in the life of the famous Duc de Montmorency, beheaded at Toulouse, and who certainly was not a man to invent foolish tales, an adventure very like yours, which happened a hundred years earlier at Cardan."

Ursula and the abbe went upstairs, and the good man hunted up a little edition in 12mo, printed in Paris in 1666, of the "History of Henri de Montmorency," written by a priest of that period who had known the prince.

"Read it," said the abbe, giving Ursula the volume, which he had opened at the 175th page. "Your godfather often re-read that passage,—and see! here's a little of his snuff in it."

"And he not here!" said Ursula, taking the volume to read the passage.

"The siege of Privat was remarkable for the loss of a great number of officers. Two brigadier-generals died there—namely, the Marquis d'Uxelles, of a wound received at the outposts, and the Marquis de Portes, from a musket-shot through the head. The day the latter was killed he was to have been made a marshal of France. About the moment when the marquis expired the Duc de Montmorency, who was sleeping in his tent, was awakened by a voice like that of the marquis bidding him farewell. The affection he felt for a friend so near made him attribute the illusion of this dream to the force of his own imagination; and owing to the fatigues of the night, which he had spent, according to his custom, in the trenches, he fell asleep once more without any sense of dread. But the same voice disturbed him again, and the phantom obliged him to wake up and listen to the same words it had said as it first passed. The duke then recollected that he had heard the philosopher Pitrat discourse on the possibility of the separation of the soul from the body, and that he and the marquis had agreed that the first who died should bid adieu to the other. On which, not being able to restrain his fears as to the truth of this warning, he sent a servant to the marquis's quarters, which were distant from him. But before the man could get back, the king sent to inform the duke, by persons fitted to console him, of the great loss he had sustained.

"I leave learned men to discuss the cause of this event, which I have frequently heard the Duc de Montmorency relate: I think that the truth and singularity of the fact itself ought to be recorded and preserved."

"If all this is so," said Ursula, "what ought I do do?"

"My child," said the abbe, "it concerns matters so important, and which may prove so profitable to you, that you ought to keep absolutely silent about it. Now that you have confided to me the secret of these apparitions perhaps they may not return. Besides, you are now strong enough to come to church; well, then, come to-morrow and thank God and pray to him for the repose of your godfather's soul. Feel quite sure that you have entrusted your secret to prudent hands."

"If you knew how afraid I am to go to sleep,—what glances my godfather gives me! The last time he caught hold of my dress—I awoke with my face all covered with tears."

"Be at peace; he will not come again," said the priest.

Without losing a moment the Abbe Chaperon went straight to Minoret and asked for a few moments interview in the Chinese pagoda, requesting that they might be entirely alone.

"Can any one hear us?" he asked.

"No one," replied Minoret.

"Monsieur, my character must be known to you," said the abbe, fastening a gentle but attentive look on Minoret's face. "I have to speak to you of serious and extraordinary matters, which concern you, and about which you may be sure that I shall keep the profoundest secrecy; but it is impossible for me to do otherwise than give you this information. While your uncle lived, there stood there," said the priest, pointing to a certain spot in the room, "a small buffet made by Boule, with a marble top" (Minoret turned livid), "and beneath the marble your uncle placed a letter for Ursula—" The abbe then went on to relate, without omitting the smallest circumstance, Minoret's conduct to Minoret himself. When the last post master heard the detail of the two matches refusing to light he felt his hair begin to writhe on his skull.

"Who invented such nonsense?" he said, in a strangled voice, when the tale ended.

"The dead man himself."

This answer made Minoret tremble, for he himself had dreamed of the doctor.

"God is very good, Monsieur l'abbe, to do miracles for me," he said, danger inspiring him to make the sole jest of his life.

"All that God does is natural," replied the priest.

"Your phantoms don't frighten me," said the colossus, recovering his coolness.

"I did not come to frighten you, for I shall never speak of this to any one in the world," said the abbe. "You alone know the truth. The matter is between you and God."

"Come now, Monsieur l'abbe, do you really think me capable of such a horrible abuse of confidence?"

"I believe only in crimes which are confessed to me, and of which the sinner repents," said the priest, in an apostolic tone.

"Crime?" cried Minoret.

"A crime frightful in its consequences."

"What consequences?"

"In the fact that it escapes human justice. The crimes which are not expiated here below will be punished in another world. God himself avenges innocence."

"Do you think God concerns himself with such trifles?"

"If he did not see the worlds in all their details at a glance, as you take a landscape into your eye, he would not be God."

"Monsieur l'abbe, will you give me your word of honor that you have had these facts from my uncle?"

"Your uncle has appeared three times to Ursula and has told them and repeated them to her. Exhausted by such visions she revealed them to me privately; she considers them so devoid of reason that she will never speak of them. You may make yourself easy on that point."

"I am easy on all points, Monsieur Chaperon."

"I hope you are," said the old priest. "Even if I considered these warnings absurd, I should still feel bound to inform you of them, considering the singular nature of the details. You are an honest man, and you have obtained your handsome fortune in too legal a way to wish to add to it by theft. Besides, you are an almost primitive man, and you would be tortured by remorse. We have within us, be we savage or civilized, the sense of what is right, and this will not permit us to enjoy in peace ill-gotten gains acquired against the laws of the society in which we live,—for well-constituted societies are modeled on the system God has ordained for the universe. In this respect societies have a divine origin. Man does not originate ideas, he invents no form; he answers to the eternal relations that surround him on all sides. Therefore, see what happens! Criminals going to the scaffold, and having it in their power to carry their secret with them, are compelled by the force of some mysterious power to make confessions before their heads are taken off. Therefore, Monsieur Minoret, if your mind is at ease, I go my way satisfied."

Minoret was so stupefied that he allowed the abbe to find his own way out. When he thought himself alone he flew into the fury of a choleric man; the strangest blasphemies escaped his lips, in which Ursula's name was mingled with odious language.

"Why, what has she done to you?" cried Zelie, who had slipped in on tiptoe after seeing the abbe out of the house.

For the first and only time in his life, Minoret, drunk with anger and driven to extremities by his wife's reiterated questions, turned upon her and beat her so violently that he was obliged, when she fell half-dead on the floor, to take her in his arms and put her to bed himself, ashamed of his act. He was taken ill and the doctor bled him twice; when he appeared again in the streets everybody noticed a great change in him. He walked alone, and often roamed the town as though uneasy. When any one addressed him he seemed preoccupied in his mind, he who had never before had two ideas in his head. At last, one evening, he went up to Monsieur Bongrand in the Grand'Rue, the latter being on his way to take Ursula to Madame de Portenduere's, where the whist parties had begun again.

"Monsieur Bongrand, I have something important to say to my cousin," he said, taking the justice by the arm, "and I am very glad you should be present, for you can advise her."

They found Ursula studying; she rose, with a cold and dignified air, as soon as she saw Minoret.

"My child, Monsieur Minoret wants to speak to you on a matter of business," said Bongrand. "By the bye, don't forget to give me your certificates; I shall go to Paris in the morning and will draw your dividend and La Bougival's."

"Cousin," said Minoret, "our uncle accustomed you to more luxury than you have now."

"We can be very happy with very little money," she replied.

"I thought money might help your happiness," continued Minoret, "and I have come to offer you some, out of respect for the memory of my uncle."

"You had a natural way of showing respect for him," said Ursula, sternly; "you could have left his house as it was, and allowed me to buy it; instead of that you put it at a high price, hoping to find some hidden treasure in it."

"But," said Minoret, evidently troubled, "if you had twelve thousand francs a year you would be in a position to marry well."

"I have not got them."

"But suppose I give them to you, on condition of your buying an estate in Brittany near Madame de Portenduere,—you could then marry her son."

"Monsieur Minoret," said Ursula, "I have no claim to that money, and I cannot accept it from you. We are scarcely relations, still less are we friends. I have suffered too much from calumny to give a handle for evil-speaking. What have I done to deserve that money? What reason have you to make me such a present? These questions, which I have a right to ask, persons will answer as they see fit; some would consider your gift the reparation of a wrong, and, as such, I choose not to accept it. Your uncle did not bring me up to ignoble feelings. I can accept nothing except from friends, and I have no friendship for you."

"Then you refuse?" cried the colossus, into whose head the idea had never entered that a fortune could be rejected.

"I refuse," said Ursula.

"But what grounds have you for offering Mademoiselle Ursula such a fortune?" asked Bongrand, looking fixedly at Minoret. "You have an idea— have you an idea?—"

"Well, yes, the idea of getting her out of Nemours, so that my son will leave me in peace; he is in love with her and wants to marry her."

"Well, we'll see about it," said Bongrand, settling his spectacles. "Give us time to think it over."

He walked home with Minoret, applauding the solicitude shown by the father for his son's interests, and slightly blaming Ursula for her hasty decision. As soon as Minoret was within his own gate, Bongrand went to the post house, borrowed a horse and cabriolet, and started for Fontainebleau, where he went to see the deputy procureur, and was told that he was spending the evening at the house of the sub-prefect. Bongrand, delighted, followed him there. Desire was playing whist with the wife of the procureur du roi, the wife of the sub-prefect, and the colonel of the regiment in garrison.

"I come to bring you some good news," said Bongrand to Desire; "you love your cousin Ursula, and the marriage can be arranged."

"I love Ursula Mirouet!" cried Desire, laughing. "Where did you get that idea? I do remember seeing her sometimes at the late Doctor Minoret's; she certainly is a beauty; but she is dreadfully pious. I certainly took notice of her charms, but I must say I never troubled my head seriously for that rather insipid little blonde," he added, smiling at the sub-prefect's wife (who was a piquante brunette—to use a term of the last century). "You are dreaming, my dear Monsieur Bongrand; I thought every one knew that my father was a lord of a manor, with a rent roll of forty-five thousand francs a year from lands around his chateau at Rouvre,—good reasons why I should not love the goddaughter of my late great-uncle. If I were to marry a girl without a penny these ladies would consider me a fool."

"Have you never tormented your father to let you marry Ursula?"

"Never."

"You hear that, monsieur?" said the justice to the procureur du roi, who had been listening to the conversation, leading him aside into the recess of a window, where they remained in conversation for a quarter of an hour.

An hour later Bongrand was back in Nemours, at Ursula's house, whence he sent La Bougival to Minoret to beg his attendance. The colossus came at once.

"Mademoiselle—" began Bongrand, addressing Minoret as he entered the room.

"Accepts?" cried Minoret, interrupting him.

"No, not yet," replied Bongrand, fingering his glasses. "I had scruples as to your son's feelings; for Ursula has been much tried lately about a supposed lover. We know the importance of tranquillity. Can you swear to me that your son truly loves her and that you have no other intention than to preserve our dear Ursula from any further Goupilisms?"

"Oh, I'll swear to that," cried Minoret.

"Stop, papa Minoret," said the justice, taking one hand from the pocket of his trousers to slap Minoret on the shoulder (the colossus trembled); "Don't swear falsely."

"Swear falsely?"

"Yes, either you or your son, who has just sworn at Fontainebleau, in presence of four persons and the procureur du roi, that he has never even thought of his cousin Ursula. You have other reasons for offering this fortune. I saw you were inventing that tale, and went myself to Fontainebleau to question your son."

Minoret was dumbfounded at his own folly.

"But where's the harm, Monsieur Bongrand, in proposing to a young relative to help on a marriage which seems to be for her happiness, and to invent pretexts to conquer her reluctance to accept the money."

Minoret, whose danger suggested to him an excuse which was almost admissible, wiped his forehead, wet with perspiration.

"You know the cause of my refusal," said Ursula; "and I request you never to come here again. Though Monsieur de Portenduere has not told me his reason, I know that he feels such contempt for you, such dislike even, that I cannot receive you into my house. My happiness is my only fortune,—I do not blush to say so; I shall not risk it. Monsieur de Portenduere is only waiting for my majority to marry me."

"Then the old saw that 'Money does all' is a lie," said Minoret, looking at the justice of peace, whose observing eyes annoyed him so much.

He rose and left the house, but, once outside, he found the air as oppressive as in the little salon.

"There must be an end put to this," he said to himself as he re-entered his own home.

When Ursula came down, bring her certificates and those of La Bougival, she found Monsieur Bongrand walking up and down the salon with great strides.

"Have you no idea what the conduct of that huge idiot means?" he said.

"None that I can tell," she replied.

Bongrand looked at her with inquiring surprise.

"Then we have the same idea," he said. "Here, keep the number of your certificates, in case I lose them; you should always take that precaution."

Bongrand himself wrote the number of the two certificates, hers and that of La Bougival, and gave them to her.

"Adieu, my child, I shall be gone two days, but you will see me on the third."

That night the apparition appeared to Ursula in a singular manner. She thought her bed was in the cemetery of Nemours, and that her uncle's grave was at the foot of it. The white stone, on which she read the inscription, opened, like the cover of an oblong album. She uttered a piercing cry, but the doctor's spectre slowly rose. First she saw his yellow head, with its fringe of white hair, which shone as if surmounted by a halo. Beneath the bald forehead the eyes were like two gleams of light; the dead man rose as if impelled by some superior force or will. Ursula's body trembled; her flesh was like a burning garment, and there was (as she subsequently said) another self moving within her bodily presence. "Mercy!" she cried, "mercy, godfather!" "It is too late," he said, in the voice of death,—to use the poor girl's own expression when she related this new dream to the abbe. "He has been warned; he has paid no heed to the warning. The days of his son are numbered. If he does not confess all and restore what he has taken within a certain time he must lose his son, who will die a violent and horrible death. Let him know this." The spectre pointed to a line of figures which gleamed upon the side of the tomb as if written with fire, and said, "There is his doom." When her uncle lay down again in his grave Ursula heard the sound of the stone falling back into its place, and immediately after, in the distance, a strange sound of horses and the cries of men.

The next day Ursula was prostrate. She could not rise, so terribly had the dream overcome her. She begged her nurse to find the Abbe Chaperon and bring him to her. The good priest came as soon as he had said mass, but he was not surprised at Ursula's revelation. He believed the robbery had been committed, and no longer tried to explain to himself the abnormal condition of his "little dreamer." He left Ursula at once and went directly to Minoret's.

"Monsieur l'abbe," said Zelie, "my husband's temper is so soured I don't know what he mightn't do. Until now he's been a child; but for the last two months he's not the same man. To get angry enough to strike me—me, so gentle! There must be something dreadful the matter to change him like that. You'll find him among the rocks; he spends all his time there,—doing what, I'd like to know?"

In spite of the heat (it was then September, 1836), the abbe crossed the canal and took a path which led to the base of one of the rocks, where he saw Minoret.

"You are greatly troubled, Monsieur Minoret," said the priest going up to him. "You belong to me because you suffer. Unhappily, I come to increase your pain. Ursula had a terrible dream last night. Your uncle lifted the stone from his grave and came forth to prophecy a great disaster in your family. I certainly am not here to frighten you; but you ought to know what he said—"

"I can't be easy anywhere, Monsieur Chaperon, not even among these rocks, and I'm sure I don't want to know anything that is going on in another world."

"Then I will leave you, monsieur; I did not take this hot walk for pleasure," said the abbe, mopping his forehead.

"Well, what do you want to say?" demanded Minoret.

"You are threatened with the loss of your son. If the dead man told things that you alone know, one must needs tremble when he tells things that no one can know till they happen. Make restitution, I say, make restitution. Don't damn your soul for a little money."

"Restitution of what?"

"The fortune the doctor intended for Ursula. You took those three certificates—I know it now. You began by persecuting that poor girl, and you end by offering her a fortune; you have stumbled into lies, you have tangled yourself up in this net, and you are taking false steps every day. You are very clumsy and unskilful; your accomplice Goupil has served you ill; he simply laughs at you. Make haste and clear your mind, for you are watched by intelligent and penetrating eyes,—those of Ursula's friends. Make restitution! and if you do not save your son (who may not really be threatened), you will save your soul, and you will save your honor. Do you believe that in a society like ours, in a little town like this, where everybody's eyes are everywhere, and all things are guessed and all things are known, you can long hide a stolen fortune? Come, my son, an innocent man wouldn't have let me talk so long."

"Go to the devil!" cried Minoret. "I don't know what you *all* mean by persecuting me. I prefer these stones—they leave me in peace."

"Farewell, then; I have warned you. Neither the poor girl nor I have said a single word about this to any living person. But take care—there is a man who has his eye upon you. May God have pity upon you!"

The abbe departed; presently he turned back to look at Minoret. The man was holding his head in his hands as if it troubled him; he was, in fact, partly crazy. In the first place, he had kept the three certificates because he did not know what to do with them. He dared not draw the money himself for fear it should be noticed; he did not wish to sell them, and was still trying to find some way of transferring the certificates. In this horrible state of uncertainty he bethought him of acknowledging all to his wife and getting her advice. Zelie, who always managed affairs for him so well, she could get him out of his troubles. The three-per-cent Funds were now selling at eighty. Restitution! why, that meant, with arrearages, giving up a million! Give up a million, when there was no one who could know that he had taken it—!

So Minoret continued through September and a part of October irresolute and a prey to his torturing thoughts. To the great surprise of the little town he grew thin and haggard.

CHAPTER XX.
REMORSE

An alarming circumstance hastened the confession which Minoret was inclined to make to Zelie; the sword of Damocles began to move above their heads. Towards the middle of October Monsieur and Madame Minoret received from their son Desire the following letter:—

My dear Mother,—If I have not been to see you since vacation, it

is partly because I have been on duty during the absence of my

chief, but also because I knew that Monsieur de Portenduere was

waiting my arrival at Nemours, to pick a quarrel with me. Tired,

perhaps, of seeing his vengeance on our family delayed, the

viscount came to Fontainebleau, where he had appointed one of his

Parisian friends to meet him, having already obtained the help of

the Vicomte de Soulanges commanding the troop of cavalry here in

garrison.

He called upon me, very politely, accompanied by the two

gentlemen, and told me that my father was undoubtedly the

instigator of the malignant persecutions against Ursula Mirouet,

his future wife; he gave me proofs, and told me of Goupil's

confession before witnesses. He also told me of my father's

conduct, first in refusing to pay Goupil the price agreed on for

his wicked invention, and next, out of fear of Goupil's malignity,

going security to Monsieur Dionis for the price of his practice

which Goupil is to have.

The viscount, not being able to fight a man sixty-seven years of

age, and being determined to have satisfaction for the insults

offered to Ursula, demanded it formally of me. His determination,

having been well-weighed and considered, could not be shaken. If I

refused, he was resolved to meet me in society before persons
whose esteem I value, and insult me openly. In France, a coward is
unanimously scorned. Besides, the motives for demanding reparation
should be explained by honorable men. He said he was sorry to
resort to such extremities. His seconds declared it would be wiser
in me to arrange a meeting in the usual manner among men of honor,
so that Ursula Mirouet might not be known as the cause of the
quarrel; to avoid all scandal it was better to make a journey to
the nearest frontier. In short, my seconds met his yesterday, and
they unanimously agreed that I owed him reparation. A week from
to-day I leave for Geneva with my two friends. Monsieur de
Portenduere, Monsieur de Soulanges, and Monsieur de Trailles will
meet me there.

The preliminaries of the duel are settled; we shall fight with
pistols; each fires three times, and after that, no matter what
happens, the affair terminates. To keep this degrading matter from
public knowledge (for I find it impossible to justify my father's
conduct) I do not go to see you now, because I dread the violence
of the emotion to which you would yield and which would not be
seemly. If I am to make my way in the world I must conform to the
rules of society. If the son of a viscount has a dozen reasons for
fighting a duel the son of a post master has a hundred. I shall
pass the night in Nemours on my way to Geneva, and I will bid you
good-by then.

After the reading of this letter a scene took place between Zelie and Minoret which ended in the latter confessing the theft and relating all the circumstances and the strange scenes connected with it, even Ursula's dreams. The million fascinated Zelie quite as much as it did Minoret.

"You stay quietly here," Zelie said to her husband, without the slightest remonstrance against his folly. "I'll manage the whole thing. We'll keep the money, and Desire shall not fight a duel."

Madame Minoret put on her bonnet and shawl and carried her son's letter to Ursula, whom she found alone, as it was about midday. In spite of her assurance Zelie was discomfited by the cold look which the young girl gave her. But she took herself to task for her cowardice and assumed an easy air.

"Here, Mademoiselle Mirouet, do me the kindness to read that and tell me what you think of it," she cried, giving Ursula her son's letter.

Ursula went through various conflicting emotions as she read the letter, which showed her how truly she was loved and what care Savinien took of the honor of the woman who was to be his wife; but she had too much charity and true religion to be willing to be the cause of death or suffering to her most cruel enemy.

"I promise, madame, to prevent the duel; you may feel perfectly easy,—but I must request you to leave me this letter."

"My dear little angel, can we not come to some better arrangement. Monsieur Minoret and I have acquired property about Rouvre,—a really regal castle, which gives us forty-eight thousand francs a year; we shall give Desire twenty-four thousand a year which we have in the Funds; in all, seventy thousand francs a year. You will admit that there are not many better matches than he. You are an ambitious girl,—and quite right too," added Zelie, seeing Ursula's quick gesture of denial; "I have therefore come to ask your hand for Desire. You will bear your godfather's name, and that will honor it. Desire, as you must have seen, is a handsome fellow; he is very much thought of at Fontainebleau, and he will soon be procureur du roi himself. You are a coaxing girl and can easily persuade him to live in Paris. We will give you a fine house there; you will shine; you will play a distinguished part; for, with seventy thousand francs a year and the salary of an office, you and Desire can enter the highest society. Consult your friends; you'll see what they tell you."

"I need only consult my heart, madame."

"Ta, ta, ta! now don't talk to me about that little lady-killer Savinien. You'd pay too high a price for his name, and for that little moustache curled up at the points like two hooks, and his black hair. How do you expect to manage on seven thousand francs a year, with a man who made two hundred thousand francs of debt in two years? Besides—though this is a thing you don't know yet—all men are alike; and without flattering myself too much, I may say that my Desire is the equal of a king's son."

"You forget, madame, the danger your son is in at this moment; which can, perhaps, be averted only by Monsieur de Portenduere's desire to please me. If he knew that you had made me these unworthy proposals that danger might not be escaped. Besides, let me tell you, madame, that I shall be far happier in the moderate circumstances to which you allude than I should be in the opulence with which you are trying to dazzle me. For reasons hitherto unknown, but which will yet be made known, Monsieur Minoret, by persecuting me in an odious manner, strengthened the affection that exists between Monsieur de Portenduere and myself—which I can now admit because his mother has blessed it. I will also tell you that this affection, sanctioned and legitimate, is life itself to me. No destiny, however brilliant, however lofty, could make me change. I love without the possibility of changing. It would therefore be a crime if I married a man to whom I could take nothing but a soul that is Savinien's. But, madame, since you force me to be explicit, I must tell you that even if I did not love Monsieur de Portenduere I could not bring myself to bear the troubles and joys of life in the company of your son. If Monsieur Savinien made debts, you have often paid those of your son. Our characters have neither the similarities nor the differences which enable two persons to live together without bitterness. Perhaps I should not have towards him the forbearance a wife owes to her husband; I should then be a trial to him. Pray cease to think of an alliance of which I count myself quite unworthy, and which I feel I can decline without pain to you; for with the great advantages you name to me, you cannot fail to find some girl of better station, more wealth, and more beauty than mine."

"Will you swear to me," said Zelie, "to prevent these young men from taking that journey and fighting that duel?"

"It will be, I foresee, the greatest sacrifice that Monsieur de Portenduere can make to me, but I shall tell him that my bridal crown must have no blood upon it."

"Well, I thank you, cousin, and I can only hope you will be happy."

"And I, madame, sincerely wish that you may realize all your expectations for the future of your son."

These words struck a chill to the heart of the mother, who suddenly remembered the predictions of Ursula's last dream; she stood still, her small eyes fixed on Ursula's face, so white, so pure, so beautiful in her mourning dress, for Ursula had risen too to hasten her so-called cousin's departure.

"Do you believe in dreams?" said Zelie.

"I suffer from them too much not to do so."

"But if you do—" began Zelie.

"Adieu, madame," exclaimed Ursula, bowing to Madame Minoret as she heard the abbe's entering step.

The priest was surprised to find Madame Minoret with Ursula. The uneasiness depicted on the thin and wrinkled face of the former post mistress induced him to take note of the two women.

"Do you believe in spirits?" Zelie asked him.

"What do you believe in?" he answered, smiling.

"They are all sly," thought Zelie,—"every one of them! They want to deceive us. That old priest and the old justice and that young scamp Savinien have got some plan in their heads. Dreams! no more dreams than there are hairs on the palm of my hand."

With two stiff, curt bows she left the room.

"I know why Savinien went to Fontainebleau," said Ursula to the abbe, telling him about the duel and begging him to use his influence to prevent it.

"Did Madame Minoret offer you her son's hand?" asked the abbe.

"Yes."

"Minoret has no doubt confessed his crime to her," added the priest.

Monsieur Bongrand, who came in at this moment, was told of the step taken by Zelie, whose hatred to Ursula was well known to him. He looked at the abbe as if to say: "Come out, I want to speak to you of Ursula without her hearing me."

"Savinien must be told that you refused eighty thousand francs a year and the dandy of Nemours," he said aloud.

"Is it, then, a sacrifice?" she answered, laughing. "Are there sacrifices when one truly loves? Is it any merit to refuse the son of a man we all despise? Others may make virtues of their dislikes, but that ought not to be the morality of a girl brought up by a de Jordy, and the abbe, and my dear godfather," she said, looking up at his portrait.

Bongrand took Ursula's hand and kissed it.

"Do you know what Madame Minoret came about?" said the justice as soon as they were in the street.

"What?" asked the priest, looking at Bongrand with an air that seemed merely curious.

"She had some plan for restitution."

"Then you think—" began the abbe.

"I don't think, I know; I have the certainty—and see there!"

So saying, Bongrand pointed to Minoret, who was coming towards them on his way home.

"When I was a lawyer in the criminal courts," continued Bongrand, "I naturally had many opportunities to study remorse; but I have never seen any to equal that of this man. What gives him that flaccidity, that pallor of the cheeks where the skin was once as tight as a drum and bursting with the good sound health of a man without a care? What has put those black circles round his eyes and dulled their rustic vivacity? Did you ever expect to see lines of care on that forehead? Who would have supposed that the brain of that colossus could be excited? The man has felt his heart! I am a judge of remorse, just as you are a judge of repentance, my dear abbe. That which I have hitherto observed has developed in men who were awaiting punishment, or enduring it to get quits with the world; they were either resigned, or breathing vengeance; but here is remorse without expiation, remorse pure and simple, fastening on its prey and rending him."

The judge stopped Minoret and said: "Do you know that Mademoiselle Mirouet has refused your son's hand?"

"But," interposed the abbe, "do not be uneasy; she will prevent the duel."

"Ah, then my wife succeeded?" said Minoret. "I am very glad, for it nearly killed me."

"You are, indeed, so changed that you are no longer like yourself," remarked Bongrand.

Minoret looked alternately at the two men to see if the priest had betrayed the dreams; but the abbe's face was unmoved, expressing only a calm sadness which reassured the guilty man.

"And it is the more surprising," went on Monsieur Bongrand, "because you ought to be filled with satisfaction. You are lord of Rouvre and all those farms and mills and meadows and—with your investments in the Funds, you have an income of one hundred thousand francs—"

"I haven't anything in the Funds," cried Minoret, hastily.

"Pooh," said Bongrand; "this is just as it was about your son's love for Ursula,—first he denied it, and now he asks her in marriage. After trying to kill Ursula with sorrow you now want her for a daughter-in-law. My good friend, you have got some secret in your pouch."

Minoret tried to answer; he searched for words and could find nothing better than:—

"You're very queer, monsieur. Good-day, gentlemen"; and he turned with a slow step into the Rue des Bourgeois.

"He has stolen the fortune of our poor Ursula," said Bongrand, "but how can we ever find the proof?"

"God may—"

"God has put into us the sentiment that is now appealing to that man; but all that is merely what is called 'presumptive,' and human justice requires something more."

The abbe maintained the silence of a priest. As often happens in similar circumstances, he thought much oftener than he wished to think of the robbery, now almost admitted by Minoret, and of Savinien's happiness, delayed only by Ursula's loss of fortune—for the old lady had privately owned to him that she knew she had done wrong in not consenting to the marriage in the doctor's lifetime.

CHAPTER XXI.
SHOWING HOW DIFFICULT IT IS TO STEAL THAT WHICH SEEMS VERY EASILY STOLEN

The following day, as the abbe was leaving the altar after saying mass, a thought struck him with such force that it seemed to him the utterance of a voice. He made a sign to Ursula to wait for him, and accompanied her home without having breakfasted.

"My child," he said, "I want to see the two volumes your godfather showed you in your dreams—where he said that he placed those certificates and banknotes."

Ursula and the abbe went up to the library and took down the third volume of the Pandects. When the old man opened it he noticed, not without surprise, a mark left by some enclosure upon the pages, which still kept the outline of the certificate. In the other volume he found a sort of hollow made by the long-continued presence of a package, which had left its traces on the two pages next to it.

"Yes, go up, Monsieur Bongrand," La Bougival was heard to say, and the justice of the peace came into the library just as the abbe was putting on his spectacles to read three numbers in Doctor Minoret's hand-writing on the fly-leaf of colored paper with which the binder had lined the cover of the volume,—figures which Ursula had just discovered.

"What's the meaning of those figures?" said the abbe; "our dear doctor was too much of a bibliophile to spoil the fly-leaf of a valuable volume. Here are three numbers written between a first number preceded by the letter M and a last number preceded by a U."

"What are you talking of?" said Bongrand. "Let me see that. Good God!" he cried, after a moment's examination; "it would open the eyes of an atheist as an actual demonstration of Providence! Human justice is, I believe, the development of the divine thought which hovers over the worlds." He seized Ursula and kissed her forehead. "Oh! my child, you will be rich and happy, and all through me!"

"What is it?" exclaimed the abbe.

"Oh, monsieur," cried La Bougival, catching Bongrand's blue overcoat, "let me kiss you for what you've just said."

"Explain, explain! don't give us false hopes," said the abbe.

"If I bring trouble on others by becoming rich," said Ursula, foreseeing a criminal trial, "I—"

"Remember," said the justice, interrupting her, "the happiness you will give to Savinien."

"Are you mad?" said the abbe.

"No, my dear friend," said Bongrand. "Listen; the certificates in the Funds are issued in series,—as many series as there are letters in the alphabet; and each number bears the letter of its series. But the certificates which are made out 'to bearer' cannot have a letter; they are not in any person's name. What you see there shows that the day the doctor placed his money in the Funds, he noted down, first, the number of his own certificate for fifteen thousand francs interest which bears his initial M; next, the numbers of three inscriptions to bearer; these are without a letter; and thirdly, the certificate of Ursula's share in the Funds, the number of which is 23,534, and which follows, as you see, that of the fifteen-thousand-franc certificate with lettering. This goes far to prove that those numbers are those of five certificates of investments made on the same day and noted down by the doctor in case of loss. I advised him to take certificates to bearer for Ursula's fortune, and he must have made his own investment and that of Ursula's little property the same day. I'll go to Dionis's office and look at the inventory. If the number of the certificate for his own investment is 23,533, letter M, we may be sure that he invested, through the same broker on the same day, first his own property on a single certificate; secondly his savings in three certificates to bearer (numbered, but without the series letter); thirdly, Ursula's own property; the transfer books will show, of course, undeniable proofs of this. Ha! Minoret, you deceiver, I have you—Motus, my children!"

Whereupon he left them abruptly to reflect with admiration on the ways by which Providence had brought the innocent to victory.

"The finger of God is in all this," cried the abbe.

"Will they punish him?" asked Ursula.

"Ah, mademoiselle," cried La Bougival. "I'd give the rope to hang him."

Bongrand was already at Goupil's, now the appointed successor of Dionis, but he entered the office with a careless air. "I have a little matter to verify about the Minoret property," he said to Goupil.

"What is it?" asked the latter.

"The doctor left one or more certificates in the three-per-cent Funds?"

"He left one for fifteen thousand francs a year," said Goupil; "I recorded it myself."

"Then just look on the inventory," said Bongrand.

Goupil took down a box, hunted through it, drew out a paper, found the place, and read:—

"'Item, one certificate'—Here, read for yourself—under the number 23,533, letter M."

"Do me the kindness to let me have a copy of that clause within an hour," said Bongrand.

"What good is it to you?" asked Goupil.

"Do you want to be a notary?" answered the justice of peace, looking sternly at Dionis's proposed successor.

"Of course I do," cried Goupil. "I've swallowed too many affronts not to succeed now. I beg you to believe, monsieur, that the miserable creature once called Goupil has nothing in common with Maitre Jean-Sebastien-Marie Goupil, notary of Nemours and husband of Mademoiselle Massin. The two beings do not know each other. They are no longer even alike. Look at me!"

Thus adjured Monsieur Bongrand took notice of Goupil's clothes. The new notary wore a white cravat, a shirt of dazzling whiteness adorned with ruby buttons, a waistcoat of red velvet, with trousers and coat of handsome black broad-cloth, made in Paris. His boots were neat; his hair, carefully combed, was perfumed—in short he was metamorphosed.

"The fact is you are another man," said Bongrand.

"Morally as well as physically. Virtue comes with practice—a practice; besides, money is the source of cleanliness—"

"Morally as well as physically," returned Bongrand, settling his spectacles.

"Ha! monsieur, is a man worth a hundred thousand francs a year ever a democrat? Consider me in future as an honest man who knows what refinement is, and who intends to love his wife," said Goupil; "and what's more, I shall prevent my clients from ever doing dirty actions."

"Well, make haste," said Bongrand. "Let me have that copy in an hour, and notary Goupil will have undone some of the evil deeds of Goupil the clerk."

After asking the Nemours doctor to lend him his horse and cabriolet, he went back to Ursula's house for the two important volumes and for her own certificate of Funds; then, armed with the extract from the inventory, he drove to Fontainebleau and had an interview with the procureur du roi. Bongrand easily convinced that official of the theft of the three certificates by one or other of the heirs,—presumably by Minoret.

"His conduct is explained," said the procureur.

As a measure of precaution the magistrate at once notified the Treasury to withhold transfer of the said certificates, and told Bongrand to go to Paris and ascertain if the shares had ever been sold. He then wrote a polite note to Madame Minoret requesting her presence.

Zelie, very uneasy about her son's duel, dressed herself at once, had the horses put to her carriage and hurried to Fontainebleau. The procureur's plan was simple enough. By separating the wife from the husband, and bringing the terrors of the law to bear upon her, he expected to learn the truth. Zelie found the official in his private office and was utterly annihilated when he addressed her as follows:—

"Madame," he said; "I do not believe you are an accomplice in a theft that has been committed upon the Minoret property, on the track of which the law is now proceeding. But you can spare your husband the shame of appearing in the prisoner's dock by making a full confession of what you know about it. The punishment which your husband has incurred is, moreover, not the only thing to be dreaded. Your son's career is to be thought of; you must avoid destroying that. Half an hour hence will be too late. The police are already under orders for Nemours, the warrant is made out."

Zelie nearly fainted; when she recovered her senses she confessed everything. After proving to her that she was in point of fact an accomplice, the magistrate told her that if she did not wish to injure either son or husband she must behave with the utmost prudence.

"You have now to do with me as an individual, not as a magistrate," he said. "No complaint has been lodged by the victim, nor has any publicity been given to the theft. But your husband has committed a great crime, which may be brought before a judge less inclined than myself to be considerate. In the present state of the affair I am obliged to make you a prisoner—oh, in my own house, on parole," he added, seeing that Zelie was about to faint. "You must remember that my official duty would require me to issue a warrant at once and begin an examination; but I am acting now individually, as guardian of Mademoiselle Ursula Mirouet, and her best interests demand a compromise."

"Ah!" exclaimed Zelie.

"Write to your husband in the following words," he continued, placing Zelie at his desk and proceeding to dictate the letter:—

"My Friend,—I am arrested, and I have told all. Return the certificates which uncle left to Monsieur de Portenduere in the will which you burned; for the procureur du roi has stopped

"You will thus save him from the denials he would otherwise attempt to make," said the magistrate, smiling at Zelie's orthography. "We will see that the restitution is properly made. My wife will make your stay in our house as agreeable as possible. I advise you to say nothing of the matter and not to appear anxious or unhappy."

Now that Zelie had confessed and was safely immured, the magistrate sent for Desire, told him all the particulars of his father's theft, which was really to Ursula's injury, but, as matters stood, legally to that of his co-heirs, and showed him the letter written by his mother. Desire at once asked to be allowed to go to Nemours and see that his father made immediate restitution.

"It is a very serious matter," said the magistrate. "The will having been destroyed, if the matter gets wind, the co-heirs, Massin and Cremiere may put in a claim. I have proof enough against your father. I will release your mother, for I think the little ceremony that has already taken place has been sufficient warning as to her duty. To her, I will seem to have yielded to your entreaties in releasing her. Take her with you to Nemours, and manage the whole matter as best you can. Don't fear any one. Monsieur Bongrand loves Ursula Mirouet too well to let the matter become known."

Zelie and Desire started soon after for Nemours. Three hours later the procureur du roi received by a mounted messenger the following letter, the orthography of which has been corrected so as not to bring ridicule on a man crushed by affliction.

To Monsieur le procureur du roi at Fontainebleau:

Monsieur,—God is less kind to us than you; we have met with an irreparable misfortune. When my wife and son reached the bridge at Nemours a trace became unhooked. There was no servant behind the carriage; the horses smelt the stable; my son, fearing their impatience, jumped down to hook the trace rather than have the coachman leave the box. As he turned to resume his place in the carriage beside his mother the horses started; Desire did not step back against the parapet in time; the step of the carriage cut through both legs and he fell, the hind wheel passing over his body. The messenger who goes to Paris for the best surgeon will bring you this letter, which my son in the midst of his sufferings desires me to write so as to let you know our entire submission to your decisions in the matter about which he was coming to speak to me.

I shall be grateful to you to my dying day for the manner in which you have acted, and I will deserve your goodness.

Francois Minoret.

This cruel event convulsed the whole town of Nemours. The crowds standing about the gate of the Minoret house were the first to tell Savinien that his vengeance had been taken by a hand more powerful than his own. He went at once to Ursula's house, where he found both the abbe and the young girl more distressed than surprised.

The next day, after the wounds were dressed, and the doctors and surgeons from Paris had given their opinion that both legs must be amputated, Minoret went, pale, humbled, and broken down, accompanied by the abbe, to Ursula's house, where he found also Monsieur Bongrand and Savinien.

"Mademoiselle," he said; "I am very guilty towards you; but if all the wrongs I have done you are not wholly reparable, there are some that I can expiate. My wife and I have made a vow to make over to you in absolute possession our estate at Rouvre in case our son recovers, and also in case we have the dreadful sorrow of losing him."

He burst into tears as he said the last words.

"I can assure you, my dear Ursula," said the abbe, "that you can and that you ought to accept a part of this gift."

"Will you forgive me?" said Minoret, humbly kneeling before the astonished girl. "The operation is about to be performed by the first surgeon of the Hotel-Dieu; but I do not trust to human science, I rely only on the power of God. If you will forgive us, if you ask God to restore our son to us, he will have strength to bear the agony and we shall have the joy of saving him."

"Let us go to the church!" cried Ursula, rising.

But as she gained her feet, a piercing cry came from her lips, and she fell backward fainting. When her senses returned, she saw her friends—but not Minoret who had rushed for a doctor—looking at her with anxious eyes, seeking an explanation. As she gave it, terror filled their hearts.

"I saw my godfather standing in the doorway," she said, "and he signed to me that there was no hope."

The day after the operation Desire died,—carried off by the fever and the shock to the system that succeed operations of this nature. Madame Minoret, whose heart had no other tender feeling than maternity, became insane after the burial of her son, and was taken by her husband to the establishment of Doctor Blanche, where she died in 1841.

Three months after these events, in January, 1837, Ursula married Savinien with Madame de Portenduere's consent. Minoret took part in the marriage contract and insisted on giving Mademoiselle Mirouet his estate at Rouvre and an income of twenty-four thousand francs from the Funds; keeping for himself only his uncle's house and ten thousand francs a year. He has become the most charitable of men, and the most religious; he is churchwarden of the parish, and has made himself the providence of the unfortunate.

"The poor take the place of my son," he said.

If you have ever noticed by the wayside, in countries where they poll the oaks, some old tree, whitened and as if blasted, still throwing out its twigs though its trunk is riven and seems to implore the axe, you will have an idea of the old post master, with his white hair,—broken, emaciated, in whom the elders of the town can see no trace of the jovial dullard whom you first saw watching for his son at the beginning of this history; he does not even take his snuff as he once did; he carries something more now than the weight of his body. Beholding him, we feel that the hand of God was laid upon that figure to make it an awful warning. After hating so violently his uncle's godchild the old man now, like Doctor Minoret himself, has concentrated all his affections on her, and has made himself the manager of her property in Nemours.

Monsieur and Madame de Portenduere pass five months of the year in Paris, where they have bought a handsome house in the Faubourg Saint-Germain. Madame de Portenduere the elder, after giving her house in Nemours to the Sisters of Charity for a free school, went to live at Rouvre, where La Bougival keeps the porter's lodge. Cabirolle, the former conductor of the "Ducler," a man sixty years of age, has married La Bougival and the twelve hundred francs a year which she possesses besides the ample emoluments of her place. Young Cabirolle is Monsieur de Portenduere's coachman.

If you happen to see in the Champs-Elysees one of those charming little low carriages called 'escargots,' lined with gray silk and trimmed with blue, and containing a pretty young woman whom you admire because her face is wreathed in innumerable fair curls, her eyes luminous as forget-me-nots and filled with love; if you see her bending slightly towards a fine young man, and, if you are, for a moment, conscious of envy—pause and reflect that this handsome couple, beloved of God, have paid their quota to the sorrows of life in times now past. These married lovers are the Vicomte de Portenduere and his wife. There is not another such home in Paris as theirs.

"It is the sweetest happiness I have ever seen," said the Comtesse de l'Estorade, speaking of them lately.

Bless them, therefore, and be not envious; seek an Ursula for yourselves, a young girl brought up by three old men, and by the best of all mothers—adversity.

Goupil, who does service to everybody and is justly considered the wittiest man in Nemours, has won the esteem of the little town, but he is punished in his children, who are rickety and hydrocephalous. Dionis, his predecessor, flourishes in the Chamber of Deputies, of which he is one of the finest ornaments, to the great satisfaction of the king of the French, who sees Madame Dionis at all his balls. Madame Dionis relates to the whole town of Nemours the particulars of her receptions at the Tuileries and the splendor of the court of the king of the French. She lords it over Nemours by means of the throne, which therefore must be popular in the little town.

Bongrand is chief-justice of the court of appeals at Melun. His son is in the way of becoming an honest attorney-general.

Madame Cremiere continues to make her delightful speeches. On the occasion of her daughter's marriage, she exhorted her to be the working caterpillar of the household, and to look into everything with the eyes of a sphinx. Goupil is making a collection of her "slapsus-linquies," which he calls a Cremiereana.

"We have had the great sorrow of losing our good Abbe Chaperon," said the Vicomtesse de Portenduere this winter—having nursed him herself during his illness. "The whole canton came to his funeral. Nemours is very fortunate, however, for the successor of that dear saint is the venerable cure of Saint-Lange."

Milton Keynes UK
Ingram Content Group UK Ltd.
UKHW030623061024
449204UK00004B/360